Critical Perspectives on Canadian Theatre in English
General Editor Ric Knowles

2005

volume one — *Aboriginal Drama and Theatre*, ed. Rob Appleford
0-88754-792-3

volume two — *African-Canadian Theatre*, ed. Maureen Moynagh
0-88754-794-X

volume three — *Judith Thompson*, ed. Ric Knowles
0-88754-796-6

2006

volume four — *Feminist Theatre and Performance*, ed. Susan Bennett
0-88754-798-2

volume five — *George F. Walker*, ed. Harry Lane
0-88754-800-8

volume six — *Theatre in British Columbia*, ed. Ginny Ratsoy
0-88754-802-4

2007

volume seven — *Queer Theatre*, ed. Rosalind Kerr
0-88754-804-0

volume eight — *Environmental and Site Specific Theatre*, ed. Andrew Houston
0-88754-806-7

volume nine — *Space and the Geographies of Theatre*, ed. Michael McKinnie
0-88754-808-3

PLAYWRIGHTS CANADA PRESS
416-703-0013 • orders@playwrightscanada.com • www.playwrightscanada.com

African-Canadian Theatre

Critical Perspectives on Canadian Theatre in English

volume two

Critical Perspectives on Canadian Theatre in English
volume two

African-Canadian Theatre

Edited by Maureen Moynagh

Playwrights Canada Press
Toronto • Canada

African-Canadian Theatre © Copyright 2005 Maureen Moynagh
The authors assert moral rights.

Playwrights Canada Press
215 Spadina Avenue, Suite 230, Toronto, Ontario CANADA M5T 2C7
416-703-0013   fax 416-408-3402
orders@playwrightscanada.com • www.playwrightscanada.com

CAUTION: The essays in this book are fully protected under the copyright laws of Canada and all other countries of The Copyright Union. No part of this book, covered by the copyright hereon, may be reproduced or used in any form or by any means—graphic, electronic or mechanical—without the prior written permission of the authors. Any request for photocopying, recording, taping or information storage and retrieval systems of any part of this book shall be directed in writing to Access Copyright, 1 Yonge St., Suite 1900, Toronto, Ontario CANADA M5E 1E5 416-868-1620.

Playwrights Canada Press acknowledges the financial support of the Canadian taxpayer through the Government of Canada Book Publishing Industry Development Programme (BPIDP) for our publishing activities. We also acknowledge the Canadian and Ontario taxpayers through the Canada Council for the Arts and the Ontario Arts Council.

Cover image: Jin-me Yoon, between departure and arrival, 1996/1997. Partial installation view, Art Gallery of Ontario. Video projection, video montage on monitor, photographic mylar scroll, clocks with 3-D lettering, audio. Dimensions variable. Courtesy of the artist and Catriona Jeffries Gallery, Vancouver.
Production Editor/Cover Design: JLArt

Library and Archives Canada Cataloguing in Publication

African-Canadian theatre / edited by Maureen Moynagh.

(Critical perspectives on Canadian theatre in English ; v. 2)
Includes bibliographical references.
ISBN 0-88754-794-X

1. Canadian drama (English)--Black Canadian authors--History and criticism. 2. Black Canadians in literature. 3. Theater--Canada--History. I. Moynagh, Maureen Anne, 1963- II. Series.

PS8163.A37 2005   C812.009'896   C2005-902775-4

First edition: May 2005
Printed and bound by Hignell Printing at Winnipeg, Canada.

Table of Contents

General Editor's Preface	iii
Acknowledgements	v
African-Canadian Theatre: An Introduction by Maureen Moynagh (2005)	vii
The Growth and Development of Black Theatre in Canada: A Starting Point by Robin Breon (1988)	1
Must All Blackness Be American? Locating Canada in Borden's *Tightrope Time* or Nationalizing Gilroy's *The Black Atlantic* by George Elliott Clarke (1996)	11
"From twisted history": Reading *Angélique* by Alan Filewod (2001)	29
"There's magic in the web of it": Seeing Beyond Tragedy in *Harlem Duet* by Margaret Jane Kidnie (2001)	40
"This history's only good for anger": Gender and Cultural Memory in *Beatrice Chancy* by Maureen Moynagh (2002)	56
Dramatic Instabilities: Diasporic Aesthetics as a Question for and about Nation by Rinaldo Walcott (2004)	80
A Particular Perspective: (Re)Living Memory in George Boyd's *Wade in the Water* by Rachael Van Fossen (2004)	92
Sex and the Nation: Performing Black Female Sexuality in Canadian Theatre by Andrea Davis (2005)	107
Suggested Further Reading	123
Notes on Contributors	129

General Editor's Preface

Critical Perspectives on Canadian Theatre in English sets out to make the best critical and scholarly work in the field readily available to teachers, students, and scholars of Canadian drama and theatre. In volumes organized by playwright, region, genre, theme, and cultural community, the series publishes the work of scholars and critics who have, since the so-called renaissance of Canadian theatre in the late 1960s and early 1970s, traced the coming-into-prominence of a vibrant theatrical community in English Canada.

Each volume in the series is edited and introduced by an expert in the field who has selected a representative sampling of the most important critical work on her or his subject since circa 1970, ordered chronologically according to the original dates of publication. Where appropriate, the volume editors have also commissioned new essays on their subjects. Each volume also provides a list of suggested further readings, and an introduction by the volume's editor.

It is my hope that this series, working together with complementary anthologies of plays published by Playwrights Canada Press, Talonbooks, and other Canadian drama publishers, will facilitate the teaching of Canadian drama and theatre in schools, colleges, and universities across the country for years to come. It is for this reason that the titles so far selected for the series—*Aboriginal Drama and Theatre, African-Canadian Theatre, Judith Thompson, George F. Walker, Theatre in British Columbia, Feminist Theatre and Performance, Space and the Geographies of Theatre, Environmental and Site Specific Theatre,* and *Queer Theatre*—are designed to work as companion volumes to a range of Canadian drama anthologies recently published or forthcoming from the country's major drama publishers that complement them: *Staging Coyote's Dream: An Anthology of First Nations Drama in English* (Playwrights Canada, 2003); the two volumes of *Testifyin': Contemporary African Canadian Drama* (Playwrights Canada, 2000, 2003); *Judith Thompson: Late 20th Century Plays* (Playwrights Canada, 2002); the various collections of plays by George F. Walker published by Talonbooks; *Playing the Pacific Province: An Anthology of British Columbia Plays, 1967-2000* (Playwrights Canada, 2001), and other projected volumes. I hope that with the combined availability of these anthologies and the volumes in this series, courses on a variety of aspects of Canadian drama and theatre will flourish in schools and universities within Canada and beyond its borders, and scholars new to the field will find accessible and comprehensive introductions to some of the field's most provocative and intriguing figures and issues.

Finally, the titles selected for *Critical Perspectives on Canadian Theatre in English* are designed to carve out both familiar and new areas of work. It is my intention that the series at once recognize the important critical heritage of scholarly work in the field and attempt to fill in its most significant gaps by highlighting important work from and about marginalized communities, work that has too often been neglected in courses on and criticism of Canadian drama and theatre. In its nationalist phase in the late 1960s and 70s, English-Canadian theatre criticism tended to neglect work by women, by First Nations peoples and people of colour, by Gay, Lesbian, Bi- or Transsexual artists, and by those working in politically, geographically, or aesthetically alternative spaces. While respecting, honouring, and representing important landmarks in Canadian postcolonial theatrical nationalism, *Critical Perspectives on Canadian Theatre in English* also sets out to serve as a corrective to its historical exclusions.

Ric Knowles

Acknowledgements

In assembling the materials for this collection, I have incurred numerous debts and obligations both to individuals and institutions. The University Council for Research at St. Francis Xavier University provided a grant that enabled me to hire my research assistant *extraordinaire*, Janette Fecteau, who has very ably assisted me in preparing the manuscript. Ric Knowles, general editor of the Playwrights Canada Press books *Critical Perspectives on Canadian Theatre in English*, has consistently provided good advice and unflagging support over the course of this project. The contributors graciously granted permission for their articles to be reprinted, as did, where applicable, institutional holders of copyright.

    Robin Breon's article "The Growth and Development of Black Theatre in Canada: A Starting Point," originally published in *Theatre History in Canada* 9.2 (Fall 1988): 216-28, is reprinted by permission of *Theatre Research in Canada*, edited by Bruce Barton. George Elliott Clarke's article "Must All Blackness be American? Locating Canada in Borden's *Tightrope Time* and Gilroy's *The Black Atlantic*," published in *Odysseys Home: Mapping African Canadian Literature* (Toronto: U of Toronto P, 2002), 71-85, is reprinted by permission of George Elliott Clarke. (The *Odysseys Home* chapter is a lightly revised version of the essay as first published in *Canadian Ethnic Studies* 28.3 [1996]: 56-71.) Alan Filewod's article "'From twisted history': Reading *Angélique*," originally published in *Siting the Other: Re-Visions of Marginality in Australian and English-Canadian Drama*, edited by Marc Maufort and Franca Bellarsi (Bruxelles: PIE-Peter Lang, 2001), 279-290, is reprinted by permission of PIE-Peter Lang S.A. Margaret Jane Kidnie's article "'There's magic in the web of it': Seeing Beyond Tragedy in *Harlem Duet*," originally published in *The Journal of Commonwealth Literature* 36.2 (2001): 29-44, is reprinted by permission of *The Journal of Commonwealth Literature*, edited by John Thieme, and now published by Sage Publications Ltd. Maureen Moynagh's article "'This history's only good for anger': Gender and Cultural Memory in *Beatrice Chancy*," originally published in *Signs: A Journal of Women in Culture and Society* 28.1 (Autumn 2002): 97-124, is reprinted by permission of *Signs*, © 2002 by The University of Chicago. Rinaldo Walcott's article "Dramatic Instabilities: Diasporic Aesthetics as a Question for and about Nation," originally published in *Canadian Theatre Review* 118 (Spring 2004): 99-106, is reprinted by permission of *Canadian Theatre Review*, edited by Ric Knowles. Another version of Rachael Van Fossen's article "A Particular Perspective: (Re)Living Memory in George Boyd's *Wade in the Water*" first appeared as "Literary Connections: A Theatrical Review of George Boyd's *Wade in the Water*" in *Kola* 16.2

(Fall 2004): 48-79. Andrea Davis's essay "Sex and the Nation: Performing Black Female Sexuality in Canadian Theatre" is published here for the first time.

African-Canadian Theatre: An Introduction

by Maureen Moynagh

> Modern African-American drama… arises in the fluid space between dream and reality, measuring their distance as a mode of historical critique while seeking their reconciliation as a means of cultural realization.
> —Kimberly W. Benston 25

While there is a great deal to distinguish African-Canadian from African-American theatre and drama, the terms of Kimberly Benston's description of the drama of the Black Arts Movement are broadly apt for characterizing the guiding passions of much contemporary African-Canadian drama. One of the most exciting bodies of theatrical production and dramatic writing that is being produced in Canada right now is African-Canadian theatre. Not only is it animated by energies at once utopian and critical, its bid for "cultural realization" is carried forward through the collective and transformative possibilities of theatrical form. From re-iterations of verse drama to the vernacular rhythms of dub theatre, African-Canadian dramaturgy, in all its diversity, engages audiences in a dialogue with black Canadas [1] both historical and contemporary. Nor is African-Canadian theatre a recent phenomenon; black performance has a long history in this country. Yet, as Djanet Sears points out in the introduction to her groundbreaking two-volume anthology of African-Canadian drama, *Testifyin': Contemporary African Canadian Drama*, African-Canadian theatre and drama risk succumbing to "the serious patterns of omission in the documentation of African Canadian cultural production" (i) that beset all facets of African-Canadian artistry. Like Sears's anthology, this collection of essays aims to resist those patterns of omission by presenting scholarly essays that historicize black performance and analyse plays by African-Canadian writers.

There is no single way of describing or defining African-Canadian theatre, or more particularly the black Canadas that the theatre practitioners, theatre institutions, playwrights, and performance traditions represented here address. African-Canadian theatre might best be described as what Stephen Slemon, in another context, termed "a set of engaged differences" (320). In what follows I will endeavour to set out a historical framework for thinking about African-Canadian theatre and performance, and to identify at least some of the "differences" that engage African-Canadian playwrights.

Performing Blackness/Black Performance

Any consideration of the history of African-Canadian theatre ought, I think, to begin by historicizing the performance of blackness in the nation. This means taking account of the impact of North American slavery on public perceptions and dominant representations of blackness. In Nova Scotia, for instance, ads in newspapers for fugitive slaves, cartoons in the *Canadian Illustrated News* depicting black Nova Scotians in the market place, or the caricatures of blacks and the apologia for slavery in Thomas Chandler Haliburton's *Clockmaker* sketches combine to give a clear sense of a colonial social order built on slavery, even if the institution itself was contested.² In this context, the "memorials" presented to colonial governors of the province by aggrieved blacks seeking redress for the injustices committed against them might justifiably be regarded as a kind of performance, if one understands performance as both performa*tive* in the way of a speech act and, as Richard Schechner does, as the "restoration of behavior." Joseph Roach elaborates: "'Restored behavior' or 'twice-behaved behavior' is that which can be repeated, rehearsed, and above all *recreated*," and since "no action or sequence of actions may be performed exactly the same way twice[,] they must be reinvented or recreated at each appearance" (46). Performance, then, in taking up cultural behaviours and reproducing them, forges a space for creative interventions in the public sphere. It is important to understand performance in these terms, which encompass but are not limited to the theatre, because they take in the wider social and historical contexts for theatrical performance, and because theatre was for so long in the hands of the dominant social groups in Canada—and arguably still is. The link Roach makes between performance and cultural memory foregrounds the contested terrain on which any performance takes place. Again, the Nova Scotian example is instructive. George Elliott Clarke notes that the government in Shelburne "passed an ordinance in 1789 'forbidding negro dances and frolicks'" (*Fire* 12). These kinds of strictures on black performance attest to the perceived potency of black communities' expression, even as they supply evidence of the social forces working to contain that expression.

A more theatre-centred approach that yields important insights into the ways blackness was performed and read by nineteenth-century audiences is offered by Stephen Johnson in his study of what came to be known as "The Tom Show." Performances of the stage version of Harriet Beecher Stowe's immensely popular and influential novel *Uncle Tom's Cabin* at Toronto's Royal Lyceum in 1853, 1854, 1856, 1857, and 1860 attest that Canadian audiences were as captivated by the sentimental abolitionist melodrama as other northerners in North America. Johnson notes that there is evidence that street performances of The Tom Show took place as well, suggesting an even broader appeal and one likely to have carried beyond the urban centre of Toronto (56). It is in the actual performance practices that one can get a sense of the ideological scripting of blackness for consumption in Canada West in the period between the 1850 Fugitive Slave Law and the Civil War in the United States, a period which saw increased numbers of fugitive slaves arriving in Canada. Johnson notes a sharp divergence in the presentation of the characters George and Eliza Harris, who escape slavery, and Tom, who does not. The actors playing George and Eliza wore light tan makeup as visual evidence of their white ancestry, and they spoke using the mainstream conventions of American English. Tom, in contrast, wore black cork makeup and used the staged Black English familiar to audiences from minstrel shows. As Johnson puts it, "The visual and aural statement made by these theatrical conventions… was that 'fugitive slaves' had white ancestry, and that it was the white ancestry that was 'escaping slavery'" (57), thus allowing European settlers in Canada West to feel moral satisfaction at the idea that Canada was a haven from slavery without the threat of an unassimilable otherness. The effect of this performance tradition is to situate blackness outside of the nation, something that contemporary African-Canadian dramatists and theatre professionals continue to address.

Another performance tradition contemporaneous with The Tom Show was of course minstrelsy, the "entertainment of choice in North America from the 1840s through the 1870s" (Johnson 58). In fact, "[t]he stage conventions" in The Tom Shows, Eric Lott notes, "were clearly those of minstrelsy" (211). As late as 1884, Callender's Colored Minstrels performed to a sold-out house in the Academy Hall in Halifax (Winks 294), and there are records of minstrel shows in venues throughout what came to be known as Upper and Lower Canada in the nineteenth century. Clarence Bayne reports that both the Odd Fellows Hall and the Garrick Theatre Club in Montreal served as venues for minstrelsy in the 1850s, including for black troupes like the Real Ethiopian Serenaders from Philadelphia (34). As Bayne, Winks and others have observed, these caricatured performances of blackness rehearsed racist stereotypes (Bayne 34; Winks 294-95), and they were met with resistance by some black communities. There is clear evidence that members of Toronto's black community, for instance, found the representation of blackness in minstrelsy demeaning; they petitioned city council annually from 1840 to 1843 to prohibit touring minstrel shows (Johnson 60; Breon).[3] Lott's recent study of minstrelsy, *Love and Theft: Blackface Minstrelsy and the American Working Class*, emphasizes the ambiguities of this performance tradition in its staging of blackness. As the title implies, in the minstrel tradition, blackness is an object of white desire as much as it is an object of appropriation and commodification, and if minstrelsy was built on "the white commodification of black bodies," black performers themselves sometimes acted as conduits for introducing black performative practices into minstrelsy in what Lott characterizes as "a way of getting along in a constricted world" (39). Lott's focus is exclusively on the United States; one cannot simply assimilate his conclusions to the Canadian context, but there are continuities as well as disruptions in these performance traditions across the Americas. Johnson's reading of The Tom Show suggests there was a peculiarly Canadian form of ambivalence toward blacks: they were desirable as evidence of Canadian moral superiority vis-à-vis the United States, but not particularly welcome as full and equal citizens.

Of course, members of black communities across the country were not merely reactive to dominant representations of blackness, but undertook to establish an independent relationship to theatre and performance. As a number of commentators have pointed out, the black church was and, in fact, remains a tremendously important institution whose functions are social as well as religious (Breon; Mortley 30; Borden

42; Henry 31). There is also evidence of black theatre groups operating independently of the church dating back to the early nineteenth century in Halifax, Toronto, and Vancouver, as well as in small communities like North Buxton and Amherstburg (Berger 355). Breon notes an 1849 production of Thomas Otway's *Venice Preserved* by the Toronto Coloured Young Men's Amateur Theatrical Society, offering what is arguably a clear riposte to the contemporary minstrel show tradition with its insistence on limited emotive and dramatic registers for black performance. In the twentieth century, community groups like the Excelsior Debating and Dramatic Club of Montreal, created in 1933; the Trinidad and Tobago Association Drama Committee, founded by Clarence Bayne and Arthur Goddard in 1964; the Inglewood Community Players of Nova Scotia, founded in 1967, ran the gamut from performance in the service of community development to laying the ground for professional theatre and mounting productions like Inglewood's *Coming Here to Stay*, a play about nineteenth-century black refugees to Nova Scotia, that won awards in the Regional Finals of the Dominion Drama Festival (Borden 41).

As professional theatre began to develop across the country after the Second World War, some of the "first truly professional Black theatre[s] in Canada" began to emerge (Breon). In 1942 in Montreal, the Negro Theatre Guild opened with a production of Marc Connelly's *The Green Pastures*, ironically a play whose representation of blackness qualifies it as a "near-minstrel show" (Lott 7). Originally produced in 1929, the play was wildly successful with American audiences, and for Yale Drama School graduate, Don Haldane, then artistic director of the Negro Theatre Guild, the play may well have seemed a logical choice. In 1949, the Guild presented Eugene O'Neill's play *The Emperor Jones* at the Dominion Drama Festival in Toronto. The first "legitimate" American play to cast a black actor in a major role, *The Emperor Jones* was ambivalently received by African-American theatre practitioners and cultural critics in the 1920s and 1930s (Steen 343, 346). While actors such as Paul Robeson were delighted that a major role had been scripted for black actors in a Broadway play, there was considerable discomfort with what many regarded as the play's caricatured representation of blackness.[3] The African-Canadian actors who were members of the Negro Theatre Guild may well have felt as Robeson apparently did, that plays by figures like O'Neill offered a welcome opportunity to perform their craft. At the same time, one cannot discount the role in play selection of the white theatre professionals who were members of the Guild and the board. When, in the 1960s, the board members of the Guild were all black, the Guild "started doing works that were more consistent with the interests of the new African and Caribbean immigrants—plays with Caribbean and African themes" (Bayne 34).

In the late 1960s, the Negro Theatre Guild faced pressure from the professional productions at the Revue Theatre, whose artistic director, Arleigh Peterson, regularly mounted African-American plays, and from the newly emerged Black Theatre Workshop (BTW), which eventually took its place as the premier black community theatre. From its inception, Black Theatre Workshop manifested an interest in developing original plays that spoke to the experiences of black communities in Canada, both those newly immigrated from the Caribbean and those with a much longer history in the country. BTW has maintained this tradition of support for African-Canadian play development, and has evolved strategies for operating as a professional theatre company while remaining engaged in community development.

As Black Theatre Workshop developed in Montreal, Vera Cudjoe founded Black Theatre Canada (BTC) in Toronto in 1973. In addition to producing plays by Caribbean, African-American and African-Canadian dramatists, Black Theatre Canada took young people's theatre very seriously, toured many of its productions to Toronto-area schools, ran theatre workshops, and engaged in cultural-awareness projects. A year later, one of Cudjoe's supporters and collaborators, Jeff Henry, established Theatre Fountainhead in an effort to move "toward an infrastructure based on professional merits" (Henry 31). Theatre Fountainhead opened with a production of Soyinka's *The Swamp Dwellers*, and it went on to mount productions by a wide range of writers for the theatre, including Samuel Beckett, in an effort to develop the range and skills of the black theatre professionals it sought to nurture (Henry 32). Eventually BTC and Theatre Fountainhead went the way of many black theatre groups in the country, succumbing to the pressures of financial exigency and the exhaustion of the founders.

The viability of these theatrical institutions has varied over the years, dependent as they have been on fluctuating funding and community support. Some of these difficulties no doubt attend most of the smaller theatrical companies in the country, whose portion of the grant funding emanating from the Canada Council and local arts councils is paltry. Yet, there is clearly an added dimension to the difficulties these black companies face, including assumptions on the part of funding agencies and the media about what counts as "Canadian" theatre. Still, new creative endeavours continue to emerge across the country, from David Woods's Voices Black Theatre Ensemble in Nova Scotia, to Sepia Players in Vancouver, and more recently to companies like Obsidian Theatre Company, the AfriCan Theatre Ensemble and b current in Toronto. The AfriCanadian Playwrights' Festival has, since 1997, been a triennial showcase for the work of African-Canadian playwrights, performers and theatre practitioners. According to artistic director Djanet Sears, the festival's mandate includes support for readings and productions of black plays by mainstream theatre companies, and the development of new works by African-Canadian playwrights: "The fundamental idea underpinning this mandate was that, for Black theatre to have a larger national impact, there must be more Black playwrights writing *and* getting access to those who could produce their work, at home and abroad" ("AfriCanadian" 4). The participation of internationally renowned theatre practitioners and playwrights like Derek Walcott and Yvonne Brewster, together with African-Canadian performers, writers, and directors, has had the desired effect of attracting established theatre and production companies to the work of African-Canadian playwrights, of providing the impetus for new plays, and for launching new companies like Obsidian. At the most recent Festival in 2003, scholars presented papers on black theatre history and aesthetics in several conference sessions, part of an effort to provide a forum for reflection on theatrical practice.

Approaching African-Canadian Theatre

As Helen Gilbert and Joanne Tompkins point out, theatre offers playwrights and theatre practitioners a range of strategies that enable them to "rework a historical moment or a character or an imperial text or even a theatre building" (1). While "re-acting (to) empire," to borrow Gilbert and Tompkins's phrase, is certainly not the only concern of African-Canadian theatre, the postcolonial strategies Gilbert and Tompkins identify are to be found in African-Canadian drama and theatrical practice. Plays such as Gale's *Angélique*, Clarke's *Beatrice Chancy*, Boyd's *Consecrated Ground*, and Seremba's *Come Good Rain* rework a historical moment in order to challenge historical oppressions, exclusions and atrocities through enactments of cultural memory. Similarly, plays like Moodie's *Riot*, Philip's *Coups and Calypsos* and Sears's *The Adventures of a Black Girl in Search of God* employ specific historical moments— the 1992 riots in Los Angeles following the acquittal of the police officers who beat Rodney King, and in Toronto following the acquittal of a police officer who shot a black man; the 1990 coup attempt in Trinidad; and the renaming of Negro Creek in Ontario—as points of departure for the themes these playwrights address. Sears's *Harlem Duet* reworks both a character and an imperial text. In order to "exorcise [the] ghost" ("nOTES" 14) of Shakespeare's *Othello*, Sears stages the story of Othello's first wife, Billie. As M.J. Kidnie observes in her contribution to this collection, the play does not merely resituate and reduce the stature of this canonical character; through the relationship between Billie and Othello, *Harlem Duet* also "articulates incompatible, yet intellectually considered and passionately held, stands on race relations" and Sears's dramaturgy expresses the impasse formally. Finally, theatrical practice enables postcolonial re-enactment of the sort Azra Francis accomplished without altering a word of the script in his staging of *A Midsummer's Night Dream*, offering a new iteration of the play by employing a Caribbean setting.

The use of postcolonial strategies by African-Canadian playwrights and directors also points up a crucial feature of African-Canadian theatre, what we might think of as its global positioning. African-Canadian theatrical practice is informed by the theatrical traditions and dramatic canons of African America, of the Caribbean, of Africa, and of Black Britain, which are themselves in constant intercultural dialogue with one another and with European and Euro-American theatrical models. This is not to suggest that national theatre institutions, funding bodies, and dramatic corpuses are negligible, or that the work of African-Canadian dramatists does not enact/perform the "nationally local"; it is rather to acknowledge the transnational dialogue that pervades both theatrical practice and the dramatic imaginary. One need only note the role played by African-American and Caribbean theatre practitioners in the development of Black Theatre Canada, the participation of Paul Carter Harrison, Ricardo Khan, Yvonne Brewster and Derek Walcott at the AfriCanadian Playwrights' Festivals, or the diverse origins of the founding members of Obsidian Theatre, which includes artists from Nigeria, the UK, the US, the Caribbean, and Canada, to recognize the cosmopolitan composition of African-Canadian theatre. African-Canadian productions of plays like Ntozake Shange's *for colored girls who have considered suicide/when the rainbow is enuf*, Athol Fugard's *Siswe Bansi is Dead* (The Sepia

Players), Wole Soyinka's *The Swamp Dwellers* (Theatre Fountainhead), August Wilson's *The Piano Lesson* (Obsidian Theatre) not only offer Canadian audiences access to world theatre, they offer more or less explicitly African-Canadian articulations of these works.

Equally important is the extent to which African-Canadian plays or workshopped productions have travelled. Jamaican playwright Trevor Rhone's play *Old Story Time* was workshopped as *Story Oh* by Black Theatre Canada before it was staged in the Caribbean and the UK. Djanet Sears's *Harlem Duet* was workshopped at the Joseph Papp Public Theater in New York before its 1997 premiere Nightwood Theatre production at Tarragon Theatre in Toronto. Recently *Harlem Duet* returned to New York for a production at the Blue Heron Arts Center in 2002. NourbeSe Philip's *Coups and Calypsos* was produced in London in 1999, the same year that it premiered in Toronto. Lorena Gale's *Angélique* premiered at the Pan Canadian playRites Festival in Calgary in 1998 and subsequently travelled to Detroit and New York. George Elliott Clarke's *Whylah Falls* premiered in Halifax in 1997 in an Eastern Front Theatre production, and in 2002 it was produced at the Teatro Carlo Goldoni in Venice. Even as it gains a certain coherence from the national context of its performance and/or composition, African-Canadian drama is informed by these global or transnational connections.

Engaging the Nation

> If one stands on the dark side of the nation in Canada everything looks different.
> —Himani Bannerji 104

Alan Filewod argues that "Canadian theatre can as a whole be considered as a metaperformance that enacts crises of nationhood" (*Performing* xvii). One need only consider a few examples of the ways blackness intersects with both historical and contemporary narratives of nation to get a sense of the ways African-Canadian theatre enacts a kind of category crisis. In the nineteenth century, the dominant historical narrative of citizenship in the Canadian context, as scholars ranging from Carl Berger to Daniel Coleman have demonstrated, centred on white Loyalist brothers, wedding "peace, order and good government" to whiteness and a normative masculinity. This is not to say that black Loyalists and other blacks fleeing slavery in the US were left out of the script entirely; black and First Nations "brothers" were crucial to the imagining of Canadian national identity, for the white Loyalists were scripted as the protectors of "their" black and native (step-)brothers. In this narrative, black and Native Canadians function as the warrant of Canadian citizenship on moral grounds; they are present to demonstrate the moral superiority of Canadian brothers in contrast with their US counterparts. The Tom Show is clearly compatible with this narrative of nation, as Stephen Johnson has shown. The performances of black theatre groups like the Toronto Coloured Young Men's Amateur Theatrical Society, on the other hand, place black actors in leading roles, implicitly re-scripting the racialized national drama.

The responses in the mainstream media and by producer Garth Drabinksy to black community protests of the Livent production of the Rogers and Hammerstein musical *Showboat* in Toronto in 1993-94 mark a more recent contest over the place of blackness in the nation, or put differently, over what Leslie Sanders has characterized as "a Canadian adoption of the American racial script" (108). In this instance, it seems that the notion of American exceptionalism serves to underwrite both the history of race relations depicted in the musical and to determine the appropriate geographic boundaries of resistance to racism. Sanders characterizes Livent's position in this way: "African American history, it is implied, is the history of all Africans in the New World, there is room for no other. Yet African American resistance is represented as necessary there, given African American realities, but unnecessary in Canada" (109). To add insult to injury, positive reception of the play from African American audiences when the production moved to Broadway was held up as evidence of the erroneous reading of the play by Toronto's black community (110).[4] Yet these positions were vociferously resisted by black Canadian cultural producers, by other members of the black community, and by their allies, who insisted that there is a place for anti-racist critique in Canada, and no place for reproducing popular racism.

What these two cases underscore are the ways that the complex dialogue between play, production, and audience is conducted within the framework of historically available understandings of what it means to belong to the nation. Both in its representation of historic struggles over the place of blacks in the nation, and in its performance of heterogeneous black identities with ties to imagined communities both national and diasporic, African-Canadian theatre enacts a particular subset of "crises of nationhood." Several of the essays in this volume seek to address the ways that African-Canadian plays stage a critical engagement with the category of nation. In his essay, Alan Filewod argues that Lorena Gale's *Angélique* "unsettl[es]… the dominant myth of liberal multiculturalism" and he notes that the play's "theatrical history signals alarms about the inability of Canadian theatre culture to accept radical revisioning." By examining the history of the play's development alongside its production history, Filewod is able to identify a serious anomaly: despite a lengthy list of pre-production workshops and staged readings, publications and awards, *Angélique* has only had one professional Canadian production. Filewod offers a number of possible explanations for this extraordinary situation, but he concludes that the play has failed to secure additional Canadian productions because it "uses the moment of performance to destabilize the narratives that have historically secured Canadian nationhood."

African-Canadian theatre also engages with the nation by means of a creative and committed refashioning. As Diana Brydon puts it, "Black intellectuals… have been in the forefront of such a search for new ways of conceiving citizenship, both local and global. They are creating new kinds of national belonging and new modes of identification and community-building…" (113). In my essay on gender and cultural memory in George Elliott Clarke's *Beatrice Chancy*, I argue that the act of "diva citizenship" undertaken by Clarke's tragic heroine can be read as staging just such an alternative mode of identification, as performing a new kind of national belonging.

One might make a similar argument about the implicit insistence in Andrew Moodie's *Riot* on the national belonging of black immigrants originally from the Caribbean and Africa alongside "indigenous" blacks in Canada. As Rinaldo Walcott puts it in his essay, Moodie may be said to script "different kinds of attachment to the nation" and implicitly to "trouble previous definitions of Blackness in Canada (at least on the stage)." In *Wade in the Water*, George Boyd stages the psychological journey of an ex-slave from the United States to Nova Scotia and ultimately to Sierra Leone, and while this is obviously a diasporic journey, it is one that has a particular national significance, especially for African-Nova Scotians, as it rehearses the ambivalent place in the Canadian nation assigned to Black Loyalists and refugees. In her essay about Boyd's play, Rachael Van Fossen suggests that "By ending [the protagonist] Nelson's quest in Sierra Leone, and calling it 'home,' *Wade in the Water* lends credence to [George Elliott] Clarke's assertion that Boyd prefers, in his drama, a black nationalist option."

George Elliott Clarke offers another take on the question of nation in his essay on Walter Borden's *Tightrope Time*. Widespread tendencies in the work of both African-American cultural producers and in the mainstream Canadian literary establishment to deny the specificities of Canadian blackness produce what Clarke terms "the dynamic dilemma of African-Canadian culture." By examining the ways Borden revises and adapts elements of Lorraine Hansberry's *A Raisin in the Sun*, Clarke argues that despite Borden's clear indebtedness to an African-American "model," his play produces an "African Canadianité." In fact, Clarke finds a specifically Canadian treatment of the elements derived from Hansberry in Borden's play. He argues, for instance, that in its dramaturgical departure from social realism and in its opting for a more metaphysical approach to the experience and conception of "race" *Tightrope Time* reveals its Canadianness.

Apart from the plays themselves, there is an institutional dimension to this question of national identification and belonging. The material support made available to playwrights and theatre companies for play development and production implicitly arbitrates between competing understandings of "Canadian" theatre, as do theatre critics and scholars. Ann Wilson gets at something of what is at stake in her introduction to a special issue of *Canadian Theatre Review* on theatre and nationalism, when she asks: "Given that the majority of plays presented in professional venues in this country are written by white men (and if you look at works on Canadian theatre, these are the ones which are discussed), does this suggest that a truly Canadian perspective is gendered male and racially inflected as white?" (3). As Wilson observes, blunt questions like this one point to the relationship between narratives of nation and those who occupy positions of power (3). Rather than operating from the assumption that the category of nation can tell us anything coherent about a body of dramatic writing or theatrical practice, contemporary theatre critics are beginning to interrogate the category. As Robert Wallace has pointed out, the critical assumption "that theatre can be 'representative' of the country implicitly entails an idea of cultural homogeneity that no longer applies in Canada, if it ever did" (108). Many of the plays that are considered in the essays collected in this volume both challenge any notion of cultural homogeneity in Canada and insist on a heterogeneous representation of African-Canadians.

The Diasporic Imagination

> It ain't where you're from, it's where you're at.
> —Paul Gilroy 121

Although nation and diaspora are sometimes treated as though they were opposing categories, their relationship is much more nuanced and complex. Given that so much of contemporary African-Canadian experience is shaped by the ties that African Canadians continue to have with other nations in the Americas and in Africa, it is not surprising that many plays by African-Canadian writers treat diasporic themes. In doing so, these playwrights implicitly re-shape the African diaspora from a Canadian perspective, even as they imagine a Canadianness informed by diasporic identifications. Brydon puts it this way:

> ...although border theories, diasporic studies, and globalization pose different kinds of necessary challenges to "the idea that literature exists in a national framework," in Canada they are also forcing fundamental rethinkings of nation, belonging, and community, rather than leading toward any kind of simply conceived "postnational" world. (114)

In this view, diasporic thinking informs and challenges the category of nation but does not simply wish the latter away.

Djanet Sears's *Harlem Duet* is an obvious place to begin a discussion of the diasporic imagination in African-Canadian drama, and not only because of its Harlem setting at the corner of Martin Luther King and Malcolm X Boulevards. As Peter Dickinson points out, the play engages with two other postcolonial rewritings of *The Tempest*, Aimé Césaire's *Une tempête* and Murray Carlin's *Not Now, Sweet Desdemona*, as well as with the debate between Octave Mannoni and Franz Fanon about colonial psychoses. At the same time, Dickinson argues, *Harlem Duet* invites comparison with such African-Canadian plays as George Elliott Clarke's *Whylah Falls*, ahdri zhina mandiela's *dark diaspora... in dub*, or M. NourbeSe Philip's *Coups and Calypsos* (193), all of which also manifest a diasporic consciousness. The play also puts "Canada" back into the diaspora, as it were, both through the naming of Billie's father and through "his sudden arrival from Nova Scotia [which serves] to remind both his daughter and the New York audiences that were among the first to view early versions of the play that there are other historically entrenched—if geographically marginal—Black communities in North America besides Harlem" (Dickinson 194).

In his contribution to this collection, Rinaldo Walcott boldly asserts that "Black Canadian theatre is forged and performed within the context of a diasporic sensibility and/or consciousness." Taking as his premise the notion that diaspora is a source of political "commentary on nationally local and global conditions," Walcott examines a wide range of plays for the ways that they use diaspora to "[problematize] the cultural and historical mechanics of belonging." At the same time, Walcott recognizes that plays such as ahdri zhina mandiela's *dark diaspora… in dub*, Andrew Moodie's *Riot*, and George Boyd's *Consecrated Ground*, to name only a few of those he takes up, speak in their various ways to the nation as well. Canada is clearly marked out as a site of black migration in mandiela's *dark diaspora*; Toronto is explicitly identified as the staging ground for heterogeneous black identities in Moodie's *Riot*; and Boyd's commemoration of Africville in *Consecrated Ground* speaks both to the violence of the nation state and to global patterns of black disenfranchisement.

As Walcott makes clear, many works by African-Canadian playwrights manifest a diasporic imagination, even where the emphasis ultimately falls on forging a specifically African-*Canadian* cultural identity. George Elliott Clarke's *Whylah Falls*, for instance, while it stages a poet's journey homeward, figures this Africadian community as "a snowy, northern Mississippi," (Clarke, *Whylah Falls* 223) draws extensively on the blues, and represents the narrator as an "ex-African-American-Cuban sailor." Others are more evidently invested in transnational affiliation, in belonging to a community that comes together in Canada, the staging ground for a larger multinational, multi-racial identification. Such is the case in maxine bailey and sharon m. lewis's *sistahs*, where a Trinidadian-Canadian, her daughter, her Jamaican-Canadian lover, her mixed race half-sister, and her African-Canadian friend make "Wes' Indian soup" in a utopian bid to nourish "a complex, extended, non-traditional family, with its own secret language, a recipe to survive genocide" (310). In these two plays, both diaspora and nation are utopian spaces—"Whylah Falls ain't a real place," (223) Pablo tells us—loci for imagining community and performing filiation, and mounting resistance to the national and transnational forces that divide and disenfranchise.

Performing Gender, Staging Sexuality

The question of identification or belonging, of "home," is more complicated still when one factors in gender and sexuality. As the character Jean expostulates in Tony Hall's *Jean and Dinah… Who Have Been Locked Away in a World Famous Calypso Since 1956 Speak Their Minds Publicly*, "Home? Where the fock is home?" (166). Jean's interrogation of the notion of home speaks most immediately to her childhood experience of sexual abuse at the hands of an uncle, an experience that radically disrupts her connection to the familial home, but this interrogation of a woman's link to a home(land) has broader implications, as Andrea Davis demonstrates in her contribution to this collection. Davis argues that *Jean and Dinah* "allow[s] us to examine the ways in which African-Caribbean women's bodies often find themselves inscribed within a patriarchal and nationalist discourse of (un)belonging and are made to bear the scars of their nations' frustrated desires and fears." Narratives of nation articulate women's bodies in racialized as well as sexualized terms, but Hall's play exploits the creative agency that the "twice-behaved behavior" of performance opens up, allowing these characters from Mighty Sparrow's famous calypso to "talk back" and reclaim their maligned sexual and racial identities. In its attention to diasporic affiliations, *yagayah* offers another take on the scripting of black women's bodies. Davis suggests that "[b]y expanding the discussion beyond the Caribbean and locating it also within the Caribbean diaspora in Canada, debbie young and naila belvett further problematize questions of identity and belonging. For them black women's bodies become the bridge that can connect nations across geographic, political and cultural divides" even as "these divides also threaten black women's existence."

Sue-Ellen Case and Erica Stevens Abbitt's observation that "[f]eminism and performance theory share a focus on endangered and engendered live bodies" (925) has a particular resonance for African-Canadian theatre. The sexual and racial violence that slavery entailed is a central preoccupation of Gale's *Angélique* and Clarke's *Beatrice Chancy*, both of which focus on that occluded part of Canadian history and make the link, either implicitly or explicitly, to contemporary ways that black women's bodies are "endangered." In fact, the history of slavery in Canada and throughout the Americas is a touchstone for representing both the violent scripting of black women's bodies and black women's resilience and resistance in plays such as *Harlem Duet* and *sistahs* as well. Even comic treatments of gender and sexuality like '*da Kink in my hair* perform suffering and pain alongside hope and sexual fantasy.

The scripting of men's bodies, too, comes under scrutiny in several plays. Walter Borden brings a camp sensibility to his one-man performance of multiple characters, including the drag-queen Ethiopia, in *Tightrope Time*. Frederick Ward considers transgender identifications and the violence with which they are often met in *Somebody Somebody's Returning*. Andrew Moodie's *A Common Man's Guide to Loving Women* explores what Rinaldo Walcott has dubbed the "post-OJ" terrain of a pro-feminist straight masculinity. George Boyd's *Consecrated Ground* and *Gideon's Blues* also explore black heterosexual masculinity, linking it to the integrity of the black community, but according to George Elliott Clarke, "[w]hile Boyd adumbrates an African-American style cultural nationalism, he differs [from US writers] by foregrounding women, not men, as its primary exponents."

In the essays that follow, the contributors analyse these and many more aspects of contemporary African-Canadian theatre. From theatre and performance history to dramaturgical form, from cultural memory to postcolonial (re)enactments, and from diasporic aesthetics to acts of sexual reclamation, these essays address a number of important thematic and performance concerns. There is, of course, more work to be done, and if this collection can inspire more scholars to devote their energies to an engagement with African-Canadian theatre, it will have served its purpose.

(2005)

Notes

On the advice of the general editor, I have retained the spelling conventions used in the original publications for the reprinted essays. Essays that are published here for the first time, the one by Andrea Davis as well as my introduction, use the Canadian convention. The essays are presented in the order of their original date of publication.

1. I borrow the term "black Canadas" from Diana Brydon.
2. See George Elliott Clarke's essay on Haliburton, "White Niggers, Black Slaves." For a discussion of judicial efforts to undermine the institution of slavery prior to its abolition by the British government in 1834, see the essays by Barry Cahill.
3. References to Robin Breon are to the essay published here.
4. See for example Alain Locke's comments in *The New Negro*, 3.
5. See also M. NourbeSe Philip's study of the play and of African-Canadian community responses to the 1993 Toronto production, *Showing Grit: Showboating North of the 44th Parallel.*

Works Cited

bailey, maxine and sharon m. lewis. *sistahs*. *Testifyin': Contemporary African Canadian Drama*. Ed. Djanet Sears. Vol. 1. Toronto: Playwrights Canada, 2000. 277-328.

Bannerji, Himani. *The Dark Side of the Nation: Essays on Multiculturalism, Nationalism and Gender*. Toronto: Insomniac, 1999.

Bayne, Clarence S. "The Origins of Black Theatre in Montreal." *Canadian Theatre Review* 118 (2004): 34-40.

Berger, Carl. *The Sense of Power: Studies in the Ideas of Canadian Imperialism*. Toronto: U of Toronto P, 1970.

Berger, Jeniva. "Multicultural Theatre." *Oxford Companion to Canadian Theatre*. Ed. E. Benson, and L.W. Conolly. Toronto: Oxford UP, 1989. 353-57.

Borden, Walter. "Black Theatre in Nova Scotia: In Search of a Sustainable and Viable Presence." *Canadian Theatre Review* 118 (2004): 41-43.

Brydon, Diana. "Black Canadas: Rethinking Canadian and Diasporic Cultural Studies." *Revista Canaria de Estudios Ingleses* 43 (2001): 101-17.

Cahill, Barry. "*Habeas Corpus* and Slavery in Nova Scotia: R. v. Hecht ex parte Rachel, 1798." *University of New Brunswick Law Journal* 44 (1995): 179-208.

———. "Slavery and the Judges of Loyalist Nova Scotia." *University of New Brunswick Law Journal* 43 (1994): 73-134.

Case, Sue-Ellen and Erica Stevens Abbitt. "Disidentifications, Diaspora, and Desire: Questions of the Future of the Feminist Critique of Performance." *Signs: Journal of Women in Culture and Society* 29.3 (2004): 925-38.

Clarke, George Elliott. *Whylah Falls: The Play*. *Testifyin': Contemporary African Canadian Drama*. Ed. Djanet Sears. Vol. 1. Toronto: Playwrights Canada, 2000. 213-76.

———. "White Niggers, Black Slaves: Slavery, Race and Class in T.C. Haliburton's *The Clockmaker*." *Nova Scotia Historical Review* 14.1 (1994): 13-40.

———, ed. Introduction. *Fire on the Water. An Anthology of Black Nova Scotian Writing*. Vol. 1. Lawrencetown: Pottersfield P, 1991. 11-29.

Coleman, Daniel. "The National Allegory of Fraternity: Loyalist Literature and the Making of Canada's White British Origins." *Journal of Canadian Studies* 36 (2001): 131-56.

Filewod, Alan. *Performing Canada: The Nation Enacted in the Imagined Theatre*. Kamloops, BC: Textual Studies in Canada Monograph Series, 2002.

Gilbert, Helen and Joanne Tompkins. *Post-Colonial Drama: Theory, Practice, Politics.* London and New York: Routledge, 1996.

Hall, Tony with Rhoma Spencer and Susan Sandiford. *Jean and Dinah… Who Have Been Locked Away in a World Famous Calypso Since 1956 Speak Their Minds Publicly. Testifyin': Contemporary African Canadian Drama.* Ed. Djanet Sears. Vol 2. Toronto: Playwrights Canada, 2003. 157-211.

Henry, Jeff. "Black Theatre in Montreal and Toronto in the Sixties and Seventies: The Struggle for Recognition." *Canadian Theatre Review* 118 (2004): 29-33.

Johnson, Stephen. "Uncle Tom and the Minstrels: Seeing Black and White on Stage in Canada West prior to the American Civil War." *(Post)Colonial Stages: Critical and Creative Views on Drama, Theatre and Performance.* Hebden Bridge, Yorkshire: Dangaroo, 1999. 55-63.

Locke, Alain, ed. *The New Negro.* [1925] New York: Atheneum, 1968.

Lott, Eric. *Love and Theft: Blackface Minstrelsy and the American Working Class.* New York; Oxford: Oxford UP, 1995.

Mortley, Basil. "Silent Screams of the Invisible, Visible Minority: African Nova Scotian Theatre." *Canadian Theatre Review* 83 (Summer 1995): 30-35.

Philip, M. NourbeSe. *Showing Grit: Showboating North of the 44th Parallel.* Toronto: Poui Publications, 1993.

Roach, Joseph. "Culture and Performance in the Circum-Atlantic World." *Performativity and Performance.* Ed. Andrew Parker and Eve Kosofsky Sedgwick. New York and London: Routledge, 1995. 45-63.

Sanders, Leslie. "American Scripts, Canadian Realities: Toronto's *Show Boat.*" *Diaspora* 5.1 (1996): 99-118.

Schechner, Richard. *Between Theater and Anthropology.* Philadelphia: U of Pennsylvania P, 1985.

Sears, Djanet. "The AfriCanadian Playwrights' Festival." *Canadian Theatre Review* 118 (2004): 3-5.

———. Introduction. *Testifyin': Contemporary African Canadian Drama.* Vol. 1. Toronto: Playwrights Canada, 2000. i-xiii.

———. "nOTES oF a cOLOURED gIRL." *Harlem Duet.* [Winnipeg]: Scirocco Drama, 1997. 11-16.

Slemon, Stephen. "Afterword." *Is Canada Postcolonial? Unsettling Canadian Literature.* Ed. Laura Moss. Waterloo: Wilfrid Laurier UP, 2003. 318-24.

Steen, Shannon. "Racial Subjectivity and Melancholy Bodies in *The Emperor Jones.*" *Theatre Journal* 52 (2000): 339-59.

Wallace, Robert. *Producing Marginality: Theatre and Criticism in Canada.* Saskatoon, SK: Fifth House, 1990.

Wilson, Ann. "Notions of Nationalism." *Nation and Theatre.* Spec. issue of *Canadian Theatre Review* 64 (1990): 3.

Winks, Robin W. *The Blacks in Canada: A History.* 2nd ed. Montreal: McGill-Queen's UP, 1997.

The Growth and Development of Black Theatre in Canada: a Starting Point

by Robin Breon

Black theatre in Canada has a presence dating back to 1849 and perhaps further. The profile of organizations and personalities detailed in this article shows the growth of this movement since the mid-nineteenth century, as well as problems and obstacles encountered by visible minorities in their struggle to enter the mainstream of Canadian cultural life.

The growth and development of Black theatre in Canada represent a unique contribution to the cultural and artistic heritage of this country. From the earliest days of the Underground Railroad movement that helped establish communities such as Amherstburg, Dresden, North Buxton, and Chatham in southern Ontario, Black Canadians have aspired to careers in the performing arts. Like most artists, their struggle has not been an easy one, but the legacy of their contribution endures, and Canada's cultural heritage and national character are enriched because of it.

The study of Canada's Black theatre is impossible without attention to cultural institutions outside the performing arts, such as the Black church. It would be difficult to number the many actors, singers, musicians and dancers who had their first taste of performance by way of the local church. The reason for this is that although it was by nature primarily a religious institution it was also by way of practical reality a *social* institution that served a wide variety of purposes. In *The AfriCanadian Church: A Stabilizer*, Dorothy Shadd Shreve quotes theologian C. Eric Lincoln as saying: "…religion was the organizing principle around which life was structured. [The] church was [the] school, [the] forum, [the] political arena, [the] social club, [the] art gallery, [the] conservatory of music. It was lyceum and gymnasium as well as sanctum sanctorum." She goes on to state that, on the other side of the coin, the church could also act as the agent through which Blacks could be most easily manipulated or indoctrinated for the benefit of the slave owner. "On the plantation, the religion taught was liberally sprinkled with the 'duties of Christian slaves.' They were led to believe that slavery had divine sanction and that insolence was as much an offence against God as against the temporal master. As a result, Christian slaves were believed to be more docile than non-Christian ones and had a higher market value" (40).

Although the Negro people of this period were very susceptible to the consolations promised by the church, they also understood its more liberating aspects. They chose Bible stories that were analogous with the history of their own slave existence and began to act them out in simple pageants, similar in ways, perhaps, to the early medieval plays. They drew from these stories faith in the coming retribution for their oppressors and surety in the triumph of truth and justice. One of the most sublime and poetic manifestations of this form of cultural expression was of course the Negro spiritual which combined religious, social and political aspirations into one moving musical statement. Paul Robeson, the great Afro-American singer, actor and scholar—who, incidentally, enjoyed a very special relationship with Canada during his lifetime—is quoted as saying that, "Spirituals reflected all the manifestations of the Negro people's social life. Therefore, the song 'Go Down Moses,' for example, far from being a religious hymn, is rather an impassioned call to the struggle for the liberation of the Negro people" (Robeson 215).

Outside of the church, among the earliest recorded Black theatrical performances in Canada were those by The Toronto Coloured Young Men's Amateur Theatrical Society. An advertisement in the *Toronto Mirror* (9 February 1849), noted that the group would perform for three nights on 20, 21 and 22 February, and that they would be presenting *Venice Preserved* by Thomas Otway (1652-1685) along with selected scenes from Shakespeare. Although the advertisement stated that this was the organization's second Toronto appearance, no record of their first performance has yet been found.

If the Toronto Coloured Young Men's Amateur Theatrical Society chose to present a Restoration tragedy along with scenes from Shakespeare as representative of the kind of dramatic fare that would be entertaining and presumably highlight the talents of the various actors, it is also interesting to note during this same period the type of theatrical activity the Black community was fighting vehemently against. On four separate occasions in 1840, 1841, 1842, and 1843, members of the Black community petitioned the mayor's office to restrict the presentation of travelling minstrel shows which came up from the US and toured widely in Canada. These crude and vulgar presentations were advertised as portraying "the life of the Negro in song and dance." In truth they were base and dehumanizing depictions that exploited every racist stereotype of the period. During this pre-American Civil War period, the minstrel show was very popular with the pro-slavery lobby because it justified the South's most "peculiar institution." Although there were some Black minstrels who performed in these shows, the overwhelming majority of the actors were white who would "black up" with burnt cork or greasepaint and proceed to swagger across the stage in the grossest form of caricature and mimicry. Even Toronto had its "burnt cork" specialists, the most famous being "Cool" Burgess who enjoyed a North American reputation.[1]

Although Black theatrical organizations seem to be few and far between during this early period, it is interesting to note the lives of several Black Canadians who excelled in theatre and the field of popular entertainment during the last half of the nineteenth century and into the beginning of the twentieth century. One such example is the remarkable Canadian-born actor Richard B. Harrison.

Harrison was born in Ontario in 1864, the son of fugitive slaves who had fled the United States. As a boy he was noted for his poetry recitations for which he won prizes at school. He liked going to the theatre and would save up his earnings as a newspaper delivery boy in order to buy tickets. When he was seventeen, his father died and as the eldest child he took all the responsibility of family provider. He began working in hotels in Windsor and then moved to Detroit where he enrolled in the Detroit Training School of Art. He graduated from the school in 1887. In his excellent book *Shakespeare in Sable, a History of Black Shakespearean Actors*, Errol Hill informs us that Harrison became a lecturer/performer with the Lyceum Bureau of Los Angeles and went on to the touring circuit. His repertoire—fully committed to memory—included narrative poems, dialect pieces and whole plays by Shakespeare in which he acted every role. Of this period in his life, which took him on tour across the southern states, Canada, and Mexico, Harrison recorded in his diary:

> The strangest thing about it all is not that I dared to do it, but that I got audiences of my own race and kept them awake while doing Shakespeare—taking all the parts, moving from side to side of the stage or hall without letting people see that I was moving, holding them without any let-ups between bits of dialogue. I did that for twenty years all over this country, keeping at the last, seven plays and more than one hundred recitations in my mind. (qtd. in Hill 88-89)

His herculean efforts finally paid off when he was cast as De Lawd in Marc Connelly's Pulitzer Prize winning all Black play, *The Green Pastures*, which played to over two million patrons for 1,657 performances on Broadway and on tour. He was sixty-five years old when cast, and never missed a performance. The only thing that stopped him in 1935 was poor health aggravated by exhaustion. Harrison often expressed his wish to play Shakespeare on the Broadway stage but he was never offered a chance to do so. Although he was never given the opportunity to do Shakespeare on Broadway, it may have been some small consolation that he did die playing God.

While Richard B. Harrison was making his contribution to the legitimate stage, several other Black Canadians from this same region of southwestern Ontario were becoming prominent in the field of popular entertainment on the musical stages across North America. Among them was Amherstburg-born Shelton Brooks whose father, the Rev. Peter Brooks, was for a time the pastor of the Baptist Church in North Buxton. Brooks was a musician/composer best remembered for songs such as "Dark Town Strutter's Ball" along with several others including "Some of These Days," the song that made the "Red Hot Mama," Sophie Tucker, famous. Shelton Brooks played the stages of vaudeville for years and in 1922 went to Europe with Josephine Baker and Florence Mills, spending time in Paris and the UK. He appeared on the New York stage with notables such as Ted Lewis, Jack Benny and Sophie Tucker. In 1939, he moved to Los Angeles where he appeared in several Black films with Herb Jeffries and Dorothy Dandrige, among others.

The 1920s and '30s brought numerous forms of artistic growth and expression in the Black community. Perhaps what we could call the first truly professional Black theatre in Canada, The Negro Theatre Guild, emerged in Montreal in the early 1940s.

As I have already tried to point out historically, it was probably not by accident that the organization was founded in the basement of the Union United Church.

Program notes from an early production state that: "The Negro Theatre Guild was formed in 1941 by a group of young members from the community, whose creative impulse craved expression. The theatre seemed both a happy and a natural medium, providing scope for a variety of talents, yet demanding group cooperation." A press release from the Guild published in the *Montreal Star* helps outline the mandate of the organization: "To utilize the enthusiasm, sincerity and native talent of colored youth, in the presentation of plays of social value, is the principal aim of our organization. We feel that in the common struggle against fascism and Hitlerism, the Negro has not only his blood and his labor to contribute, but has a distinct cultural contribution to make" (Powell).

Appropriately enough—carrying on in the tradition of Richard B. Harrison—the Guild's first production was a mounting of Marc Connelly's play, *The Green Pastures*, featuring Charles Horrace Phillips in the lead role and directed by Don Haldane, the first Canadian graduate of the Yale School of Drama. Presented at His Majesty's Theatre in May 1942, the production was received warmly. Herbert Whittaker's review in the *Montreal Gazette* noted the extraordinary effort that was required to mount the show with its large cast, including a choir and musicians. Of Mr. Phillips in the leading role Mr. Whittaker stated: "Any account of the performance must include mention of Horace Phillips as De Lawd. It is a tremendous part in physical and emotional demands as well as religious implication, but Mr. Phillips never let it down. He played with consistent sincerity and perfect simplicity" (2).

World War II brought with it a four-year hiatus for the Guild. However, in 1946 the group made a strong comeback with the presentation of two one-act plays, *Hello Out There* by William Saroyan and Alfred Krymborg's *America, America*. The following year saw Elsie Salomon's spectacularly choreographed version of *The Congo* followed by an impressive rendering of Eugene O'Neill's *The Emperor Jones* presented at the Montreal Repertory Theatre Playhouse on Guy Street. This production was under the direction of Beatrice MacLeod and choreographed also by Elsie Salomon.

Again the progress of The Negro Theatre Guild was documented by Mr. Whittaker's review of the production for the *Gazette*. He called it "easily one of the most admirable productions of the season" and one that "reveals dramatically and visually the full force of this unique work" (6). This production also marked the emergence of a major Canadian talent in the person of Percy Rodrigues as the Emperor, Brutus Jones. Mr. Whittaker went on to note that: "No amount of understanding and imagination on the part of the directors would be enough if there was not an actor available to measure up to the magnificent role of the Emperor. In Percy Rodrigues, the Guild is fortunate enough to have found one" (6). Herbert Whittaker's colleague Sydney Johnson, drama critic for the *Montreal Daily Star*, concurred calling the production "an electrifying evening of theatre" and Mr. Rodrigues "magnificent… truly a superb performance" (6). The production was remounted in February 1949, again with Mr. Rodrigues in the title role and in the spring of that year was one of the winners at the Dominion Drama Festival.

The Negro Theatre Guild continued through the 1950s, '60s and into the early '70s, later changing its name to the Negro Theatre Arts Club of Montreal. Productions included Kurt Weill's folk opera *Down in the Valley*, original plays such as *The Plea of Orpheus* and *Little Tropics*, Pirandello's *The Vise*, *The Black Judges* (an adaptation of Gratien Gélinas' *Hier les enfants dansaient*), and others. Today the Black Theatre Workshop of Montreal continues in the pioneering tradition established by the Negro Theatre Guild in that city almost sixty years ago.

The Black theatre movement in Canada continued to play an important role during that very vibrant period in Canadian theatre history which began in the early 1970s. The wave of West Indian immigration that began in the mid sixties brought with it new artistic and cultural impulses that soon blended into the Black diaspora in Canada. In Toronto, one young Black woman from Trinidad embarked upon the difficult journey of training to become an actress.

Vera Cudjoe studied theatre and broadcasting at Ryerson and took theatre and acting classes from different instructors. Although originally trained as a registered nurse in England, Ms. Cudjoe wanted very much to pursue a career in the theatre. She soon found out that acting is a very competitive profession with never enough work to go around and for a Black woman the road was especially tough going. In order to open up more opportunities for Black actors, Cudjoe decided to form a Black theatre troupe. In 1973, with organizational help from Ed Smith who teaches Afro-American Studies at the University of Buffalo, Black Theatre Canada (BTC) was founded and officially launched. The first production was a play entitled *Who's Got His Own* by Ron Milner and directed by Smith. The play was presented for one night only to an enthusiastic audience at the Unitarian Church on St. Clair Avenue West in Toronto. The warm response encouraged Cudjoe to pursue the theatre as a career.

During this period a number of individuals were active in setting up the framework under which the new company would operate. June Faulkner (now general manager of Young People's Theatre) assisted with the technicalities of incorporating the company and forming a board of directors. The first board was composed of, among others, novelist Austin Clarke, choreographer Len Gibson and Alderman Ying Hope. Theatre artists in the Black community who came forward to lend assistance included Jeff Henry, actor and professor with York University's Theatre Arts Department; Daniel Cauldieron, writer, director and former associate producer of MTV's "Black World" television program; Len Gibson, dancer, choreographer and founder-director of his own school; Amah Harris, then a recent graduate of the University of Windsor's theatre program who was interested in children's theatre and who would also found her own company in future years; and a number of others.

From the outset the mandate and focus of Black Theatre Canada was clear. In fact it really did not differ greatly in substance from the mandate established over a half century before by those pioneering artists of the Negro Theatre Guild of Montreal;

that is, to establish a platform for the expression of Black culture in Canada and to create an environment that could offer training to the many talented actors, performers, writers, and directors who came from the Black community. It was the hope of founders that theatre would allow them not only to share their heritage with the Canadian mainstream, but also to encourage professional development to young artists who would then find themselves better prepared to compete in the arts/entertainment fields of theatre, television, radio and film. To name the artists—Black and white—who have touched base with Black Theatre Canada at some point in their careers would be too lengthy for this document, but among them are: Arlene Duncan, Marvin Ishmael, Leon Bibb, Jackie Richardson, Michael Danso, Joe Sealy, Cecile Frenette, Tom Butler, Phil Aiken, Dennis Simpson, Jim Plaxton, Diana Braithwaite, Jeff Jones, Linda Armstrong, Emerita Emerencia and many, many others. A number of these individuals have stayed in the theatre and have gone on to develop successful careers. Others have gone on to work in community and social work, education, business and politics.

The body of work produced by this organization over the last fifteen years is also quite substantial. It is further to the everlasting credit of BTC that these theatre productions, school tours, educational materials, numerous workshops and classes were produced with the most minimal amount of government and private support. Indeed, the organization has always been precariously financed and chronically underfunded by government agencies. However, in spite of this handicap their contributions have been steady, on-going and professional in quality.

Again it is not possible here in such a short space to begin to enumerate, let alone discuss, the significance of various projects at different times. That will be the business of a more lengthy paper, but I would like to refer to a few highlights from the past fifteen years.

In the area of young people's theatre, important work was initiated by Amah Harris and Daniel Cauldieron. Ten years ago, Ms. Harris began work on her cycle of plays for young people based on the Anansi African folktales. These plays were some of the very first multi-racial, cross-cultural "learning plays" to enter the Metro-Toronto school system playing to thousands of elementary students. Their popularity was so great that the company was asked to take them to Detroit to participate in the AfroAmerican Ethnic Festival where they played to an additional 35,000 children in 1979.

Also in this category is a play entitled *A Few Things About Us*, by Daniel Cauldieron, a multi-media musical foray into the "new" multicultural Toronto that has begun to flower so brilliantly over the past twenty years. This production was followed by *More About Me*, a play that emphasized the sharing of one's culture and the nature of racial discrimination. Also in the area of theatre for young people was Ed Smith's production of *Staggerlee* based on the legend of the Black cowboy by the same name.

For the adult Toronto theatre-goer there have been numerous productions over the years that have introduced new plays and playwrights as well as the classics. The Jamaican playwright Trevor Rhone (*The Harder They Come, Smile Orange*) was introduced to Canadian audiences by Black Theatre Canada in the mid-seventies. His production of *School's Out* was a popular success and was later moved to the St. Lawrence Centre for a special one-week run. In 1979 Rhone mounted a play entitled *Story Oh* in a workshop production that later became the basis for his play *Old Story Time*, also a great success throughout the Caribbean and the UK.

Other Caribbean artists who were given an opportunity to perform in Canada under the auspices of Black Theatre Canada included Jamaican folklorist Louise Bennett and Trinidadian comedian Paul Keens-Douglas who collaborated in a wonderful evening entitled *Miss Lou Meets Tim Tim*. Also in this same series of performances were Guyanese Ken Corsbie and Marc Mathews who combined their political barbs, social comment and caustic comedy into a production entitled *Dem Two in Canada*.

Children's theatre and popular drama were not the only areas of engagement for the theatre over the years. BTC also felt an obligation and a responsibility to present the classics—both Black and white. Lorraine Hansberry's benchmark play *A Raisin in the Sun*, opened in New York in 1958 and directed by Lloyd Richards, could now be classified as a play that has entered the repertory of classical Black drama. The play had not been given a Canadian production in Toronto when Vera Cudjoe chose to do it in 1978. The production featured Jackie Richardson and Arlene Duncan and was directed by Bobby Ghisays from Jamaica. It was a critical as well as a popular success. Similarly, the decision to adapt Shakespeare's *A Midsummer Night's Dream* and place it in a Caribbean setting was done with a respect and understanding for the role classical theatre plays in our society. Far from bowdlerizing the script, Azra Francis, who directed the production and who is a member of the Drama Department at the University of Windsor, set about to emphasize the cross-cultural potential inherent in the play without changing one word. The production received a Dora Mavor Moore Award in the category of Innovation and Artistic Excellence and was an historic breakthrough in the area of *non-traditional and colour-blind* casting, which is a topic of increasing concern among Canadian theatre directors and university drama departments.

The company has also not failed in its obligation to develop and present new Canadian plays over the years. In addition to the children's plays previously mentioned, a short list would include: *Layers* by Vilbert Cambridge, *Changes* by Peter Robinson, the collectively written *Bathurst Street, One More Stop on the Freedom Train* by Leon Bibb with musical direction by Joe Sealy, and *The African Roscius (Being the Life and Times of Ira Aldridge)* by Robin Breon.

In looking at the wide diaspora that makes up the cultural heritage of Black people's artistic voice throughout the world, a person must note that Black Theatre Canada has consistently been on the cutting edge of this movement in Canada. In 1986 the theatre helped to initiate and organize the Arts Against Apartheid Festival which brought to Toronto Archbishop Desmond Tutu from South Africa and international human rights activist Harry Belafonte. As part of their contribution to the festival BTC presented the play *Under Exposure* by Lisa Evans, a play that particularly emphasizes the women's struggle against apartheid in South Africa.

It should be clear at this point that my research has barely begun, relatively speaking, and that little other research has been carried out so far on Black theatre in Canada. Because of that, and my close association with Black Theatre Canada as administrative director and co-producer from 1981 through 1987, I have chosen to focus on only a small part of the history of Black theatre in Canada. There are additional organizations with parallel historical developments that also deserve mentioning; among them are Jeff Henry and the founding of Theatre Fountainhead in Toronto, Clarence Bayne's work with Black Theatre Workshop in Montreal, and the Black Cultural Centre of Halifax. But even this selects only three. There are numerous other areas where research can be done.

In conclusion, it is my feeling that a paper on this topic would not be complete without some reference to the status of Black theatre artists in Canada today. Our society is increasingly multi-racial in its composition, and the performing arts in this country should not fail to reflect that fact. We need to provide greater opportunities for visible minorities in this country to participate in the mainstream of Canadian cultural and artistic life. In the next few months, the Canadian Actor's Equity Association has announced that it will sponsor a national symposium on the topic of non-traditional and cross-cultural casting in the theatre. The University of Guelph was one of the first in this country to announce to the student body that they have officially adopted the policy of colour-blind casting in an effort to encourage visible minority participation in the theatre program there. These are steps in the right direction but there is more that can be done.

We should recognize that inclusion of visible minorities within the various Canadian theatres at all levels of production, including administrative, artistic, and technical areas, should be looked upon as a unique opportunity to enrich our cultural heritage and to enable the theatre to offer a true reflection of Canadian society. The results will include an expansion of the appeal of cultural institutions and a broadening of the audience base; needless to say for those with a practical mind: an increase in box office revenue.

To further this end, there is also a need to implement some kind of affirmative action program throughout the theatre arts industry. Institutions such as the Stratford and Shaw Festivals should be especially sensitive to the training and nurturing of talented actors and stage people who are from visible minorities. In addition, there should be some visible minority representation on the various arts councils and agencies (including the Ontario Arts Council and the Canada Council) that are so important in the area of funding and cultural policy making. Finally, special attention and support should be given to those organizations that have consistently provided a platform for the cultural expression of visible minorities in Canada. If I might use as an example the location where I work, hence with which I am most familiar, the various councils of Metropolitan Toronto and the Province of Ontario Government should be called upon to assist in providing proper housing for such organizations in the same substantial way they have come forward for numerous other artistic groups and social service institutions.

The history of theatre in Canada has been enhanced from its earliest beginnings by the contributions made by Black artists. With fair and equitable support and encouragement, this important segment of our society will continue to flourish and make many additional contributions in the years ahead.

(1988)

Notes

The following individuals have been extremely helpful in my research: Herbert Whittaker, drama critic emeritus, *The Globe and Mail*; Sydney Johnson, drama critic emeritus, *Montreal Daily Star*; Sylvia Warner of Montreal; Vera Cudjoe, founder and executive director of Black Theatre Canada; Azra Francis, professor of drama, University of Windsor; and Anton Wagner, associate editor of the *World Encyclopedia of Contemporary Theatre*.

[1] Colin "Cool" Burgess is the subject of a series of articles in the *Toronto Evening Telegram* which have been reprinted in a pamphlet, a copy of which is held in the theatre collection of the Metropolitan Toronto Library (O'Neill 43, 110).

Works Cited

Hill, Errol. *Shakespeare in Sable, A History of Black Shakespearean Actors.* Amherst, MA: U of Massachusetts P, 1984.

Johnson, Sydney. *Montreal Daily Star*, Apr. 1948: n.p.

O'Neill, Patrick B. *A History of Theatrical Activity in Toronto, Canada, from its Beginnings to 1858.* Diss. Louisiana State U, 1973. Ann Arbor: UMI, 1975.

Powell, S. Morgan. *Montreal Daily Star* 28 Feb. 1942: n.p.

Robeson, Paul. *Paul Robeson Speaks, Writings, Speeches, Interviews (1918-1974).* Ed. Phillip S. Foner. Larchmont, NY: Brunner/Mazel, 1978.

Shreve, Dorothy Shadd. *The AfriCanadian Church: A Stabilizer.* Jordan Station: Paideia, 1983.

Whittaker, Herbert. *Montreal Gazette* 8 May 1942: 2.

———. *Montreal Gazette* 12 Apr. 1948: 6.

Must All Blackness Be American?
Locating Canada in Borden's *Tightrope Time*,
or Nationalizing Gilroy's *The Black Atlantic*

by George Elliott Clarke

For Blair Arnold States (1959-2001)[1]

Preface

As I suggested in "Contesting a Model Blackness" [in *Odysseys Home*], a primary ontological conundrum to confront the analyst of African-Canadian literature is as obvious as it is invidious: How Canadian is it? The question is insidious, but it cannot be peremptorily dismissed, for the literature is awash in African-American and Caribbean influences. These "presences" are so palpable, so pervasive, that the literature may seldom seem "Canadian" (whatever that means) at all. This essay explores, then, the supposed alterity of African-Canadian literature, given its boldfaced absorption of African-American literary modes and models. Yet, it also scrutinizes the manner in which one specific writer, Walter M. Borden, produces *African-Canadianité* within his text, chiefly, by revising an African-American mentor. I conclude by reading Paul Gilroy's thesis *The Black Atlantic: Modernity and Double Consciousness* (1993), in the light of Borden's postcolonial practice, to examine the points where Gilroy's pronounced anti-nationalism fails to be practicable.

I

Until the onset of major black immigration from the Caribbean Basin in the mid-1950s, European Canadians imagined African Canadians as once-and-always Americans. In a 1956 magazine article, Edna Staebler ventures that some Black Nova Scotians "had a broad Southern accent" (qtd. in Dillard 517), even though the last considerable migration of African Americans to Nova Scotia occurred during the War of 1812. Two generations later, the U.S.-born, Canadian literary scholar Leslie Sanders charges that "the Canadian literary and media establishment... too often chooses to read race through the American situation..." (2). If Canadians have viewed blacks as misplaced Americans, African Americans have tended to annex African Canadians within their dominant cultural matrix. Thus, in his biography of the great African American intellectual W.E.B. Du Bois, historian David Levering Lewis asserts, with admirable aplomb, that Du Bois's Cambridge, Massachusetts landlords, John and

Mary Taylor, were "African-Americans originally from Nova Scotia" (84). African-American film historian Donald Bogle remarks that Oscar Micheaux's silent feature *The Brute* (1920) "featured boxer Sam Langford" (xvii), but Bogle overlooks Langford's Nova Scotian nativity. The Canadian backgrounds of painters Robert Duncanson and Edward M. Bannister are granted in Cedric Dover's *American Negro Art* (1960), but they remain strictly "American Negroes" (25, 27, 11). The erasures continue. The 1996 Filmakers Library catalogue lists Africadian Sylvia Hamilton's National Film Board of Canada documentary "Speak It! From the Heart of Black Nova Scotia" (1993) under the rubric "African-American Studies" (2). At other times, African Americans reject African Canadians as representing some aberrant version of *blackness*. Thus, U.S. historian Robin Winks tells us that "Reverend Wilton R. Boone, who came from Massachusetts, returned there because he found the customs of the country [African Baptist Nova Scotia] too different to accept" (346).

These bold denials of what I term *African-Canadianité* illuminate the dynamic dilemma of African-Canadian culture. Euro-Canadian critics often consider it as *Other*, while African-American (and Caribbean) critics read it—unabashedly—as a bastard version of their own. To complicate matters further, African Canadians often utilize African-American texts and historical-cultural icons to define African-Canadian experience (which can seduce the unwary into believing that no uniquely African-Canadian perspective exists).[2] Examples are legion. In the pages of the *Atlantic Advocate*, a black community newspaper issued in Halifax, Nova Scotia, between 1915 and 1917, one finds the poetry of African-American writer Paul Laurence Dunbar juxtaposed with surveys of race progress in the United States. In October 1968, Stokeley Carmichael (Kwame Turé), the charismatic Black Power orator, toured Halifax, unnerving whites and inspiring blacks to adopt militant stances, a process intensified by the visit, the following month, of two members of the radical, U.S.-based Black Panther Party.[3] Spectacularly, in Toronto, in May 1992, black youths rioted in sympathy with those who had taken to the streets in Los Angeles. Awad El Karim M. Ibrahim reports, in his 2000 sociological study "'Hey, ain't I Black too?': The Politics of Becoming Black," that "a group of continental *francophone African* youths, living in a metropolitan city in southwestern Ontario" (111, italics added), in the latter 1990s, demonstrated "an *identification* with and a *desire* for North American Blackness" (111, italics in original). Remarkably, the youths articulate a *specific* interest in *African-American* cultural styles. One stresses that "Black Canadian youths are influenced by the *Afro-Americans* because of popular " culture" (124); another announces, bluntly, "We identify ourselves more with the Blacks of America" (125).

Too, most African-Canadian writers, whether native-born or immigrant, eye African-American culture with envy and desire. Novelist Cecil Foster, a Barbados native, defends the attractiveness of African-American culture for African Canadians, stressing that, if Black Canadian artists have developed African-American sensibilities in place of a strong Canadian consciousness, well, *c'est la vie*.

> Also, I do not have any problem whatsoever in laying claim to black icons from any place in the world. I feel they are all common property and we can use them…. Should I disown a Martin Luther King or a Malcolm X? Other cultures don't. English writers—even those who are living here in Canada—can deal with Chaucer and the pre-Chaucerian writers, and Shakespeare. (21)

Rejecting interviewer Donna Nurse's argument that "African-American culture fails to reflect accurately the black Canadian experience," Foster insists that "the reality for many blacks in Canada may be closer to what they see in the streets of New York or Los Angeles than what many people assume as being their reality" (21). Given the gravitational attractiveness of Black America and the repellent force of frequently racist Anglo-Canadian (and Québécois *de souche*) nationalisms, African-Canadian writers feel themselves caught between the Scylla of an essentially U.S.-tinctured cultural nationalism and the Charybdis of their marginalization within Canadian cultural discourses that perceive them as "alien."[4] Hence, African-Canadian writers are forced to question the extent and relevance of their Canadianness (that notoriously inexpressible quality).

Yet, African Canadians cannot avoid assimilating African-American influences, for both African Canada and African America were forged in the crucible of the slave trade, an enterprise the British aided, abetted, and affirmed, then suppressed, then finally abolished in 1833. Before the American Revolution, New World Africans—both slaves and freeborn—were probably traded (or migrated) up and down the Atlantic coast, given the existence of New World African English in both the American South and Nova Scotia.[5] Linguist J.L. Dillard confirms that "the literary evidence… provides a clear picture of a continuum of eighteenth, nineteenth, and twentieth century Black English from the American South to Nova Scotia, with no great break in such places as New York City, Boston and Connecticut…" (517).[6] Thus, both African Canada and African America originated in the working out of the global fate of the British Empire; both arose (with the exception of communities situated in Hispanic and francophone locales) in a colonial, English milieu.[7]

Certainly, anglophone African Canada can trace its origins to the arrival, following the American Revolution, of roughly 3,400 African Americans (or "Anglo-Africans," to use the nineteenth-century term). These Black Loyalists opposed the Revolution, supported Britain, and, in the aftermath of the republican victory, were accorded refuge in Nova Scotia and New Brunswick. Significantly, those who did not come as the chattel of white Loyalists, but as free persons—the majority—did so because they rejected a Revolution waged to secure a theoretically egalitarian society which still promised to oppress people of African (and First Nations) ancestry. Another 2,000 African Americans were settled in Maritime Canada following the War of 1812, while tens of thousands of others found asylum in Montréal, southern Ontario, and even Saltspring Island, British Columbia, in the years between the passage of the Fugitive Slave Law (1850) and the end of the American Civil War (1865). African Canada was created, then, by the struggle to extinguish slavery—both in

British North America (where it had "withered away" by the early 1800s, while still remaining legal) and the United States—and to secure a free "homeland" for blacks. It is, then, a kind of inchoate, New World version of Liberia, the African "Canaan" or "free state" organized by anti-slavery African Americans.

Too, African Canada and African America share a history of marginality that has impinged on the constructions of their literatures. Both entities resist the fugues of racial erasure indulged in by mainstream Canadian and American critics. African-American *and* African-Canadian writers create "texts that are double-voiced in the sense that their literary antecedents are both white and black [texts], but also modes of figuration lifted from the black vernacular tradition" (Gates xxiii). For both *états*—African Canada and African America—the development of usable identities, in the face of strong, countervailing, imperial(ist) influences, has driven their histories. Close readings of African-Canadian literature can spotlight, moreover, the manner in which post-colonial theory can be applied to ever-smaller units of "mass" identity. For one thing, ethnic texts are, writes Joseph Pivato, "on the periphery of this North American margin," Canada, which "is itself marginal" from "the perspective of the literary traditions of Europe…" (44). Hence, as Canada seeks to establish its difference from the United States, so does Québec confront English Canada, and so do, in turn, Haïtian emigrés challenge the dominant Québécois culture.

II

This constant regression of post-colonial politics, its shrinkage about each particularity, also governs the construction of African-Canadian literature. This point is underlined by a contemporary Africadian drama, *Tightrope Time: Ain't Nuthin' More Than Some Itty Bitty Madness between Twilight and Dawn* (1986), by Walter M. Borden (b. 1942), an Africadian poet and actor of African-American descent. Borden proves himself to be a deft post-colonial exploiter of the "parent" culture of African America, one who engenders a Canadian *différence* (that race-conflicted, native sensibility), even while he confiscates significant African-American intertexts. In Borden, one finds, as does Margery Fee in her analysis of Australian/Aboriginal literary duality, "the use of repetition to effect a reversal… [T]hrough signifying, power relations are changed through the signifier's clever (mis)use of someone else's words" (18-19). Borden pursues a tradition in which Canadian writers strive "to forge new meanings out of foreign links and foreign chains" (Trehearne 320).

A truly one-man show, *Tightrope Time* was selected to represent Canada at the International Multicultural Festival in Amsterdam in 1987. Composed of two acts (of fourteen and nine scenes respectively), the drama's printed text of 1986 includes a dozen photographs of Borden playing each of the drama's twelve characters. (In order of appearance, they are the Host, the Old Man, the Minister of Justice, the Minister of Health and Welfare, the Child, the Old Woman, the Pastor, the Minister of Defence, the Minister of the Interior, Adie, Ethiopia [a "drag queen"], and Chuck.) *Tightrope Time* does not stage a single protagonist, but rather a *bizarrerie* of speakers delivering a pot-pourri of monologues, blending song, poetry, and prose. This *bigarré* semi-musical, blending Jacques Brel *chansons*, African-American spirituals and blues, Top 40 pop (circa 1978), and other music, is unified, though, by recurrent discussions of identity and consciousness. These overarching interests are broached and buttressed by felicitously utilized African-American interpolations.

Principally, Borden sounds the work of celebrated playwright Lorraine Hansberry (1931-65), both directly and indirectly. Hansberry's best-known work, *A Raisin in the Sun* (1959), treats the desire of the Younger family to escape the claustrophobic poverty of their apartment, where "[t]*he sole natural light the family may enjoy in the course of a day is only that which fights its way through [a] little window*" (12, italics in original). Borden bypasses this limited setting to explore, instead, "the mansions of my mind" (13). Hansberry regards the move from a blighted apartment to a hitherto segregated suburban neighbourhood as illustrative of the progressive amelioration of the Youngers' and, allegorically, the African-American, condition. Borden evades such plain social realism, however, opting instead for intellectual abstractions. His difference is enunciated at once. *A Raisin in the Sun* opens with the preparation of a breakfast of fried eggs, but "Tightrope Time" debuts with the Host's *recollection* of a like breakfast as he launches into a philosophical reverie. Borden's first, indirect allusion to Hansberry's work stresses, then, not the nobility-versus-indignity it privileges, but rather the casualness of causality:

> Born on some forgotten *FRY*day,
> That's *FRY*day with a '*y*',
> Not *FRI*day with an '*i*',
> At half past discontent,
> Mama sat down on life's sidewalk,
> Spread her legs
> And pushed one ain't-no-problem time;
> And spewed me there
> Where *MAYBE-YOU-WILL-CHILE BOULEVARD*
> Cuts across *MAYBE-YOU-WON'T-CHILE AVENUE*,
> And Indifference sauntered by
> To serve as midwife,
> To wrap me in my soul and say:
> You are Nature's love-chile—
> And Freedom is your father. (14)

Borden's speaker is disengaged from active, socio-political struggle; rather, he emphasizes, in an almost neo-Neo-Platonist manner, the "many mansions/in the complex of my mind" (13). The gallery of speakers in *Tightrope Time* depicts a multiply divided consciousness. The function of the Host is, in fact, to provide the cranial space—a cabinet of Dr Borden, if one likes—in which the motley'd monologuers can assemble. If Hansberry promotes laudable black bourgeois aspiration, Borden expresses a kind of quixotic black psychoanalysis. If Hansberry may be related to the liberal "uplift" slogans of the early twentieth-century African-American leader Booker

T. Washington, Borden seems closer to the existentialist *cum* Freudian stance of Frantz Fanon.

Borden imports Hansberry directly into his work in 1.2, where he rechristens the "Hermit"—a character from an early draft of *Raisin*[8]—as the "Old Man." Save for this single—and signal—alteration, Borden reprints Hansberry's speech for the "Hermit" with uncompromised fidelity: "And so, to escape time, I threw my watch away. I even made a ceremony of it. I was on a train over a bridge… and I held it out the door and dropped it" (Borden 16; Hansberry, *Be* 3). The arty speech that Hansberry omitted from her most successful play is precisely (or perversely) the one that Borden feels compelled to use in his own.[9] Tellingly, rather than appropriating a discourse from the finished, realist version of *Raisin*, Borden cribs Hansberry's more philosophical musing on time. Even as he honours Hansberry, Borden dissents from her dramaturgy, scribing a metaphysical stance to her more physical focus on place and race.

Yet, Borden's predilection for ideas over ideals manifests his *Canadian* sensibility, for Canadian poets have often mingled the "Aesthetic" with "committed and realistic poetry" (Trehearne 314). The result is what Québécois literary scholar Clément Moisan calls "strange and esoteric poetry" (30), and what Anglo-Québécois critic Louis Dudek names as "poetry… almost surrealist in its contortions, and well-nigh private in its subjectivity" (161). Indeed, "its metaphysical searchings and symbolic profundities cannot hope for a contact with… 'the common reader'" (Dudek 161). For Norman Newton, Canadian poetry stresses "a fondness for ornate and colourful language" (8). Anglo-Canadian poetry tends to exalt the absurd and the abstract—even when the poets themselves believe they are being plain and down-to-earth. In Anglo-Canadian poetry, the "vernacular" is interpreted by professors of literature. Accordingly, Borden's verse, though accessible, ransacks the Byzantine lexicon of Beat cant as often as it does that of black populist directness: "let emptiness come sneak into my solitude/& ravage all my dreams/& bittersweet rememberings of yesterday/ when all my thoughts were young as innocence itself/& love & understanding flowed from me like *MAN-AH* was completely in control" (62). Suitably then, Borden opts to read Hansberry in academicist terms.[10] He closes his use of her Hermit (his Old Man), then, by calling for the playing of a song, "The Old Folk," recorded by Brel, accompanied by the sound of a clock ticking "*in syncopation with the music*" (16, italics in original). These absurdist touches are Borden's invention. Hence, *Tightrope Time* enacts a revisioning of Hansberry's *Raisin*, dismissing her "realism" and ghetto setting to dramatize, instead, the unreal "inscape" of identity.

Borden's adoption of Hansberry's Hermit hints, too, that *Tightrope Time* is only tangentially about "race;" or, rather, that it avoids dissecting "race" in any stock sociological-empirical fashion. For instance, the Old Man's penultimate speech in 1.2 turns, not on explicit concerns about "race" or racism, but, instead, on one concrete and two abstract nouns—*piece(s)*, *time*, and *value*—a trinity of tropes that presides over the play: "I am afraid men invent time*PIECES* [time*pieces*]; they do not invent time. We may give time its dimensions and meaning;[,] we may make it worthless or important or absurd or crucial. But,[ ] ultimately,[ ] I am afraid it has a value of its own" (Borden

16; Hansberry, *Be* 4). Borden absorbs Hansberry's academic musings and terms, detecting in them corollaries for his interests. This fact is clarified by his use of the word(s) *piece(s)*. Though the term occurs in contexts that can allude to Hansberry, they are wholly Borden's own. In 1.4, the Minister of Health and Welfare relates that his dream "dried up, just like that raisin in the sun" (24), a clear reference to Hansberry as well as to African-American poet Langston Hughes (1902-67);[11] then the Minister continues on to assert that "painful thoughts rummage through/the few last pieces of my heart" (24) and that he seeks "bits and pieces of love/that I have known" (25). Borden shifts from the specific concerns of both Hansberry and Hughes to anatomize alienation. In fact, the African Americans are sounded only after the Minister declares that "this celebration is not so much an historical documentation of the quest of a people for a place in the Nova Scotian or indeed the Canadian mosaic, as it is an illumination of the resiliency of the human spirit" (22). An abstract universalism takes precedence, thus, over African-American utterance—even though, paradoxically, Hansberry herself is the source of the notion of "the resiliency of... this thing called the human spirit" (Borden 80; Hansberry, *Be* 256). This pattern recurs in 1.4, where Hansberry is again directly quoted. This time, Borden seizes a passage from Hansberry's *The Sign in Sidney Brustein's Window* (1964), uttered by Brustein, a white ex-fighter for social justice, who feels compelled to re-enter the fray:

> I care. I care about it all. It takes too much energy *not* to care. Yesterday, I counted twenty-six gray hairs on the top of my head all from trying *not* to care…. The *why* of why we are here is an intrigue for adolescents; the *how* is what must command the living. Which is why I have lately become an insurgent again. (Borden 25; Hansberry, *Be* xvi)

Just as Hansberry's Brustein continues to struggle for social liberation, so does Borden's Minister of Health and Welfare, this Canadian liberal, decide to shore pieces—of love, of heart—against his potential ruin. Borden's transference of words written for a Euro-American character to the mouth of a Black Canadian, is, once again, a universalist gesture. His audacious reconfiguration of Hansberry's words accents their innate universality. Racial identities are collapsed within his enveloping view that "the human spirit has no special resting place. It will find a lodging wherever it is received" (22). Thus, Borden dislodges Hansberry from an easy essentialism or empty liberalism, choosing to use her words to gird his interest in the "mansions of the mind," that is to say, the multiple addresses where "the human spirit" may dwell.

Toward the conclusion of the play, Borden utilizes the term *pieces* one last time, citing Hansberry's rhetorical question "*Life?*" and her reply, "Ask those who have tasted of it in pieces rationed out by enemies" (Borden 80; Hansberry, *Be* 256; italics in originals). Ironically, *Tightrope Time* is itself just such a *piece* of theatre, just such a "*PIECE OF RESISTANCE*" (62, italics in original), to use an epithet that Borden ascribes to Ethiopia, his transvestite character, for it flouts both racism and homophobia.

18   African-Canadian Theatre

This last point necessitates a brief examination of Borden's use of *value*, another term that he teases from Hansberry, his putative precursor. His assault on prejudice is predicated upon its reduction of the worth of human beings. When Borden utilizes (with slight amendments) Hansberry's comment that time "has a value of its own" (Borden 16; Hansberry, *Be* 4), he lets it follow the Host's act of satiric self-evaluation:

> I read the other day
> That, on the open market,
> I'm worth about five ninety,
> Allowing for inflation.
> But that's alright—
> I'd hate to think
> That I was priced beyond accessibility. (13)

To Hansberry's insight that time possesses its own value, independent of socially imposed, ideological criteria, Borden adds the body. He goes on to besiege racial (and, thus, physical) devaluations throughout his play:

> A second glance, however,
> Reveals a flaw in pigmentation,
> So, regretfully you must look for me
> In the *reduced for clearance* section. (13)

In 1.7, the Host recalls a childhood incident in which his mixed-race heritage resulted in his receiving a "high"—but unsought and racially inflected—e/valuation:

> i knew that there was something wrong
> the day i watched my living room become
> an auction block;
> [and a visitor]
>   ...called my blue eyes,
>   honey hair and
>   mellow/yellow presence
>   A WONDERMENT! (30, italics in original)

Throughout *Tightrope Time*, Borden juxtaposes "face" value and "soul value," specifying that the oppressed are those "who have no place/the ones who have no face" (32), whose value, then, is little. They are "*CHEAP GOODS*" (34, italics in original) to be bought up by Death. In 1.10, the Host remembers an Old Woman who spent her days "*puttin' the pieces together*" of a patchwork quilt (36, italics in original), and whose speech reiterates the connections between time and value. The Old Woman notes that "*the young folks*" are "*wastin' all that precious time/at tryin' to be what other folkses want*" (38, italics in original). The loss of time, of life, is affiliated with trying to live according to false notions of one's worth. The Minister of the Interior, in 1.14, restores value, lustre, to *blackness* by producing a roster of worthies whom, he alleges, have been wrongly claimed to be white, including Queen Charlotte Sophia (the spouse of King George III), the Queen of Sheba, Ludwig von Beethoven, and Charles

XIV of Sweden, to name but a few (55-6). Poetically, Borden "borrows back" these "credits to the race."

Not only does Borden rescue the devalued black body, he also redeems that of the homosexual. If act 1 centres—albeit usually obliquely—on "race," act 2 considers sexuality—the repressed side of black self-consciousness. Here Borden revalues, in order, Adie, a female prostitute; Ethiopia, a Queer transvestite; and Chuck, a hustler. Ethiopia disparages hypocritical, bourgeois sexual mores, declaiming, "& *HAPPY DAYS*/unsanitized for early prime time viewing/meant more than suckin' lollipops out back behind some diner/but no one really thought that we was fuckin' up/*TRADITION*/cuz/no one saw/no decrease in/the surplus population" (62, italics in original). Chuck augments the currency of his Queer body by coupling coitus with money:

> I don't fuck for I.O.U.'s
> > for Master Charge
> > or Visa
> Just hard old cash… (65)

In a sense, here, Borden conducts a radical raid on Hansberry, for he drafts her voice, that is to say, her insight into *value*, for a liberatory movement for which it was not, perhaps, primordially intended.

The most ostentatious broadside against devaluation in act 2 speaks, though, to "race." At the conclusion of 2.7, a "tired and beaten" black mother, whose innocent son has been slain by a paranoid white man,

> Slowly turn[s] the pages
> Of some book,
> And look[s] at all the faces
> Of those selected few
> Thought worthy of being voted
> As the Mother of the Year…
> Worthy
> Because of all her suffering…
>
> And she tently [*sic*] [takes] a pencil
> And mark[s] the letter X
> Beside the picture of
> Rose Kennedy! (77)

The passage is a damning indictment of self-devaluation—the manner in which oppression replicates itself.

While Hansberry becomes a useful means of debuting the motifs of fragmentation (*piece*[*s*]), time, and value, Borden domesticates or nationalizes her work, wresting it from its African-American context and recasting it in Canadian terms. For instance, he transforms her sentence "O, the things that we have learned in this unkind house that we have to tell the world about" (Borden 79; Hansberry, *Be* 256) from a commission to young African-American writers to tell of the African-American experience into a commission to *all* to practise humane behaviour. Specifically, he translates her metaphor for a racist America, that "unkind house," into a metaphor for the "cage" that is the self-imprisoned consciousness (Borden 79). The resistance valued by Borden is not achieved merely by denouncing social ills, but also by refusing any facile quotation of Hansberry. He changes the name of one of her characters, alters, by proxy, the race of another, and quarantines her more abstract, less social realist, work. By recontextualizing her work to suit his own needs, Borden renders Hansberry a "Canadian" writer.

III

Borden's reforms of Hansberry, his major African-American influence, must be read in the context of an intra-racial post-coloniality. Certainly, his emphasis on "piecing together" his patchwork drama reinforces Paul Gilroy's notion that "even where African-American forms are borrowed and set to work in new locations they have often been deliberately reconstructed in novel patterns that do not respect their originators' proprietary claims…" (98). Moreover, Borden's post-coloniality, *vis-à-vis* African-American texts, pushes him to adopt a contestatory stance, for this is the condition of the ex-centric writer. No matter how deep lies the commitment to imitate the "parent" culture, any "imitation" must always be different—and critical—because of its temporal lateness, its automatic status as "post." Max Dorsinville maintains that all emerging literatures suffer a similar condition of lateness. Yet, his notion that postcolonial writers are merely "indigenous writers hypnotized by the cult of metropolitan 'models'" (201) is contestable. The standard practice of these writers—which Borden's (mis)use of Hansberry illustrates—is to revise original influences or intertexts. (Cogent here is Trehearne's proviso that "Influence" can be a "dependence" "avidly sought, a life-giving transfusion of order and authority when no such order [is] provided by the [native] environment, or by the present means of mastering it" [8].) In other words, Borden does not—and cannot—read Hansberry in the same way as would an African American. His acts of quotation represent not, then, abject capitulation to metropolitan forces (Halifax succumbing—finally—to New York City), but (im)polite subversion; his "lateness" is a marginal position that permits radical reinterpretation of the "original" source. Eyed from this perspective, the margin is a time-devoid centre in which literary forms and movements coexist in democratic chaos; it becomes a location where the neoclassical can jar against the surreal, the sonnet clang against the haiku, and dead authors possess the living. Thus, Borden's text can be read as exemplifying the ability of temporally "late" Canadian writers to adapt a variety of European and American forms and influences to their unique contexts—of environment, history, and language, including different forms of English. *Tightrope Time* testifies to such hybridity or *bricolage*. This peripherally situated text becomes a homeplace where African American literature—in its northern, existentialist exile—is assimilated, domesticated, into a Canadian context. Borden's relationship to Hansberry affirms, too, Harold Bloom's thesis regarding, as Stephen Sicari puts it, "an Oedipal struggle between a great precursor poet and his follower" (38). If "the later poet looks for (and discovers) places where the precursor fails to communicate to a [contemporary] reader… and requires 'updating' by the [contemporary] poet" (Sicari 221 n6), then Borden amends Hansberry similarly, translating her (African-)American obsessions into (African-)Canadian ones. He observes, wryly, that "Black folks always seem to get those/Hand-me-down revisions!" (72). Borden's rewriting of Hansberry demands a theory of post-colonial "placement" and "displacement," one which recognizes that the supposed recipient of meaning (the "colonial") can instead become its bestower (the resister, the newly subjectivized).

Gilroy himself needs to tussle more muscularly with this imperial-colonial dialectic. He argues that texts like that of Borden represent the "unashamedly hybrid character… of black Atlantic cultures," which thus confound "any simplistic (essentialist or anti-essentialist) understanding of the relationship between racial identity and racial non-identity" (99). He forgets, though, that cultural nationalism never entirely evaporates, even when techniques of "creolisation, métissage, mestizaje, and hybridity" (2) are in play, as in Borden. *Au contraire*, it is exactly the use of forms of *bricolage* that allows new understandings of the native (or post-colonial) culture to be articulated. When Borden reads Hansberry (and Hughes and James Weldon Johnson)[12] into his own Canadian text, his *Africadianité* is not reified but reinforced.

Borden's practice serves to highlight, then, a few of the *a priori* aporias in Gilroy's vaunted text, *The Black Atlantic* (1993), which undertakes, like *Tightrope Time*, to dissent from "Americocentricity" (Gilroy 191). The notion that authentic *blackness*— or *Africanité*—is implicated, ontologically and epistemologically, with some subtle sense of 100 percent Americanism challenges all other would-be national(ist) versions of *blackness*. Gilroy attempts to dismantle the "U.S. first" conception of "blackness" by constructing a "transcultural, international formation [called] the black Atlantic" (4), which consists of African communities in the United States, the Caribbean, Britain, and Africa. While Gilroy omits Canada (this gap in his map replicates a suspiciously "Americocentric" blindness), his "Pan-Atlanticism" is intended as a panacea for the "ever-present danger" of "ethnic absolutism" (5), or larval nationalism, especially "the easy claims of African-American exceptionalism" (4). Yet, Gilroy's project is fraught with contradiction. His very formulation, "the black Atlantic," resurrects a Pan-Africanism that almost dare not speak its name. As well, his decentring of African-American culture is intended to shift attention to the Caribbean-British contributions to Pan-African culture. Fundamentally, then, Gilroy, like Borden, poses this question: Must all blackness be American? But Gilroy's attempt to naysay this interrogative, while simultaneously vetoing cultural nationalism, scores his project with irrepressible self-negations.

Blatantly, Gilroy ups old-fashioned nationalism when he announces that "the dependence of blacks in Britain on black cultures produced in the new world has recently begun to change" (86). He relishes "the current popularity of [pop music acts] Jazzie B and Soul II Soul, Maxi Priest, Caron Wheeler, Monie Love, the Young Disciples, and others in the United States" because it confirms that during the 1980s "black British cultures ceased to simply mimic or reproduce wholesale forms, styles, and genres which had been lovingly borrowed, respectfully stolen, or brazenly high-jacked [*sic*] from blacks elsewhere" (86). This inchoately neo-nativist pronouncement denies the truth that, as Borden's work demonstrates, utterances of "un-American" *blackness* often represent deliberate "deformations" or reformulations of African-American cultural productions (which Gilroy admits when he treats the "hybridity" of black Atlantic cultures). [13]

In addition, Gilroy's effort to dispense with African-American parochialism is complicated by his decision to focus his analyses on African-American writers and intellectuals, namely, Frederick Douglass, Martin Robinson Delany (who may also be classified as African-Canadian), Du Bois, Richard Wright, James Baldwin, and Toni Morrison. Though Gilroy essays, valiantly, to set these figures in a Pan-Atlantic context, he nevertheless succumbs to ideas that, once again, Americanize blackness. For example, Gilroy lauds Richard Wright's insight that "the word Negro in America means something not racial or biological, but something *purely social*, something made in the United States" (qtd. in Gilroy 149, italics in original), seeing in it an "anti-essentialist conception of racial identity" (149). But if the Negro is, as Wright thought, "America's metaphor" (qtd. in Gilroy 149), then is not all *blackness* (i.e., *négritude*) deemed American? If so, then (an American) essentialism lives. Gilroy even urges that "in Wright's mature position, the Negro is no longer just America's metaphor but rather a central symbol in the psychological, cultural, and political systems of the West as a whole" (159). An American conception of *blackness* is made to dominate the entire Occident, thus situating U.S. definitions at the centre of diasporic African experience, the very fate that Gilroy had sallied forth to avoid. The only possible counterweight to this *de facto* dictatorship of influence is precisely the cultural nationalism that Gilroy, haphazardly and haplessly, both disparages and embraces, but that Borden, quietly, consistently—"Canadianly"—employs.

Despite the blithe assurance of some liberal theorists that the post-national Brave New World Order has arrived, Gilroy's infuriatingly mercurial struggle to displace "Americocentrism" with his dream of "the black Atlantic" demonstrates that nationalism persists. For one thing, as Elizabeth Alexander sees, "there is a place for a bottom line, and the bottom line… argues that different groups possess sometimes subconscious collective memories which are frequently forged and maintained through a 'storytelling tradition,' however difficult that may be to pin down, as well as through individual experience" (94). Though the scholarly voodoo of the notion of "collective memories" is regrettable, Alexander reveals a strong reason for the continued vibrancy of "tradition," of group identities, namely, the primacy of shared (narrative) experience as the locus of "national" feeling. Pivato concurs with this precept, urging "the history of this century demonstrates that a distinctive culture is vital to the life of a people; it survives beyond language, beyond geography and beyond political states" (252). What one must seek is the lyricism of cultural difference, not the mere prose of cultural diversity. [14] Consequently, the canon of "African-Canadian literature" emerges when a writer or a critic declares his or her membership in that tradition. Such new canons are also created, though, through acts of resistive appropriation—the mandatory practice of Borden, the muddled practice of Gilroy. This fate cannot be evaded.[15] All narrative pursues an original identity, and poetry declares it.

This declaration can be heard within the basic lineaments of a language. It sounds even within the history of Black English in Nova Scotia—or "Africadia"…

(1996)

Notes

[1] This paper was first read on the occasion of the 13th Biennial Meeting of the Association for Canadian Studies in the United States, in Seattle, Washington, on 16 November 1995. I am indebted to Professor Joseph Pivato and to Professor Arnold "Ted" Davidson (1936-99) for their suggestions for revisions. I dedicate this essay to the memory of Blair Arnold States, my cousin and mixed-race Africadian, who could "pass" for white, but was *culturally* black, who was Canadian, but also profoundly African-American in his orientations.

[2] André Alexis believes that "black Canadians have yet to elaborate a culture strong enough to help evaluate the foreignness of foreign [i.e., American] ideas" (20). Yet, this presumed instance of Americanization is simplistic: though African-American culture enjoys wide currency among African Canadians, they—we—remain a distinct group.

[3] See Bridglal Pachai 247-9.

[4] Joseph Pivato observes that "Canadian [thematic criticism] has not been open to ethnic texts since it cannot accommodate them into such national myths as the two solitudes, the ellipse with two centres, or the garrison" (72).

[5] Dillard also states that "slaves were transferred from one place to another, as from Nova Scotia to Surinam... quite freely in the eighteenth century" (513). Before the American Revolution, then, there was likely a good measure of black travel—voluntary and involuntary—between the Thirteen Colonies and Nova Scotia.

[6] In his study of the ways in which francophone African youth in Franco-Ontarian high schools "become Blacks" (111), Awad Ibrahim demonstrates that many of his subjects "articulated their identification with Black America through the re/citation of rap [music] linguistic styles" (125). They even eschewed the "highly valued symbolic capital" of "*le français parisien* (Parisian French)" (122) in favour of "Black Stylized English" (119), a way of saying, argues Ibrahim, "'I too am Black'" (119). His study illustrates, then, the steady circulation of specifically *African-American* styled English among black newcomers to Canada, despite their francophone and direct-from-Africa backgrounds. In this new sense, too, Dillard's "continuum" of North American Black English continues...

[7] Philip Brian Harper urges that while "the situation of black Americans [cannot] be posited unproblematically as a colonial one, its historical *sine qua non*—the slave trade—can certainly be considered as a manifestation of the colonizing impulse" (253 n26).

[8] See Hansberry, *To Be Young, Gifted and Black*, 3-4.

[9] Hansberry considered her work "genuine realism," which she defined as depicting "not only what *is* but what is *possible*... because that is part of reality too" (*Be* 228). She also speculated that "ours [i.e., black theatre] ...will be a theatre *primarily* of

emotion" (*Be* 211). Hansberry's adoration of realism and empiricism explains her omission of the Hermit's unrealistic speech from *Raisin*, but this fact also throws into even starker relief Borden's inclusion of the discourse in his play and his employment of expressionist theatrical techniques and devices.

[10] I refer here to John Matthews's theory that Canadian poetry prefers "Academic" over "Popular" modes of discourse. See my article "Contesting a Model Blackness" (27-70), particularly Part III.

[11] Hansberry reproduces Hughes's famous poem "Harlem" (1951) as an epigraph to *Raisin in the Sun* (whose title is derived from a line in the poem) and also in a 1964 letter to the editor of the *New York Times* in support of the civil rights movement (*Be* 20-1). (To read a copy of the poem, see *The Langston Hughes Reader: The Selected Writings of Langston Hughes* [New York: George Braziller, 1958], p. 123). Borden also reproduces the poem in its entirety, using its hint of menace to preface the Minister of Justice's discussion of the demise of his "dream," which "had something to do with my trying, in quite a humble way, to make this world a better place in which to work—and play" (22, 24).

[12] Borden reprints the whole of "The Prodigal Son," a sermon-poem by African-American poet James Weldon Johnson (1871-1938), in 1.11, and accords this piece to the Pastor. Borden is largely faithful to Johnson's text, but he introduces a few alterations. He increases the stanza breaks, thus yielding sixteen stanzas to Johnson's thirteen. He confers extra articles, pronouns, adverbs, and adjectives upon some lines. For instance, Johnson's line "That great city of Babylon" (23) becomes, in Borden's treatment, "That great, great city of Babylon" (44). Likewise, Johnson's line "And he went to feeding swine" (24) is transformed by Borden to read, "And he went down to feeding swine" (44). Such relatively minor redactions are accompanied by three ampler interventions by Borden. Johnson's "stopped" (23) becomes "passed" in "And he passed a passer-by and he said" (Borden 44). Johnson's "you've" (25) becomes the more idiomatic "you" in "Today you got the strength of a bull in your neck" (Borden 45). Dramatically, Borden affixes two new lines to the conclusion of the penultimate stanza of Johnson's poem:

> You'll have a hand-to-hand struggle with bony Death,
> And Death is bound to win,
> *Make no mistake about it;*
> *Old bony Death is bound to win.* (Borden 45, italics added)

Borden's revisions of Johnson's already speakerly text intensify its oratorical power. Moreover, the line "In my father's house are many mansions" (Johnson 24; Borden 45) accents Borden's strategy of presenting the psyche as the "Host" of various speakers. See Borden 43-5; Johnson 21-5.

[13] Thus, Gilroy's text is an anthology of antitheses. His wilful pleasure in the success of Black British art adumbrates a vision of the resistive workings of cultural nationalism that he seeks, elsewhere, to undercut.

[14] Sneja Gunew distinguishes between *difference* and *diversity* in a vital passage in her foreword to Pivato's *Echo: Essays on Other Literatures* (1994):

> Like Homi Bhabha, my sympathies have always been with *cultural difference* as distinct from *cultural diversity*: an insistence on the untranslatability or incommensurability of cultural difference. For me, this is most clearly apparent in my own studies of Aboriginal epistemologies. I am trying to hear and acknowledge the difference rather than attempting to equate it with known elements in more familiar epistemologies. To put it another way, it is the opposite of the old humanist assumption that all human experience is essentially the same. (20-21)

[15] The construction of any particular artistic tradition requires, as well, the articulation of nationalism, even if merely *naïf*.

Works Cited

Alexander, Elizabeth. "'Can you be BLACK and look at this?': Reading the Rodney King Video(s)." *Black Male: Representations of Masculinity in Contemporary American Art.* Ed. Thelma Golden. New York: Whitney Museum of Modern Art, 1994. 91-110.

Alexis, André. "Borrowed Blackness." *This Magazine* 28.8 (May 1995): 14-20.

Bogle, Donald. Introduction. *A Separate Cinema: Fifty Years of Black Cast Posters.* By John Kisch and Edward Mapp. New York: Noonday, 1992. xiii-xxxiii.

Borden, Walter. *Tightrope Time: Ain't Nuthin' More Than Some Itty Bitty Madness Between Twilight and Dawn. Callboard* 34.2 (Sept. 1986): 8-81.

Clarke, George Elliott. "Contesting a Model Blackness: A Meditation on African-Canadian African-Americanism, or the Structures of African-Canadianité." *Odysseys Home: Mapping African-Canadian Literature.* Toronto: U of Toronto P, 2002. 27-70.

Dillard, J.L. "The History of Black English in Nova Scotia—a first step." *Revista Interamericana Review* 2.4 (Winter 1973): 507-20.

Dorsinville, Max. *Caliban Without Prospero: Essay on Québec and Black Literature.* Erin, ON: Porcépic, 1974.

Dover, Cedric. *American Negro Art.* New York: New York Graphic Society, 1960.

Dudek, Louis. "Poetry in Canada." 1962. *In Defence of Art: Critical Essays and Reviews.* By Louis Dudek. Ed. Aileen Collins. Kingston, ON: Quarry, 1988. 160-62.

Fee, Margery. "The Signifying Writer and the Ghost Reader: Mudrooroo's *Master of the Ghost Dreaming* and *Writing from the Fringe.*" *Australian and New Zealand Studies in Canada* 8 (Dec. 1992): 18-32.

Filmakers Library Catalogue. *Deep River/Strong Currents: Films and Videos about the African-American, Afro-Caribbean and African Experience.* New York: Filmakers Library, [1996].

Foster, Cecil. "A Long Sojourn." Interview with Donna Nurse. *Books in Canada* 24.6 (Sept. 1995): 18-21.

Gates, Henry Louis, Jr. *The Signifying Monkey: A Theory of Afro-American Literary Criticism.* New York: Oxford UP, 1988.

Gilroy, Paul. *The Black Atlantic: Modernity and Double Consciousness.* Cambridge, MA: Harvard UP, 1993.

Gunew, Sneja. "Foreword: Speaking to Joseph." *Echo: Essays on Other Literatures.* By Joseph Pivato. Toronto: Guernica, 1994. 7-31.

Hansberry, Lorraine. *A Raisin in the Sun*. [1959.] New York: New American Library/Signet, [1966?].

———. *To Be Young, Gifted, and Black: Lorraine Hansberry in Her Own Words*. Adapted by Robert Nemiroff. Englewood Cliffs, NJ: Prentice-Hall, 1969.

Harper, Philip Brian. "Nationalism and Social Division in Black Arts Poetry of the 1960s." *Critical Inquiry* 19.2 (Winter 1993): 234-55.

Ibrahim, Awad El Karim M. "'Hey, ain't I Black too?': The Politics of Becoming Black." *Rude: Contemporary Black Cultural Criticism*. Ed. Rinaldo Walcott. Toronto: Insomniac, 2000. 109-36.

Johnson, James Weldon. *God's Trombones: Seven Negro Sermons in Verse*. New York: Viking, 1927.

Lewis, David Levering. *W.E.B. Du Bois: Biography of a Race, 1868-1919*. New York: Holt, 1993.

Matthews, John. *Tradition in Exile: A Comparative Study of Social Influences on the Development of Australian and Canadian Poetry in the Nineteenth Century*. Toronto: U of Toronto P, 1962.

Moisan, Clément. *A Poetry of Frontiers: Comparative Studies in Quebec/Canadian Literature*. Victoria, BC: Porcépic, 1983.

Newton, Norman. "Classical Canadian Poetry and the Public Muse." 1972. *Colony and Confederation: Early Canadian Poets and Their Background*. Ed. George Woodcock. Vancouver, BC: UBC P, 1974. 7-23.

Pachai, Bridglal. *Beneath the Clouds of the Promised Land: The Survival of Nova Scotia's Blacks, Vol. II: 1800-1989*. Halifax, NS: Black Educators Association of Nova Scotia, 1990.

Pivato, Joseph. *Echo: Essays on Other Literatures*. Toronto: Guernica, 1994.

Sanders, Leslie. "Blackness Repossessed." Letter. *This Magazine* 29.2 (Aug.1995): 2.

Sicari, Stephen. *Pound's Epic Ambition: Dante and the Modern World*. SUNY Series, The Margins of Literature. [Ed.] Mihai I. Spariosu. Albany, NY: SUNY P, 1991.

Trehearne, Brian. *Aestheticism and the Canadian Modernists: Aspects of a Poetic Influence*. Montreal and Kingston, ON: McGill-Queen's UP, 1989.

Winks, Robin W. *The Blacks in Canada: A History*. 1971. Montreal and Kingston, ON: McGill-Queen's UP, 1997.

"From twisted history": Reading *Angélique*

by Alan Filewod

In the introduction to her anthology, *Testifyin': Contemporary African Canadian Drama*, Djanet Sears makes the important point that "any informal examination into Canadian Theatre will likely reveal an absence of African Canadians as contributors altogether" (i). Taking this point a step further, the absence of African-Canadian artists in the narrative of theatre history signals a more profound absence in the national imaginary. Historically, the notion of "Canadian Theatre," which conjoins two unstable terms, has always meant an imagined theatre projected within (and often inhibited by) the material theatre of the day. This idea of the imagined theatre brings into play the entire realm of theatre culture that is quoted, implied and legitimised by the theatre as it is understood at any given historical moment. At the same time, the imagined theatre brings into play the theatre that it rejects. If the theatre enacts the national imaginary, the absences which it frames—historically and materially—are equally constitutive of theatre culture. "Canadian theatre" can in this way be understood as a history of absences: the actual theatre culture of the moment always refers to an imagined theatre that defers realisation.

I make this point to introduce Lorena Gale's *Angélique*, because in both its narrative performance strategies and its production history, the play exposes the crises of contemporary Canadian theatre as it seeks to re-imagine the nation that it enacts. *Angélique* represents to my mind the most remarkable and important play staged in Canada in the late 1990s. Its vision of Canadian history is unsettling to those raised in the dominant myth of liberal multiculturalism, and its theatrical history signals alarms about the inability of Canadian theatre culture to accept radical revisioning.

Angélique is a product of the theatre enterprise that developed in Canada to model the liberal pluralist nation. Lorena Gale, herself a theatre worker, has for over twenty years pursued a career as an actor, director and now playwright in a theatre enterprise that affords few possibilities for African-Canadian women. Since an early draft of her play won a national playwriting award in 1995, it has moved through the entire realm of possibilities offered by the informal network of play development programmes that function as the dramaturgical crucible—the research and development laboratory—of Canadian theatre. *Angélique* has evolved through a long sequence of seven different workshop productions, leading to a culminating fully staged production in Alberta Theatre Projects' renowned playRites programme. The whole prehistory of *Angélique* is worth restating here, because it clearly shows on the one hand the systemisation of play development, and on the other the somewhat disconcerting end result. Here follows the production prehistory, as compiled by the playwright:

1995	Excerpt published in *Canadian Theatre Review*.
	Monologue published in *Another Perfect Piece: Monologues From Canadian Plays* (Playwrights Canada).
	Winner, Du Maurier National Playwriting Competition.
	Workshop/staged reading, Women in View Festival, Vancouver.
	Workshop/reading, Nightwood Theatre Company, Groundswell Festival, Toronto.
1996	Workshop/staged reading, Spring Writes Festival, Vancouver.
	Excerpt published in *Beyond the Pale: Dramatic Writings by First Nations Writers and Writers of Colour* (Playwrights Canada).
1997	Workshop production, On the Verge Festival, National Arts Centre, Ottawa.
	Presentation, 4th International Women Playwrights Conference, Galway, Ireland.
	Workshop production, Celafi Festival/First Afri-Canadian Playwrights Conference, Canadian Stage, Toronto.
	Production draft development, Banff Centre for the Arts, Playwrights Colony.
1998	Staged reading, Calypso Productions, Dublin, Ireland.
	Professional premiere, Pan Canadian playRites Festival, Alberta Theatre Projects, Calgary.
	Nomination, Outstanding New Play, Betty Mitchell Awards, Calgary.
2000	Journal publication, *Canadian Theatre Review* (CTR 100).
	Book publication, Playwrights Canada.

This seems, by any account, a distinguished pedigree for a new play, with prestigious publications, workshops at the National Arts Centre and Canadian Stage Company, and a premiere at the most respected new play showcase in Canada. But there are two ways to read this history. The first is as an accumulation of distinction, the second as a tier of absences. Few plays "arrive" on the canonising stage with this degree of distinction. This represents the kind of history that would seem to record the efforts and investments (of time, of labour, of creativity, and of money) of a great number of people, all of whom appear committed to putting *Angélique* on the stage. But since its Alberta premiere, *Angélique* has not appeared on a stage in Canada. It has, however, appeared twice in the United States, with productions in Detroit and New York, where, in both cases, African-American theatre is an established fact. This might seem to suggest that *Angélique* "speaks" to audiences drawn from the African diaspora, but the fact that the play appears to have better chances of production in the United States than in Canada suggests as well that it summons an *imagined* audience in Canada, that the productions that *it does not receive* are as important to an understanding of the play as those that actually take place.

Why, after such a long workshop history, has *Angélique* not been programmed on the main stage of a major theatre in Canada? We can only guess, but the expected answer would be that artistic directors are too cautious, that *Angélique*'s enactment of nation and history is too "risky." From there, it is not too far a step to surmise—perhaps cynically—that Lorena Gale has written a play that satisfies the needs of play development bodies, but not of institutional theatres. By hosting a workshop of the play, Canadian Stage receives the credit for sponsoring it without actually having to produce it or invest financial risk in it. This cynical reading implies that *Angélique* functions as a value-producing commodity in an economy of reputation.

There may be some truth in this, but I tend to another interpretation, which gives the play and the author more agency. *Angélique* is a genuinely radical statement that uses the moment of performance to destabilise the narratives that have historically secured Canadian nationhood. And in the same way, it destabilises structures of critical authority: it forces the critic, the "I" that authorises value, into a personal response. There is a moment in the first scene of the play, in which the character of François Poulin de Francheville, speaking from Gale's imagined New France in 1730, describes his first sight of Angélique, the African (descended) slave whom he has been invited to buy:

> So I said I'd take a look. What does it cost to look?
> ANGÉLIQUE *in shadows.*
> The figure of this fine creature could not but attract my particular notice. She was standing off to the side with some others. Perfectly straight... with the most elegant shapes that can be viewed in nature. Her chestnut skin shone with double lustre. Her large ebony eyes with their inward gaze. Her proud face... immobile... I don't know... (7)

In a similar complex of fascinated desire, the play itself attracts the "particular notice" of the critical eye that presumes to survey and value theatrical commodities. And just as François' capturing "notice" of Angélique's blackness takes him to the point where language fails, so too does the blackness of the play paralyse critical discourse. One of the lessons of *Angélique*, a lesson that runs through much African-Canadian drama, is that the Canadian imaginary marks its limitations with the notion of the black other. Blackness may be a shifting, plural and historically contingent category, but it always functions as the border. Angélique is one of several slaves in the play, each captured by a different system of servitude—Claude, the French indentured servant, has traded freedom for opportunity; Manon, the aboriginal slave, thinks of herself as free because she is in her own land. But Angélique comes to believe that neither she nor her children will ever negotiate a place in this new country: there will always exist a blackness that borders the map of the cultural imagination.

Critical authority ruptures when reading *Angélique*, because Lorena Gale exposes the structures of power and desire which have erased African presence from the Canadian imaginary, and in the performative structures of the play she implicates the audience in that erasure. The fact of imagining the play in that sense verifies the story it tells, and if we accept the story, then we must also accept that we are produced by the structures that have denied the story, that we are part of it, that, as Gale tells us in her stage directions, "*Then is now. Now is then*" (6). Other "thens" cross through the play, awakened by the politics of reception; the one that frames my own reception is a dimly remembered Halifax school yard in the late 1950s, where white and black kids looked at each other across a playground that was in practice segregated. In a very real sense, *Angélique* plays in the space between those gazes.

Lorena Gale juggles boldly with a complex of uncomfortable and disconcerting subjects, beginning with the fact of slavery in the pre-Canadian colonies. The dominant narratives of Canadian history condemn slavery as an American institution, preferring instead to construct Canada as a haven of liberty and justice. *Angélique* indicts the past as much more complex and contradictory. Perhaps the most harrowing aspect of the play's historical vision is the complexity of the slave system which it exposes—a system where aboriginal First Peoples and Africans are caught in a web of slavery, where commodity slavery and indentured servitude intertwine, where slavery is systematically enforced through rape. In a stylistic frame that offsets cool distance with intense emotion, the play exposes the psychology of a slavery so abject that a mother cannot bear to see her children grow into it, and ensures they do not. The historical episode recalled (and reclaimed) by the play concerns the execution by hanging of a young woman in Montreal in 1734 on charges of setting a fire that ripped through the city. In a community where slavery fulfills no economic purpose—except in an economy of status and distinction—Angélique is a "gift" from François to his embittered wife Thérèse (who, as Angélique will do, mourns a dead child). But as Thérèse well knows, Angélique is in fact François' gift to himself.

The substructure of the play exposes a complex world in which Angélique is a diasporic voice who is ironically more European than many of the proto-Québécois amongst whom she lives. She is an African who has never seen Africa; instead, she has been "imported" from Madeira, taken from a context of slavery that at the very least offered the comfort of family. As she tells César, an American-born slave with whom she is expected to produce children for the slave market, "We toiled for them. Yes! But it was work. Just work. Hard work is a part of life. And at least we were together... I cannot understand this coldness and this cruelty. I may have always been a slave. But I did not feel like one until I came to this land..." (15). From the island of Madeira, Angélique could "imagine I could see the land of my ancestors" (15). In the middle of the North American continent, she cannot: all that she can envision is a future of rape and brutality, for herself and her children. This loss of any sense of a future (which corresponds in fact to the erasure from the social imaginary) is the condition which separates the African slaves from the indentured French servants and aboriginal slaves who share their toil. In the span of the play, Angélique brings five children into the world. None lives very long. In one of the most harrowing moments of the play, Angélique sits alone with her first infant—whose fair complexion excites gossip and speculation among the townsfolk. To the accompaniment of a "new heart beating," she tells the baby a long, lyrical and mythic story about the origin of the world and the separation of the originary, "seamless" and profound darkness, and about the light it birthed:

Light
was now everywhere.
Cutting through the darkness
with the sharpness of an axe.
Cruelly
severing
the umbilicus between them.

Darkness
was so blinded by the light
she could no longer
see.
And so
retreated.
To where she could have some sense of
herself.
Though light still
pierced
her.
As a reminder that
It
now
ruled
every
thing.

Light and darkness.

That
is how the two became separate
forces.
In constant
opposition.
Light
in the forefront
and darkness…
waiting…
on the edge
of everything. (13)

At the end of the story, with a tenderness that is hard to witness—the more so because we see it coming—Angélique does what we know she must do, and gently smothers the baby, with the words, "Fly home and greet the darkness. There are others waiting there. Mama loves you and will join you soon" (13). Perhaps the most disconcerting thing about this moment is that it occurs fairly early on in the play, not as the tragic climax of a sentimentalised plot, but as an almost routine incident of daily life.

But routine as it may seem, the birth and death of this first child transforms Angélique. When she first arrives in New France, she is still able to envision futurity. She is introduced to her new slavery as a worker—and the stage directions remind us that "*Unless otherwise stated, in every scene in which the slaves are present they are working*" (6). Angélique meets her new mistress on this ground of work and duty (with the play of anachronism that is so crucial to Gale's argument):

> THÉRÈSE. Beds each morning, change the linen every other day or so. Bathrooms every other morning. Vacuum the main living spaces, bedroom, living room, stairs daily… Don't worry, we have a deluxe machine. I hear it makes vacuuming a breeze… Floors swept and washed every day. Waxing every third week. Are you getting all this…?
> ANGÉLIQUE. *(eager to please)* Oui, Madame.
> THÉRÈSE. I am very sensitive to dust. You'll have to dust each day. Metal and wood surfaces polished. Mirrors and windows clear. Without streaks…
> ANGÉLIQUE. Oui, Madame.
> THÉRÈSE. Let's see. What else is there? Laundry, including dry cleaning, is Tuesday and Friday. Hand washing daily. Mending as necessary. Marketing is Saturday.
> ANGÉLIQUE. Oui, Madame. (7)

The depersonalised nature of this work deceives Angélique. It promises a secure structure of duty which can be separated from the self and in effect disguises slavery as a "job." Thus in the next scene, we witness Angélique "moving through space in an abstracted dervish of cleaning" to the sound of urban club "jungle" music on a boom box. "This time," she tells herself, "will be different":

> This time,
> I will be treated with loving kindness and understanding.
> I will work hard.
> From sun to sun.
> Do exactly as I'm told.
> I will perform each duty with pride and obedience.
> I will maintain their order.
> Everything will go smoothly.
> I'll know my place.
> I will give freely of myself.
> Repaying their humanity with loyalty.
> Earning their protection
> And their care.
> They'll wonder how they ever lived without me. (8)

This promise of a humanised life that enables private subjectivity is almost immediately extinguished by rape, which makes explicit the fact that Angélique's "job" is to be a commodity and an actor in François' private theatre of desire. Gale shows this suppression of self in a theatricalised demonstration of the way in which rape eradicates the illusions of autonomy. In this gestic demonstration, the instrument of sexual torture is the corset in which François dresses Angélique. François masks his sexual ownership in his erotic fantasy of seduction, and in this dramaturgy of desire and power, Angélique experiences a deceptive illusion of freedom:

> *From behind, FRANÇOIS reaches around and removes ANGÉLIQUE's uniform, revealing period undergarments beneath her modern clothing. He then commences to dress her up again, only this time, in period clothing. ANGÉLIQUE does not resist.*
> ANGÉLIQUE. A dog barking… A baby crying… Footsteps… The
>   wind whistling low and breathy…
> *THÉRÈSE enters and watches in the shadows.*
> ANGÉLIQUE. The faint creek of wood giving way to weight…
>   Someone stepping stealthily on the fourth floorboard
>   before the doorway to my room.
>   There is no sneaking in this house where every
>   sound
>   betrays…
>   A cat scrowling…
>   Perhaps the dog has caught the cat.
>   Or maybe
>   the cat has caught the dog.
> *FRANÇOIS places a corset on ANGÉLIQUE.*
>   I could leave here. Right now…
> *She takes a step away from him. Then another and another. Which has the effect of tightening the corset.*
>   I am walking towards the door… I open it… I step outside and…
> *She falls forward. Her arms spread like a bird. She is kept aloft by the laces of the corset which FRANÇOIS holds like reins on a wild horse. But he doesn't notice anything happening with her. He pumps her, like he is fucking her from behind.*
>   I'm freeeeeeee! I'm free! I'm free! I'm free! Look at meeee…! I'm
>   running through the gates of the city. I'm racing across the land.
>   I'm floating across the big river. I am washed up on the shores of
>   my beloved Madière…
> *He pulls her back to him and ties the corset.*
>   But I am not really out there… (15-16)

The birth of her child projects this dehumanisation into a future of erasure and despair, and it leads Angélique to her own understanding of radicalism as an existential choice. Lorena Gale never shows us whether Angélique actually starts the fire that begins and ends the play, but she shows how she might have, and replays the voices that condemn her. Before the fire, Angélique seeks escape. When François dies (after drinking water that may have been deliberately contaminated by the slaves), Thérèse makes plans to sell Angélique, and the need to escape becomes urgent. Angélique has fallen in love with Claude, who fuels her hopes of escape by telling her of the free Blacks whom he has seen in New England. He promises to escape with her, but defers until the night of the fire. For Claude, escape is about opportunity: "In New France, I'll never be more than peasant scum who signed five years of his life away for some new clothes, a few sacks of grain and a stony piece of land that may never bear fruit. But in New England, or farther south, there's no telling what a man could make of himself" (23). What Angélique does not see is that Claude dreams of becoming another François, that his dream of power and wealth reiterates the conditions that have enslaved her.

The consuming fire that offers Angélique escape, but leads to her execution, starts with a pail of hot coals which we see Angélique take from Claude:

> ANGÉLIQUE. Love… I had almost forgotten it felt like… freedom.
> CLAUDE. Soon. *(he exits leaving the pail with ANGÉLIQUE)*
> ANGÉLIQUE. How long can I wait? Each minute brings me closer to a living death. And I'm alive. I am alive!
> His touches burn, sear, scorch, igniting fire deep inside where pain and ice had been. And I feel… heat, life, force, power, black and strong.
> She envies that. Cold, passionless bitch. Just like her bastard husband. Both sucking. Sucking life. Denying life.
> No! I am not a chair, a sack of grain or a calf to be fattened and sold for slaughter. I am alive. And loved. And I can't wait… any longer.
> *Smoke begins to fill the stage.*
> THÉRÈSE. Fire!
> ANGÉLIQUE. Fire!
> IGNACE. Fire!
> CÉSAR. Fire!
> *Pandemonium breaks out. Church bells ringing, people shouting, panicking. The actors run around and organize themselves into a line in which buckets pass from person to person. ANGÉLIQUE is at the end of the line. Buckets pass swiftly and desperately from person to person. CLAUDE enters picking his teeth and watches silently for a moment. ANGÉLIQUE turns to grab another bucket, sees CLAUDE and instead grabs CLAUDE's hand.*
> ANGÉLIQUE. Now?
> CLAUDE. Now! (23-24)

As they make their bid for freedom, we observe the testimony of witnesses, all of whom implicate Angélique. In alternating scenes, Angélique and Claude find themselves lost in the winter bush; they celebrate their freedom by making love, but as Angélique sleeps, Claude deserts her because "with you, I'll always be running" (26). When she awakes, she is arrested, tortured (this we hear from the voices of witnesses) and the play ends with its beginning: then is now, and Angélique is hanged.

In its subject matter and its theatrical technique alike, *Angélique* works a ruthlessly effective critique of the naturalised fictions that historical narrative so often conceals. The conventional mode of historical narrative in the theatre—at least on Canadian stages—is one in which revelations of past crime speak to present injustice. The mapping of past and present tends to result in a "living history" form of dramatic realism that dehistoricises the past. Lorena Gale deliberately dismantles this convention with a strategic play of spectatorial politics in which every moment of the drama is constructed through frames of testimony and witnessing. In her introductory directions, Gale writes that "*Although the specifics are not written into the text, what can be explored is the concept of witnessing. As servants and slaves are essentially invisible, experiment with who sees what, knows what, etc*" (6). This notion of witnessing, of observation and testimony, is built into the performance text of the play. It destabilises the receptive experience of the audience through anachronism, ambiguity and contradiction. Not knowing whom to believe, we depend on visual evidence. But the visual evidence of *Angélique* functions as deliberately unsettling.

In *Angélique* the past crime is not only slavery—humanised and perhaps in danger of being sentimentalised in the tragic history of one woman—but the erasure of it from dominant historical narratives. To address this, Gale intervenes in the structures of historical representation, to turn history on its head. In her cast list, she pointedly describes Angélique as "*a slave, in a history book*" (6), and throughout the play we are confronted with the construction of history as a textual frame that can be manipulated to reveal or suppress. Characters move from period to contemporary dress; language shifts from conventionalised "historical" realism to contemporary idiom, and our points of historical reference are destabilised by the intrusion of artifacts of modernity (a computer, a bic lighter, a boom box) into the imagined past. Angélique herself begins and ends the play with a book in hand—the book in which she has been reduced to a minor note and, through the agency of the play, restored.

To this end, Gale plays with the technologies of authentification that verify representations in popular culture, but at the same time construct the "twisted history" that Angélique, in her closing speech, condemns, and which condemns her. By taking to its logical next step the common trope of historical melodrama, in which the past is always a costumed present, the intrusion of the world of the audience into the action of the play through the tactical planting of anachronisms naturalises the representation of the past. But at the same time, this play of anachronism denaturalises the past by exposing the limits and erasures of historical narration.

As audiences imagined in the theatre by the play, we witness Lorena Gale's interventions in what we take to be our shared history; as participants in the drama, we are the constructed witnesses to the monologues, addresses and testimonies of her characters. In this duality, the foundational concept of witnessing itself shifts, as what begins as an act of resistance becomes a medium of oppression. The act of witnessing that is so instrumental to the survival of enslaved peoples is also the act that legitimises the oppressive power of the slave-owners. To this end, video screens on the stage reinforce what Gale herself refers to as "documentary" evidence, when the characters testify to Angélique's (alleged) guilt. That such mediatised authenticity is as much a part of the "twisted history" as the records themselves, Gale makes clear by her passing allusion to the hyperbolic media coverage of the O.J. Simpson case:

> *On all screens.*
> REPORTER. In dramatic new developments in the O.J.... I mean Marie Joseph Angélique case... four-year-old Amable Le Moine was brought before the court. Amable, daughter of Alexis Le Moine Monière, brother-in-law of Madame de Francheville, who swore under oath to tell the truth, testified that on the day of the fire she saw the negress, Marie Joseph Angélique, carrying a coal shuttle up to the attic. (25)

In the structure of complicity fixed by the returned gaze of the testifying characters and the audience, Angélique must be condemned, as she recognises at the end of the play. She exists only to be systematically erased. This is in fact the opening moment of the play which the rest of the action restores. The play begins with Angélique dancing, book in hand, as a depersonalised, authentifying voice-over gradually removes her from the historical record:

> SFX
> And in seventeen thirty-four a Negro slave set fire to the City of Montreal and was hanged.
> in seventeen thirty-four a Negro slave set fire to the City of Montreal and was hanged.
> seventeen thirty-four a Negro slave set fire to the City of Montreal and was hanged.
> a Negro slave set fire to the City of Montreal and was hanged
> slave set fire to the City of Montreal and was hanged
> set fire to the City of Montreal and was hanged
> fire to the City of Montreal and was hanged
> to the City of Montreal and was hanged
> City of Montreal and was hanged
> Montreal and was hanged
> and was hanged
> was hanged
> hanged. (6)

In the play, Lorena Gale restores Angélique in the historical narratives that supply the national imaginary with evidence of its origins; *with* the play, she challenges the theatre profession—and its authorising structures of value and critical reception—to recognise that "we" are invested in the erasure of African-Canadian experience, and that like François, we take "particular notice" of blackness for reasons we seldom choose to examine. *Angélique* activates a crisis in critical response, because it calls on us to confront the sliding glances of racism, the twisted and unspoken histories, the boundaries that we do not admit because they have been erased, the lost Angéliques in our shared history. No play in recent years has so deeply affected my sense of self as *Angélique*, a play of lost futures enacted on the stages of imagined theatres.

(2001)

Works Cited

Gale, Lorena. "Angélique." *Canadian Theatre Review* 100 (Fall 1999): 5-27.

———. *Angélique*. Toronto: Playwrights Canada, 2000.

Sears, Djanet, ed. *Testifyin': Contemporary African Canadian Drama*. Vol. 1. Toronto: Playwrights Canada, 2000.

"There's magic in the web of it": Seeing Beyond Tragedy in *Harlem Duet*

by Margaret Jane Kidnie

African-Canadian playwright Djanet Sears explains in three of her numbered "nOTES" that preface the earliest printed edition of *Harlem Duet* that she writes for the theatre as a form of political resistance:

> 23 I have a dream. A dream that one day in the city where I live, at any given time of the year, I will be able to find at least one play that is filled with people who look like me, telling stories about me, my family, my friends, my community. For most people of European descent, this is a privilege they take for granted.
>
> 24 Like Derek Walcott, I too have no choice. I must write my own work for the theatre. I must produce my own work, and the work of other writers of African descent. Then my nieces' experience of this world will almost certainly be different from my own.
>
> 25 But where do I start? How do I find the words? ("nOTES oF a cOLOURED gIRL" 14)

Harlem Duet was inspired by Shakespeare's *Othello*, a canonical, and in Sears's eyes, disturbing treatment of African identity that had persistently haunted her professional career as a dramatist and actor. She sets out to "exorcise this ghost" by telling the story of Othello's first wife, Billie ("nOTES" 14). This piece for five Black actors first performed in Toronto in 1997 offers a challenging exploration of the impact of race and gender relations on the lives of people of African descent in Canada and the United States today. *Harlem Duet*, described by Sears as "a rhapsodic blues tragedy," gives material form to her resolve to transform political anger into artistic creativity: "For the many like me, black and female, it is imperative that our writing begin to recreate our histories and our myths, as well as integrate the most painful of experiences [...] In a very deep way, I feel that I am in the process of giving birth to myself. Writing for the stage allows me a process to dream myself into existence" ("nOTES"14-15).

The drama opens with a Prologue in which Billie learns that Othello has fallen in love with another woman. The play's Harlem setting thereafter shifts across three distinct historical moments: the years leading up to Emancipation (1860-62), the Harlem Renaissance (1928), and the present day. The two central characters, Billie and Othello, feature in all three strands, and the crisis that arises from Othello's sudden revelation is complicated each time by the spectre of inter-racial desire—the realization that his new lover, Mona, is White. Mona never bodily enters the performance space, a marked contrast to Shakespeare's treatment of the character of Desdemona, and her few lines are delivered as an off-stage voice. Sears in fact marginalizes the White community altogether, thus offering the spectator, as Leslie Sanders notes, a new and unfamiliar perspective on Othello's actions: "[Othello] no longer is seen as an alien in a white world, but rather as a member of the black community who is dazzled by whiteness and follows it away from the community's place and space. The Othello of *Harlem Duet* is far from heroic; as a result the canonical Othello is greatly diminished" (558). While Sanders is right to emphasize the importance of Sears's decision to locate the action within a Black, rather than White, community, the conflict between Billie and Othello, on the one hand, and the impact of *Harlem Duet* on our perception of *Othello*, on the other, constitute more complex sets of relations than this initial analysis of character might suggest. The play's originality rests in the particular way it articulates incompatible, yet intellectually considered and passionately held, stands on race relations.

The present-day Othello justifies his turn towards the White community in terms of a politics of integration, asserting that "[l]iberation has no colour," and citing the words of Martin Luther King to affirm that "at a deeper level we're all the same" (55).[1] He identifies not specifically as a Black man, but as a member of the human race, arguing that Billie's advocacy of a distinctive Black identity ignores the fact that African history and Black personhood have been disentangled in the West through a steady process of education and cultural assimilation. As he explains to Billie during an argument prompted by the news that he and Mona are engaged to be married,

> [M]y culture is not my mother's culture—the culture of my ancestors. My culture is Wordsworth, Shaw, "Leave it to Beaver," "Dirty Harry" […] I mean, what does Africa have to do with me. We struttin' around professing some imaginary connection for a land we don't know. Never seen. Never gonna see. (73)

But leaving Billie also represents for Othello a break with the stifling personal limitations he feels as a Black man in a relationship with a Black woman. The Black feminist message, according to his experience of it, is that "Black men are poor fathers, poor partners, or both" (70). White women, not prejudiced by these particular gender assumptions, are better able to support and encourage his ambitions. Mona thus embodies for Othello the enigmatic allure of the unknown, the as yet intangible promise of what he can achieve as a man: "Our experiences, our knowledge transforms us," he says. "That's why education is powerful, so erotic. The transmission of words from mouth to ear. Her mouth to my ear. Knowledge. A desire for that distant thing I know nothing of, but yearn to hold for my very own" (73).

Othello rejects as inadequate and unfulfilling a racial identity that in his opinion tries to define him as a member of a disadvantaged minority (73). "Some of us," he says in frustration, "are beyond that now. Spiritually beyond this race shit bullshit now. I am an American" (73-74). The idea that colour might be only skin deep prompts from Billie, however, a literally visceral response: "The skin holds everything in. It's the largest organ in the human body. Slash the skin by my belly and my intestines fall out" (44). This assertion of her ancestral heritage as destiny is given powerful voice near the end of the play when Billie, either suffering a complete nervous breakdown or poisoned by her own magic, observes of herself, "Trapped in history. A history trapped in me" (101). Billie's view is that Othello is selling out Black culture and heritage in a misguided effort to gain White respect. In her eyes, he embodies the caricature offered by their landlady, Maji, of the educated Black man who tries to "White wash" his life: "Booker T. Uppermiddleclass III. He can be found in predominantly White neighborhoods. He refers to other Blacks as 'them'. His greatest accomplishment was being invited to the White House by George Bush to discuss the 'Negro problem'" (66). The moral force of Billie's position is undermined, however, by concerns voiced by her family and closest friends about what seems to be an all-consuming obsession with race: "Do you know who you are anymore? [...] Racism is a disease my friend, and your test just came back positive" (103, see also 31). This highly charged stand-off between Billie and Othello, turning on the question of whether to live according to a separatist or integrationist racial politics, is never conclusively resolved in favour of either side.

A useful way to begin examining Sears's treatment of this political dilemma is through reference to Jean-François Lyotard's philosophy of the differend. This concept, at its most basic level, describes any argument in which opponents find themselves unable to resolve their differences justly due to the lack of a shared system of thought by which to arbitrate the conflict. Importantly, as Lyotard emphasizes, "[o]ne side's legitimacy does not imply the other's lack of legitimacy" (*The Differend* xi). Neither perspective can be assessed, or even articulated, in the other's idiom, and therefore to apply "a single rule of judgment to both [parties] in order to settle their differend as though it were merely a litigation would wrong (at least) one of them (and both of them if neither side admits this rule)" (Lyotard, *The Differend* xi).[2] This analysis of the peculiar nature of the differend suggests the possibility that Billie and Othello lack the language even to debate their differences, and that the tactics they adopt to negotiate their dispute are not only insufficient, but unjust.

The confrontation that results from the news of Othello's impending marriage in the present day, an episode stretched over three scenes, is significant in this respect as it ends with Billie staring at Othello in silence as he lectures her at length on Black/White relations (68-74). Silence, in an instance of the differend, is a negative phrase signalling that something remains to be said, but lacks, as yet, means of expression. The inability to put that phrase immediately into words, and another's unwillingness to acknowledge that inability within the idiom currently in use, constitutes what Lyotard calls a wrong [*tort*] (*The Differend* 13). The awareness that Billie has a response, but not one that can be expressed using Othello's genre of discourse, is brought home in performance when Othello's monologue is interrupted by an anachronistic scene set in 1928 (act 1.8) in which Billie, holding a bloodied razor, presses her own views in a non-linear, counter-rational stream of free associations as Othello lies motionless at her feet:

> Deadly deadly straw little strawberries it's so beautiful you kissed my fingers you pressed this cloth into my palm buried it there an antique token our ancient all these tiny red dots on a sheet of white my fingernails are white three hairs on my head are white the whites of my eyes are white too the palms of my hands and my feet are white you're all I'd ever and you my my I hate Sssshh. (72)

The abrupt and disturbing shifts in context and tone between scenes seven and nine throw into relief the strategies according to which each character pursues conflict resolution: whereas Othello enforces his views through verbal domination, Billie resorts to physical violence. In the present-day action, she works destructive magic on the strawberry-spotted handkerchief given to her by Othello as a wedding present, and which she presents as being "fixed in the emotions of all [his] ancestors:"

> The one who laid the foundation for the road in Herndon, Virginia, and was lashed for laziness as he stopped to wipe the sweat from his brow with this kerchief. Or, your great great grandmother, who covered her face with it, and then covered it with her hands as she rocked and silently wailed, when told that her girl child, barely thirteen, would be sent 'cross the state for breeding purposes [...] And more... so much more. What I add to this already fully endowed cloth, will cause you such...... such... Wretchedness. (75-76)

Billie imposes on her former lover through magic the generations of anguish summoned up by the handkerchief, a cultural identity she insists they share: "Fight with me. I would fight with you... Suffer with me... I would suffer—" (76). Each of these two characters thus responds to the differend by resorting to victimization of the other. This impasse between them finds expression in *Harlem Duet* on the level of form through Sears's unique and disorienting dramaturgy.

Each scene opens with brief audio recordings of landmark moments in African-American history accompanied by blues music performed by cello and bass. The spectator variously hears, amongst other clips, passages from the speech Martin Luther King gave at the March on Washington, phrases from the Emancipation Proclamation, Christopher Darden's request to O.J. Simpson to try on the bloodied glove, Paul Robeson welcoming the opportunity to play Othello in England, and Malcolm X on the need to build strong Black communities. These diverse voices, which become dissonant and distorted before the scenes immediately leading up to Billie's mental breakdown (act 2, scenes 4-7), provide a historically resonant, but inconsistent and even self-contradictory, counterpoint to the dramatic action, implicitly extending the scope of Billie's and Othello's argument from a private to a public forum.

The dramatic action builds on the alienating effect of these polyphonic fragments by multiplying the characters of Billie and Othello across distinct historical moments. Sears indicates elsewhere that this structure and its handling in performance is central to the play's thematic concerns: "There [had to] be a way not only to have three time periods but to go back and forth through them, not have a moving set, and not have huge changes in the cyc[lorama].... [U]sing three time periods was very important. It gave depth that I wanted. It supported many layers of the play, of the language, and of the contradictions around race" ("The Nike Method" 25). Each of the narrative strands shares with the others certain common features: a love affair between Othello and Billie, a strawberry-spotted handkerchief, inter-racial desire and the politics of such desire in American culture, and violent marital breakdown. The script states that the speech prefixes "Him" and "Her," and "He" and "She" signify Othello and Billie as portrayed in the 1860 and 1928 plot strands respectively. The instant recognition of the actors' bodies in performance—the realization that the same two actors portray Billie and Othello in all three settings—creates the sense that we are witnessing a single story, stretched across time.

The shaping of recurrent moments between the independent strands further contributes to this impression of narrative unity. Act 1.2, the first scene set in the nineteenth century, stages the original moment of betrothal between Othello and Billie. Kissing Billie's fingers, Othello places in her hand a white silk handkerchief spotted with "little strawberries," telling her that it is a family heirloom given to him by his mother, and from him to her as "an antique token of our ancient love" (35). "There's magic in the web of it," Othello responds when Billie sighs, "It is so beautiful." The young lovers then plan their escape to freedom in Canada where they will live together forever in "[a] big house on an emerald hill." The scene concludes with the performance of a ritualized and private sexual exchange between the two lovers, during which Othello, kissing Billie as he offers a metaphorical topography of her body, is figured as a prospector exploring America (36).

Moments and phrases of this scene resonate elsewhere in the play. The Prologue, set in a tiny Harlem dressing room in 1928, opens with Billie holding the handkerchief and asking Othello, "Remember… Remember when you gave this to me? Your mother's handkerchief. There's magic in the web of it. Little strawberries. It's so beautiful—delicate. You kissed my fingers…and with each kiss a new promise you made…swore yourself to me…for all eternity…remember?" (21). Billie's repeated injunction to "remember" in the strand set in 1928 thus anticipates the betrothal dramatized two scenes later in a different, chronologically earlier, strand. Further resonances of act 1.2 are heard in act 1.4, a scene set in a late twentieth-century Harlem apartment that closes with a slightly adapted version of the lovers' "prospecting" ritual (58). Not only, therefore, is the linear progression of the opening scenes disrupted, with the betrothal situated after Othello's betrayal of his original promise to Billie, but what progression we are able to reconstruct from the fragments takes place across the three interwoven historical strands. The mental activity required of the spectator to piece together these non-sequential fragments creates the effect of an overarching narrative—*Harlem Duet*—both spanning and unifying the historical strands.

But at the same time that these three stories are drawn together through the recognition of such features as actors' bodies, personal names, or similarities in the dramatic action, jarring differences systematically undermine the possibility of organizing the fragments into a coherent whole. The characters embraced by the name "Othello," for example, are variously a slave, a minstrel, and a university lecturer. They are all identifiably "Othello," and yet they are also independent characters who respond to issues of race and gender relations within specific sets of historical and social conditions. This sense that the three versions are not self-identical is further developed by the various outcomes of each narrative: in the 1860-62 strand the staging implies that Othello has been hanged, but we remain unclear at whose hands; in the 1928 strand Billie sinks a straight-edged razor into her lover's throat; while in the strand set in the present, Billie is admitted to a psychiatric ward and Othello exits their apartment to enter Shakespeare's play, placing a call on his mobile to another member of faculty, Chris Yago.

The conviction that these stories can be resolved into a single narrative is troubled by other slight, but insistent, inconsistencies in the narrative action.

Act 2.7 dramatizes in the present day the vow of eternal love first witnessed at act 1.2. Viewing the Harlem apartment that will become their home and dreaming of the time when they will be able to afford "A big house […] On a rolling emerald hill," Othello spontaneously asks Billie to jump the broom with him:

> Think them old slaves had rings? Slave marriages were illegal, remember. This broom is more than rings. More than any gold. *(He whispers.)* My ancient love. (107)

Verbal echoes between act 1.2 and act 2.7—"My ancient love," "A big house […] On a rolling emerald hill"—suggest that these two betrothal scenes, albeit widely separated in Sears's play and taking place in different historical moments, are versions of the same key event which ultimately leads to the lovers' tragedy. Again, as in the previous examples of resonances of act 1.2 elsewhere in the play, the spectator is implicitly encouraged to formulate correspondences between the scenes in an effort to draw the fragments together into a single story. But this later version of the betrothal scene, crucially, does not include Othello's gift of the handkerchief.

We know as early as act 1.10 that Billie received this gift at some point during the strand set in the present because the stage directions indicate that she "*picks up a large white handkerchief with pretty red strawberries embroidered on it*" (75). Holding the handkerchief, presumably the same theatrical property first seen in act 1.2, she prepares to work magic on it that will cause all who touch it to come to harm: "Othello? […] Once you gave me this handkerchief. An heirloom. This handkerchief, your mother's… given by your father. From his mother before that. So far back… And now…then…to me" (75). This speech echoes Othello's words from the betrothal scene set in 1860:

> It was my mother's. Given her by my father… from his mother before that. When she died she gave it me, insisting that when I found…chose…chose a wife…that I give it to her…to you heart. (35)

The language of Billie's soliloquy at act 1.10 suggests that she was not only given the handkerchief by Othello, but given it in a manner similar, if not identical, to the manner in which "Him" gives "Her" the gift in act 1.2. And yet the betrothal scene between Billie and Othello as actually played out at act 2.7 omits any mention of the handkerchief. The gift of the heirloom remains an aporia in the present-day action that cannot be supplemented through recourse to the other two strands, the 1928 version failing to dramatize the scene, the 1860 version presenting the progression of events in a manner that just fails to fit.

The bewildering conclusion to which spectators are led is that the various strands represent—simultaneously—a single transhistorical plot, and three independent sequences of events. The dramatic structure of *Harlem Duet* fosters the unshakeable belief that the scenic fragments can be reassembled as a narrative unity, while at the same time denying the satisfaction of seeing that goal ever accomplished. In short, the play powerfully forces upon its audience the pre-cognitive *feeling* of the differend, a sensory, rather than intellectual, experience of the confrontation of irreconcilable differences typical of what Lyotard terms sublime art. As James Williams explains it, this affect "halts our drives to understand, to judge and to overcome. It does not so much cancel them as leave them in suspense by welding to them feelings that indicate that a difference is impassable…. [Sublime art does] not fall prey to the precept of logic that we cannot be in a state of simultaneous hope and despair" (4). The structural indeterminacy of *Harlem Duet* unsettles efforts to ignore or falsely patch over the lack of shared ground between Billie and Othello; more than that, it enables the realization that there exists an excess beyond what they—and we—are currently able to communicate.

Afrika Solo, Sears's first play for the stage, offers a fictionalized account of the playwright's year-long journey through Africa in search of an answer to the question, "Where the hell am I from?" (40). This early drama, conceived in large part as a solo performance and first performed in 1987 with Sears herself playing the central character, focusses on the protean identity of the individual subject, and explores the complexities of African-Canadian identity in the context of Sears's own multicultural background, born to a Jamaican mother and Guyanese father, and raised both in Britain and Canada.[3] *Harlem Duet* shifts the emphasis from one to two voices: the focus no longer rests on identity as role-play, but on the reciprocal relationship between the identities of subject and other as given shape by the postmodern event. It is in this respect that the sensation generated by Sears's drama of an as yet indiscernible excess in the confrontation of irreconcilably opposed structures is of most effect.

One response to opposed structures—that adopted by both Billie and Othello—is to attempt to regulate the outcome of the conflict, to impose common ground where none exists, through the violent application of idioms that silence the other. An alternative response, however, is to refuse to dominate what we cannot yet know. Subject and other participate in a relationship of mutual influence, and the identity of each adapts in response to spontaneous, unpremeditated events in directions that necessarily cannot be predicted or rationalized. In a case of the differend, this dynamic model of political resistance is seen as preferable to—even more ethical than—the forcible imposition of alternative, but eventually equally oppressive, idioms. This is the tactic by which conflicting conceptions of race and gender are handled in the duet played out between Sears and Shakespeare. Sears avoids the stand-off staged between Billie and Othello by weaving her own story in and around the canonical text, loosening, rather than trying to contradict or overthrow, Shakespeare's tragic vision of inter-racial desire. Crucially, since the dramatic structure of *Harlem Duet* requires each spectator to construct his or her own provisional and subjectively-determined networks of potential links between interconnected but non-identical parts, the precise outcome of this collision of texts is beyond Sears's control. The performance event impacts on and potentially modifies, in a manner that cannot be determined prior to the encounter, a web of reciprocally influenced and influencing identities that extends to include Sears, Shakespeare, *Harlem Duet*, *Othello* and most importantly, the spectator.

Such radical indeterminacy lends implicit significance to Sears's apparently incongruous decision to set each of the three narrative strands in a fixed geographical location. Modern-day Harlem is portrayed as a unique space in which people of African descent pursue their lives and culture almost entirely free of White influence. Filled with "Black bookstores. Black groceries […] Black banks. Black streets teeming with loud Black people listening to loud Jazz and reggae and Aretha" (106), Harlem is a dream—or illusion (66)—powerful enough to inspire the imaginations of African-Canadians such as Billie and her father, both of whom independently make the trip to Harlem just to walk through its streets (57, 79). Harlem stands not merely for a distinctive Black identity, but for pride in that racial identity. This is made clear in the Prologue, a scene set in the second quarter of the twentieth century during the Harlem Renaissance: "Harlem's the place to be now," Billie tells Othello. "Everyone who's anyone is coming here now. It's our time. In our place. It's what we've always dreamed of… isn't it?" (21). This shared dream, however, is one from which Othello increasingly distances himself. The idea of Harlem becomes in their relationship a troubled cultural and geographical signifier: whereas Billie celebrates it as a "sanctuary" (106), Othello dismisses it as a "reservation" (56). Harlem as urban space and dramatic setting thus symbolizes the lovers' ideological differences about racial assimilation.

But while the action of *Harlem Duet* is set entirely in New York City, and its immediate political preoccupations are American, the play's narrative horizon is oriented toward Maritime Canada. In the plot strand set in the days of American slavery Billie and Othello plan to run away and cross the border to Canada, a dream that is abandoned only when Othello falls in love with Miss Dessy, his White owner. Nova Scotia's history as a "haven for slaves" is mentioned twice in the present-day strand, both times in the context of the decision made years previously by Billie's father—who is also called Canada—to move his family back to Dartmouth after his wife's death (45, 82). Canada explains that this decision to leave the Bronx was motivated by his inability to cope with his sudden loss: "What's that them old slaves used to say? 'I can't take it no more, I moving to Nova Scotia'" (82). Struggling to come to grips with her own recent separation from Othello, Billie herself considers moving home to Dartmouth (65, 82). Nova Scotia thus holds out to the characters—whether they actually get there or not—the promise of an escape from suffering: "Canada freedom come." [4]

This presentation of Nova Scotia as a Black homeland is complicated, however, by the actual, and troubling, history of the African-Canadian experience over the past three centuries. Nova Scotia is home to the first free Black community in Canada, a legacy that dates back to the late eighteenth century when slaves who defected to the British to fight against the Americans during the War for Independence were relocated along with other Loyalists to the Maritime provinces (Walker, *The Black Loyalists* x, 11-12). Assured that they would be granted the rights of British subjects, the Black Loyalists soon learned that their treatment in Canada would not be appreciably different from life in slavery (Walker, *The Black Loyalists* 57). In particular, the land guaranteed to them by the British administration, land required to safeguard their freedom from White control, was not forthcoming: "the promise of land took on the meaning of a Promised Land, a place where their spiritual and temporal security would be realised. By 1791 many of [the Black Loyalists] had come to doubt that Nova Scotia could be that Promised Land" (Walker, *The Black Loyalists* 87). A second wave of slaves who resorted to the British standard during the War of 1812, similarly in search of a life free of bondage, arrived in Halifax in 1815. Once again, the Black refugees suffered deprivation and racial injustice. Economic discrimination, geographical and cultural isolation from the White community, and the practice of slavery in Nova Scotia into the nineteenth century thus set in place the foundations for the construction of a distinct African-Canadian identity which, by the twentieth century, was most readily and visibly associated with a fifteen-acre settlement called Africville (Clairmont and Magill 25-42; Walker, "Allegories" 156).

Founded in the mid-nineteenth century on the Bedford Basin across the bridge from Dartmouth and on the northern periphery of the city of Halifax, Africville grew over the approximately 125 years of its existence into a community of about eighty families (Clairmont and Magill 1-2, 29-30). Without water, sewerage, or lighting, and unprotected by emergency fire services, Africville over the years became identified by Blacks and Whites as "the slum by the dump," a Black ghetto on the margins of respectable society (Clairmont and Magill 1-2, 93-99, 108-31). The site was finally bulldozed in the mid-1960s as part of an urban relocation programme. But the memory of Africville has assumed a powerful iconic status since the late 1960s with the emergence of a more politicized Black consciousness:

> The community has continued to exist despite its physical destruction, and it is taken now as a symbol of the unconquerable black spirit in Nova Scotia... [Africville's] refusal to die has forced a reconsideration and ultimately a recognition of the powerful community orientation of black history in Canada". (Walker, "Allegories" 155) [5]

Harlem Duet's evocation of Nova Scotia as a refuge for Blacks wishing to escape the circumstances of their lives in the United States is thus the source of qualified optimism, conjuring up a rich and uniquely Canadian history of Black identity and multicultural relations that emphasizes, in particular, the importance of African-Canadian community. But for Canada and his children, Billie and Andrew, Nova Scotia is not a blind utopian dream, nor even the Promised Land, but home. Early discussion of the family's connections to Dartmouth alongside a description of one of Billie's favourite meals as "[s]ome Canadian delicacy" (26) firmly establishes them as native neither to Harlem, nor indeed, to the United States. The action set in the present day takes place, for this family, in a foreign country, an important contextualizing detail that draws attention to Mona's decision in the 1928 strand to cast Othello as "the prince of Tyre" (100). Othello is given the opportunity to perform, not the great tragic roles to which he aspires—Hamlet, Othello, Macbeth—but Pericles, the lead in a Romance traditionally marginalized within the canon by reason of textual corruption and uncertain authorship.[6]

Pericles, a play that dramatizes broken families and travels far from home, shares striking similarities to *Harlem Duet*, particularly in terms of the portrayal of domestic relationships between parents and children. Canada's wife died unexpectedly, leaving behind a grieving husband, and a daughter who was too young at the time even to have memories of her mother in adulthood. Billie tells her father that she "hardly remember[s] her anymore": "I get glimpses of this ghostly figure creeping in and out of my dreams" (81). Billie and her brother, Andrew, are raised by their grandmother, while their father slips ever further away from his children through alcoholism. A motivating reason behind Othello's decision to leave Billie—his resentment at "being mistaken for someone's inattentive father" (71)—is suggestive of the damage caused by these events. Billie relates his concern in even more explicit terms: "What does [Othello] say? Now he won't have to worry that a White woman will emotionally mistake him for the father that abandoned her" (67). The history of Billie's family, like that of Pericles's family, is characterized by traumatic loss accompanied by geographical and emotional displacement.

It would be a mistake to try to map *Pericles* onto *Harlem Duet* too precisely. There is no one character that corresponds exactly to Shakespeare's hero—both Canada and Billie can seem Pericles-like in their suffering and despair. Moreover, Canada's dead wife does not return from the grave, and the reversal of family misfortunes as dramatized in Sears's play is only tentative, a closing tableau that promises hope rather than delivers joy (117). But what *Harlem Duet* takes from Shakespeare's play is a rediscovered faith in the ability to survive overwhelming personal hardship. In *Pericles*, such renewal is located in the character of Marina, the hero's daughter. Pericles sinks into a deep melancholy in the fifth act after learning of her supposed death, a mental and physical despondency that causes him to reject the words of comfort offered by the woman brought to him by Lysimachus (Shakespeare 5.1.79). But as Marina—uncertain why she feels compelled to stay—begins to relate the history of her own sufferings, Pericles slowly comes to know her. The moment of recognition between father and daughter is handled with a profound sense of wonder and awe. Pericles, mistrustful of his sudden good fortune and seeking still further confirmation of Marina's true identity, asks her to name her mother. "Is it no more to be your daughter," she answers, "than/To say my mother's name was Thaisa?/Thaisa was my mother, who did end/The minute I began" (5.1.204-7).

Harlem Duet stages a similarly pivotal scene, but here it is the father, rather than the daughter, who is at first rejected. Billie tells her father, who has suddenly surfaced in Harlem after years of separation, that she does not need or want his help: "I haven't seen you in God knows how long… And you just show up, and expect things to be all hunky dory" (96). Canada, acknowledging Billie's criticism, but, like Marina, determined to stay, delivers a long monologue in which he relates memories of Billie's childhood before her mother's death, and tells about his grief when his wife, Beryl, died. In lines that echo Pericles's dawning recognition of Thaisa in his daughter's person (5.1.101-8), Canada explains to Billie, "I kept seeing your face. It's your mother's face. You've got my nose. My mouth. But those eyes… The shape of your face… The way you're [sic] head tilts to one side when you're thinking, or just listening. It's all her" (97). In both *Pericles* and *Harlem Duet*, father-daughter reconciliation can only be effected through each character remembering back to a time before their sufferings began. Canada holds out to Billie, as Marina does to Pericles, the possibility of inner peace through patience and forgiveness. "I just wanted to come," he tells his daughter, taking her in his arms when his words die away:

> I just wanted to come. And I know I can't make everything alright. I know. But I was there when you arrived in this world. And I didn't think there was space for a child, I loved your mother so much. But there you were and I wondered where you'd been all my life, like something I'd been missing and didn't know I'd been missing. And I don't know if you've loved anybody that long. But behind your mother's face you're wearing, I still see the girl who shrieked with laughter, and danced to the heavens sometimes… (98)

For refugee Black Americans in the eighteenth and nineteenth centuries, the idea of Canada represented full citizenship, land, and the promise of a new life, an idealism given voice in *Harlem Duet* by the slaves' dream of "a white house, on an emerald hill" (35). But in the strand set in modern-day Harlem, in the aftermath of centuries of personal disappointments and frustrated ambitions, African hopes of freedom from suffering are no longer pinned on a geographical, but on a spiritual, destination. This reorientation is embodied in the character of Billie's father. Billie, tellingly, never does flee to Canada—Canada comes to her. The promise of new beginnings, key to the regenerative power of Shakespeare's late plays, is evoked in the final scene of *Harlem Duet* when Canada tells his daughter-in-law that he plans to stay in Harlem indefinitely: "Oh, I don't think I'm going anywhere just yet—least if I can help it," he says. "Way too much leaving gone on for more than one lifetime already" (117).[7]

Othello, as noted previously, exits Sears's play to enter a different drama in which his first wife has no place. *Harlem Duet*, however, is "Billie's story" (Sears, "nOTES" 15). Symbolically set "at the corner of Martin Luther King and Malcolm X boulevards," Billie's story is a fable of race and gender relations in the late-twentieth century able to affirm neither her own nor Othello's perspective, but the crossroads between them. The potential stalemate implicit in such a view is countered, however, by the manner in which Sears evokes the bitter-sweet tone of Shakespeare's late plays, a genre positioned between comedy and tragedy, to suggest that there exist possible—albeit as yet indiscernible—ways forward for her protagonist. *Harlem Duet* is a postmodern narrative that loosens existing systems of race and gender oppression, systems in which Shakespeare's *Othello* is intimately implicated, by reaching towards unknown idioms. The urgent need for such idioms in Western society is brought home by Billie's dream in Harlem hospital. The dream is about her psychiatrist, Lucinda—a White doctor:

> Lucinda was sitting at the edge of a couch and I asked her a question. But she couldn't couldn't answer because her eyes kept flashing. Like neon lights. Flash, flash, flash. That was it. That was the dream. I knew it was important, but I didn't get it. And I told her. And she didn't get it either. But it gnawed away at me… For days… The flashing eyes. And that was it! The eyes were flashing blue. Her eyes were flashing blue. She could only see my questions through her blue eyes. (115)

In both her dream and its subsequent analysis, Billie fails to get an answer from her doctor because the very question she needs to ask cannot be phrased according to White discourse. Significantly, Billie's account of her dream occludes the question itself. Denied means of expression, this particular instance of the differend is forever silenced.

This scene in the hospital forcefully projects the debilitating challenges confronting Black female identity in the West today. Such issues are not finally resolved in Sears's play. What *Harlem Duet* does offer, and this is a feature it shares with *Pericles*, is its ability to see beyond tragedy.[8] *Harlem Duet* resists postmodern nihilism not by asserting answers to the differend, but by offering hope in face of the differend. The happy endings dramatized in Shakespeare's Romances are qualified: the lost years are never recovered, and death, in some instances, cannot be reversed. Billie's happy ending, the possibility that she might yet transcend generations of inter-racial suffering, is similarly qualified. But what sets Romance apart from tragedy is its turn away from death towards hope and creative inspiration, particularly as embodied by children. This explains the significance of Sears's decision to extend the double plot of *Pericles* to include a third generation. Billie's six-year-old niece, Jenny, is a character frequently invoked by the dialogue, although never seen on stage. Repeatedly denied access to her grieving aunt, Jenny draws pictures for Billie which she sends along with her mother: "She made them specially for you," Amah tells Billie. "She wanted to give you some inspiration. You might not be able to tell, but one's of her dancing, and the other's of her singing" (84). The scene closes in silence with Billie leaning against the closed door, studying her niece's drawings.

Harlem Duet is not, in the final analysis, about tragedy, but about the promise of renewal as pursued in the postmodernity. In "nOTES oF a cOLOURED gIRL," Sears relates witnessing her niece's birth, an experience that she describes as challenging her disbelief in miracles. One of the reasons she now writes for the stage is to create for

Qwyn a different world: "I wanted there to be no question of her right to take up space on this planet" (12).[9] Lyotard argues that postmodern art prompts the question "Is it happening?", where not only the shape of the thing coming into being, but also whether it is even coming into being, is uncertain. The production of such art is not about the achievement of mere perfection according to established standards, but about "working without rules in order to formulate the rules of what *will have been done*" ("Answering the Question" 81). *Harlem Duet* leaves us with the sensation that something is happening precisely because it cannot—as yet—be fully discerned or understood.

(2001)

Notes

I am indebted to Kristin Lucas for first bringing *Harlem Duet* to my attention, and to the McGill Shakespeare Colloquium for offering helpful comments on an orally delivered version of this paper in autumn 2000. I would also like to thank James Purkis for his incisive feedback at a late stage of the essay's development.

1. The details here of Billie's and Othello's conflicting ideological perspectives on race and gender are drawn from lengthy exchanges between the lovers set in the present day; the scenes set in the historically earlier periods tend to portray the consequences, rather than explore the politics, of their marriage breakdown.

2. Lyotard offers contract negotiation between labourers and employers as one example of the differend. The idiom of social and economic law within which disputes are regulated requires the former to speak of their labour as a commodity they own and are free to sell. So long as labourers argue within this idiom, they remain plaintiffs, and their perceived damages can be addressed through litigation. But if labourers do not accept this law as valid, then they cease to "exist within [the court's] field of reference:" their damages become a wrong [*tort*] that they are unable to prove because their evidence is non-existent—cannot be cognitively recognized—within the court's idiom. In this situation, the labourers become victims as well as plaintiffs (*The Differend* 9-10). Notably, if the situation were reversed, the contract being negotiated according to the labourers' idiom, the employers would find themselves wronged and in the position of victims: the differend points to a mutual lack of shared discourse.

3. Joanne Tompkins argues that *Afrika Solo* figures identity construction as a never-ending transformation: "The 'real' performance is endlessly deferred as Janet, who has completed her preparations for the 'role' of Djanet, is ready to go 'on,' to continue rather than complete" (36).

4. Billie delivers this line three times in the play, twice in the strand set in 1860, and once in the present day (35, 63, 115).

5. George Elliott Clarke's two-volume edited collection, *Fire on the Water: An Anthology of Black Nova Scotian Writing*, makes available to modern readers selected African-Acadian [sic] literature dating from the eighteenth century to the present day, and builds on what Clarke describes as a developing awareness amongst African-Acadian writers of a sense of belonging to "a literary *family*" (11).

6. Othello's ambitions to the classical stage are made clear in the dialogue. Claiming he is "of Ira Aldridge stock," he quotes *Hamlet* (99), rehearses Othello's defence before the Venetian council (113), and "long[s] to play the Scottish king" (99).

7. Sears explains in an interview with Ric Knowles that the character of Billie's father was a late, but to her mind, essential, addition to the play: "I paid for this man to read the part of Canada, the father. But I don't know why the character came, I just

knew he had to be there and I don't know now how the play could have done without him" ("The Nike Method" 26).

8 This analysis of *Pericles*'s dramatic effect can be traced to G. Wilson Knight's essay on the play (65). The passage is discussed and developed in the introduction to F.D. Hoeniger's New Arden edition of *Pericles* (ixxxv).

9 This sentiment paraphrases the last sentence of the Afterword to *Afrika Solo*, a line that describes how Sears felt about herself while living in Africa: "For the first time in my life, I felt I had a right to take up space on this planet, and it felt good" (101).

Works Cited

Clairmont, Donald H. and Dennis William Magill. *Africville: The Life and Death of a Canadian Black Community*. 1974. 3rd ed. Toronto: Canadian Scholars' Press, 1999.

Clarke, George Elliott. *Fire on the Water: An Anthology of Black Nova Scotian Writing*. 2 Vols. Lawrencetown Beach, NS: Pottersfield, 1991, 1992.

Hoeniger, F.D. Introduction. *Pericles*. By William Shakespeare. NewArden Shakespeare. London: Routledge, 1969. xiii-xci.

Knight, G. Wilson. *The Crown of Life*. London: Methuen, 1947.

Lyotard, Jean-François. "Answering the Question: What Is Postmodernism?" Trans. Régis Durand. *The Postmodern Condition: A Report on Knowledge*. Trans. Geoff. Bennington and Brian Massumi. Foreword Fredric Jameson. Minneapolis: U of Minnesota P, 1997. 38-46.

———. *The Differend: Phrases in Dispute*. 1983. Trans. Georges Van Den Abbeele. Minneapolis: U of Minnesota P, 1988.

Sanders, Leslie. "*Othello* Deconstructed: Djanet Sears' *Harlem Duet*." *Testifyin': Contemporary African Canadian Drama*. Ed. Djanet Sears. Vol 1. Toronto: Playwrights Canada, 2000. 557-60.

Sears, Djanet. *Afrika Solo*. Toronto: Sister Vision, 1990.

———. *Harlem Duet*. Scirocco Drama, 1997.

———. "nOTES oF a cOLOURED gIRL: 32 sHORT rEASONS wHY i wRITE fOR tHE tHEATRE." *Harlem Duet*. Scirocco Drama, 1997. 11-16.

Sears, Djanet and Alison Sealy-Smith. "The Nike Method:" Interview with Ric Knowles. *Canadian Theatre Review* 97 (1998): 24-30.

Shakespeare, William. *Pericles*. Ed. Doreen Delvecchio and Antony Hammond. New Cambridge Shakespeare. Cambridge: Cambridge UP, 1998.

Tompkins, Joanne. "Infinitely Rehearsing Performance and Identity: *Africa Solo* [sic] and *The Book of Jessica*." *Canadian Theatre Review* 74 (1993): 35-39.

Walker, James W. St. G. "Allegories and Orientations in African-Canadian Historiography: The Spirit of Africville." *The Dalhousie Review* 77.2 (1997): 155-77.

———. *The Black Loyalists: The Search for a Promised Land in Nova Scotia and Sierra Leone 1783-1870*. New York: Africana, 1976.

Williams, James. *Lyotard and the Political*. London: Routledge, 2000.

"This history's only good for anger": Gender and Cultural Memory in *Beatrice Chancy*

by Maureen Moynagh

National narratives are, willy nilly, acts of cultural memory, if we understand cultural memory to be about identity, values, and recollections of the past that serve the needs of the present.[1] National narratives are also, as we know, profoundly gendered.[2] Taking my cue from Lauren Berlant, who asks what it would mean "to write a genealogy of sex... in which unjust sexual power was attributed not to an individual, nor to patriarchy, but to the nation itself" (221), I want to ask what it would mean to stage an act of cultural memory in which unjust sexual power is indeed attributed to the nation and where the identity at stake is both national and diasporic. Cultural memory is a tool of the powerful as well as of the disenfranchised, and if, as Marita Sturken has argued, cultural memory "is a field of cultural negotiation through which different stories vie for a place in history" (1), it is also the case that the terms of negotiation are prejudiced in favour of the dominant group. Yet among the consequences of undertaking a genealogy of sex in the nation, Berlant argues, would be the exposure of the importance of sexual underclasses "to national symbolic and political coherence" and the establishment of an alternative historical archive, "one that claimed the most intimate stories of subordinated people as information about *everyone's* citizenship" (221). The promise, then, of articulating cultural memory with gender and race is the contestation of hegemonic narratives of nation, a splitting open of the historical sutures that close out stories of racial terror and sexual injustice, relegating them to a space beyond the body of the nation.

In this essay, I would like to transpose Berlant's inquiry to Canada and to undertake a genealogy of sex in the nation via a reading of the scripting of cultural memory in George Elliott Clarke's verse drama and opera *Beatrice Chancy* (1999). The drama is set in Nova Scotia in 1801 and combines a tale about incest and patricide with the history of slavery in the province. The title character is the daughter of a white Loyalist planter and one of his slaves; she has been raised in her father's household, educated in the ways of white folk, and treated like a prized possession. When Beatrice declares her love for another slave, however, her father's "love" is abruptly transformed: he rapes her. Beatrice, in turn, murders her father and is hanged, but not before sparking a revolt among the other slaves on the plantation. Another installment in Clarke's mythopoetic elaboration of "Africadia,"[3] *Beatrice Chancy* shares with Clarke's other poetic works and much of his literary criticism an abiding concern with the erasure of the history and, more broadly, the lived experiences of African Nova Scotians and African Canadians from the national imaginary. In contesting that erasure, Clarke has created works in a range of media, from the printed page to theatre, radio, film, and most recently opera. In many of these works Clarke has undertaken to restore the lives of black women to their proper order of importance, but nowhere in so far-reaching and fundamental a manner as in *Beatrice Chancy*.

As Clarke engages in the process of what Toni Morrison in *Beloved* called "rememory," constructing a history of slavery in a nation actively invested in forgetting that slavery was ever practiced there, he seduces his audiences into an uncomfortable intimacy with public violence and compels them not only to denounce that violence but to acknowledge their complicity in it. In choosing to make his heroine the mulatta daughter of a slaveholder and the victim of incestuous rape, moreover, Clarke exposes the nation's reliance on sexual underclasses in a way that has far-reaching implications for national self-understanding. Clarke's commemoration of the experiences of slaves in Canada is not only an effort to "maintain at the centre of national memory what the dominant group would like to forget" (Singh, Skerrett, and Hogan 6), it also writes African Canadians into national narratives in a way that refuses patriarchy together with racism. In staging a drama about incest, Clarke impresses on his audiences the extent to which cultural memory work that redresses sexual and racial violence is necessarily about "everyone's citizenship." His heroine, Beatrice, performs what Berlant calls an act of "diva citizenship," staging "a dramatic coup in a public sphere in which she does not have privilege" and "calling on people to change the social and institutional practices of citizenship to which they currently consent" (223). In "indigenizing" (Findlay) a diasporic narrative, Clarke interrupts the national imaginary, disrupting its coherence with a drama that lays bare the nation's intimacy with racial and sexual violence.

Technologies of memory

Literature is but one of the technologies of cultural memory, but as a technology of memory literature resonates in multiple ways in *Beatrice Chancy*. Not only is literature Clarke's chief medium for cultural memory work, it is also arguably his medium for, as it were, communing with the dead.[4] In writing about memory and the art of memoir, Morrison observes that slave narratives represent the beginnings of black literature in the United States ("The Site of Memory" 85). Not surprisingly, memoirs and slave narratives are at the foundation of African-Canadian writing as well, as Clarke attests (*Fire* 1: 12, *Eyeing* xiv), citing John Marrant's *Narrative of the Lord's Wonderful Dealings with John Marrant, a Black (Now Going to Preach the Gospel in Nova-Scotia)* (1785); David George's *An Account of the Life of Mr. David George, from Sierra Leone in Africa...* (1793); Boston King's *Memoirs of the Life of Boston King, a Black Preacher, Written by Himself...* (1798); and Josiah Henson's *Life of Josiah Henson, formerly a Slave, now an Inhabitant of Canada* (1849). As the records of slavery and of the experiences of New World Africans more generally, these memoirs are the literary foundations of cultural memory in the African diaspora. The dual function of representing a life and speaking to injustice that characterized the slave narratives also characterizes the cultural memory work that Clarke undertakes in

Beatrice Chancy. Clarke draws directly on this body of diasporan writing; he acknowledges Harriet Jacobs's *Incidents in the Life of a Slave Girl: Written by Herself* in particular. Yet like Morrison, Clarke's interest in these texts arguably has to do with more than the historical information that they can yield. Morrison suggests that her interest in recreating accounts of slavery in fiction is to remember what the authors of the slave narratives were compelled to forget. Where for the sake of decorum the authors and editors of slave narratives scrupled to suppress the harshest details of slavery, Morrison understands her task as finding a way to "rip that veil drawn over 'proceedings too terrible to relate'" (91). Connected to this task is that of imagining an interior life, also suppressed in the slave narratives, and claiming the agency historically denied African Americans as a people. Clarke, too, tears down the veil over not only the most graphic acts of exploitation but over slavery itself. In imagining a life for Beatrice and endowing her with agency, moreover, Clarke is effectively doing double duty: remembering slavery in behalf of African Canadians and in behalf of the nation. In *Beatrice Chancy* cultural memory is performed as countermemory.

There is another way in which literature serves Clarke as a technology of memory in *Beatrice Chancy*. Not only does Clarke draw on and indigenize African diasporan works like Jacobs's *Incidents in the Life of a Slave Girl* and Frances Harper's *Iola Leroy* (1892), he borrows a story from European history and literature as well and indigenizes it twofold, making it African and Canadian. In choosing the story of Beatrice Cènci, Clarke effectively makes decorum a central preoccupation. For there can scarcely be an act more usually veiled in secrecy than incest or a figure more apt for blurring the line "between personal and national tyranny" (Berlant 232) and exposing the nation as agent of unjust sexual power. Incest is an indecorous act, but as an intimate transgression taking place "in private" it is frequently veiled in the public code of decorum that will not admit of (or to) it. The drama effectively deconstructs decorum, exposing its endless deferral of the ethical behavior in the name of which it differentiates between classes, genders, and races. A masquerade of seemliness and propriety, decorum is the guise adopted by those who would justify acts of violence and oppression conducted according to the terms of a patriarchal and racist social code. Decorum is also the refuge of those who would not see or hear of such acts but allow them to continue. Beatrice, in rising up against her violator, violates the terms of decorum, refuses its morality, and claims the justice of her actions. In this rising up, Beatrice Chancy performs an act of "diva citizenship."

In reading *Beatrice Chancy* as an act of cultural memory, as I aim to do, I am also compelled to consider the conditions of its performance. That is to say, under what circumstances does it enter into the public sphere to offer its counternarrative, to deconstruct the decorum of Canadian national narratives? One might well expect, in the case of a verse drama and opera, that performance is, quite literally, the chief mechanism for intervention. Yet the matter is not at all straightforward. To begin with, there are effectively two "versions" of *Beatrice Chancy*. The opera is not a performance of the verse drama but a production of a separately published libretto.[5] The verse drama, on the other hand, while clearly a dramatic text, is not necessarily a theatrical text.[6] There is abundant textual evidence suggesting that the drama is to be read as poetry rather than performed as a play: stage directions scan, descriptions of the characters are similarly poetic, there are photographs scattered through the volume, and the arrangement of the words on the page is frequently key to meaning. As cultural memory work, then, *Beatrice Chancy* is transmitted both by textual and performative means. Yet, if features of the verse drama are literally unperformable, they are nonetheless arguably performative in another sense. I contend that it is possible, even crucial, to speak of performance with respect to both versions of *Beatrice Chancy*.

In his elaboration of performance as a medium for cultural memory, Joseph Roach cites Richard Schechner's definition of performance as "restored behavior" or "twice-behaved behavior" and conjoins it to the theatrical concept of surrogation ("Culture" 46, *Cities* 3). Key for Roach is the constitutive impossibility of restoring behaviour, for "no action or sequence of actions may be performed exactly the same way twice; they must be reinvented or recreated at each appearance," and thus "in this improvisatory behavioral space, memory reveals itself as imagination" ("Culture" 46). For Roach, surrogation supplements Schechner's understanding of performance in its "uncanny" emphasis on reinvention, on theatrical doubling, and on "the doomed search for originals by continuously auditioning stand-ins" (*Cities* 3). There is much in Roach's elaboration of surrogation, of "the three-sided relationship of memory, performance, and substitution" (*Cities* 2), that I find suggestive for a discussion of *Beatrice Chancy*, not least his interest in how surrogation operates between cultures in what he calls the "circum-Atlantic world." Yet where Roach positions memory and performance largely outside of textual modes of cultural transmission, I would like to suggest that in the verse drama, quite as much as in the opera, Clarke is engaged in acts of surrogation.

W. B. Worthen argues persuasively that "although Roach tends to frame performance surrogation as a form of resistant remembering that is opposed to the oppressive forgetting he associates with textual transmission, the power of this sense of surrogation lies in how it reflects the transformative nature of the cultural transmission of meanings, textual as well as performative" (1101). In other words, texts and their cultural meanings are also reiterated, reinvented, and remade as they are circulated; textual studies, too, is "doomed" in its search for originals. Worthen is particularly interested in the ways that a dramatic performance may be understood as a form of surrogation, "as an act of iteration, an utterance, a surrogate standing in that positions, uses, signifies the text within the citational practices of performance" (1102). Not only are these insights helpful for understanding the significance of *Beatrice Chancy* the opera, Worthen's extension of surrogation to textual transmission offers another way of thinking about the workings of cultural memory in the verse drama as well.

Not only does Clarke reiterate and reinvent Percy B. Shelley's *The Cenci* and other literary, dramatic, and filmic versions of the Renaissance tale; not only does he reiterate slave narratives like Jacobs's *Incidents in the Life of a Slave Girl*; and not only does he refunction historical texts to his purposes, Clarke cites and signifies (on) theatrical and poetic form in his poeticized stage directions and self-conscious referencing of theatrical performance and canonical literary works throughout. While each reference has its own contextual resonance, taken together they comprise a citational practice that, like the theatrical mode of doubling, holds copy and "original" up together. This citational practice, moreover, shares with Roach's notion of surrogation the sense of cultural and ethnic difference, for, as Clarke has attested on numerous occasions, "part of [his] strategy as a writer, in responding to [his] status as the scribe of a marginal and colonized community, is to sack and plunder all those larger literatures... and to domesticate their authors and their most famous or noted lines" (Compton 143). Clarke's work, moreover, underscores what Roach describes as the mutually constitutive relationship between literature and orature, "the range of cultural forms invested in speech, gesture, song, dance, storytelling, proverbs, customs, rites, and rituals" ("Culture" 45), insofar as Clarke cites not only literary canons but what he calls "Africadian" poetry, by which he means the poetry "rooted in the voice and in [the] shared jokes, stories, proverbs" (140) of Black Nova Scotian communities. Performative in the sense of "*draw*[*ing*] *on and cover*[*ing*] *over* the constitutive conventions by which it is mobilized" (Butler 51), Clarke's poetic drama draws on conventions both of literary texts and of the ritualized practices of everyday life and speech that Roach sees as the realm of "living memory as restored behavior" (*Cities* 11). In what follows, I analyze the surrogation, the resignifying of historical and literary archives in *Beatrice Chancy,* and I then explore the citational practices that mobilize both the verse drama and the opera as technologies of cultural memory.

History, countermemory

Beatrice Chancy is set in the Annapolis Valley of Nova Scotia in 1801, where slavery remained legal, as it did in the rest of British North America, until 1834, when it was officially abolished throughout the British Empire. Both the French and English settlers practiced slavery in the colonies that were eventually to become Canada, although slavery was not to become the economic cornerstone in these northerly colonies that it was elsewhere in the Americas. In 1783 an influx of 3,000 free blacks in the wake of the American Revolutionary War, together with the more than 1,000 black slaves who accompanied white Loyalists to Nova Scotia, both augmented and destabilized what was effectively a slave society in the province. If the presence of free blacks made things easier for fugitive slaves, the practice of slavery represented a constant threat to free blacks (Walker 41). As far as white Loyalists were concerned, all blacks were fit for slavery, and a provincial social formation that slotted blacks as labourers for whites only reinforced that ideology (Mannette 111; Walker 42). Barry Cahill observes, "Like the *ante-bellum* United States, Loyalist Nova Scotia could not endure half-slave and half-free. Either the slaves would have to be emancipated, or the free Blacks would have to emigrate" ("*Habeas Corpus*" 186). In effect, something of both these alternatives came about. In 1792, a large number of free black Nova Scotians left for Sierra Leone, and from then until the arrival of black refugees between 1814-16, "Nova Scotia's residual black population was largely unfree and was concentrated in Annapolis County" (Cahill, "Slavery" 43). Meanwhile, from the late 1790s into the early 1800s, successive non-Loyalist chief justices waged what Cahill terms a "judicial war of attrition against slavery in Nova Scotia" ("*Habeas Corpus*" 182). Unable to rule on the legality of slavery as an institution, judges sought by other legal means to free those blacks jailed as fugitives even as Loyalists sought, unsuccessfully, through the Provincial Assembly, to create statutes affirming and extending slavery as a practice.

The play and the opera are historically resonant with this struggle over slavery, as well as with the broader diasporan experience of slavery in the Americas. In this way, Clarke confronts the national amnesia about slavery with the diasporan linkages the nation prefers to deny or displace to the late twentieth century. The national significance of this representation of Loyalist Nova Scotia, moreover, has in part to do with the place of the Loyalists in what historian Daniel Francis has dubbed the "myth of the master race" (52-87). One of the foundational narratives of Canada as a nation, "the myth of the master race" has to do with the fundamentally British and imperial character of Canada. Without its ties to Britain and the empire, Canada counted for little, according to the terms of this narrative, "but as part of a union of Anglo-Saxon nations, and an Empire which embraced a quarter of the world's population, Canada could participate in the great mission of spreading justice, freedom, and prosperity around the world" (Francis 63)—not to mention ensure its independence from the United States. According to the imperialist narrative of Canada as a nation, the Loyalists were "'the real makers of Canada': they were the best and the brightest that the American colonies had to offer" (56). Given that the "real makers of Canada" were frequently staunch defenders of slavery, there is an irresolvable contradiction at the heart of the national vision of Canada as a land of justice and freedom.

Gradually, as Britain's colonies claimed their independence around the world and Canadian immigration policies opened up, the myth of the master race came to be displaced by another, the myth of the Canadian mosaic, which itself evolved into the myth of multiculturalism in the wake of Prime Minister Pierre Elliott Trudeau's official 1971 policy.[7] Consistent in all of these narratives, despite the nominal embrace of diversity in the postwar and particularly post-1971 period, is a foundational racism and sexism. If the "myth of the master race" was clearly a myth about whiteness in which there was simply no place in the nation for racial others—not First Nations, not blacks, not Chinese—the postwar myths of inclusiveness could still, for different reasons, not admit of the existence of slavery. The myth of multiculturalism, on the other hand, makes claims about the cultural freedom of all Canadians, irrespective of ethnic origin, and pronounces an end to discrimination and forced assimilation.[8] According to the terms of this myth, slavery is a U.S. phenomenon; Canada's only acknowledged connection with the institution is as the terminus for the underground railway, as the geopolitical locus of the North Star and freedom. Testimony to the endurance of this popular understanding of Canada's role in the history of slavery is to be found in the Canadian Broadcasting Corporation's recent television series, "Canada: A People's History" (CBC-TV and Radio Canada 2000-2001), which passes over in silence the practice of slavery in early settlements and among Loyalist immigrants but explicitly dramatizes the arrival of black refugees under the auspices of the underground railway.

Clarke tackles the occlusion of blackness in these myths of nation both in his writing and in his critical work. "If Canada itself is a residual America," Clarke observes in a recent essay, "old-line black Canadians form a kind of lost colony of African America. The American Revolution, the War of 1812, and abolitionist agitation forged the first major African-Canadian populations" ("Contesting" 2). Yet African Canadians are a "lost colony" in another sense—lost from view. It is no exaggeration to claim that African Americans figure more frequently in the Canadian national imaginary than African Canadians, for, as Clarke notes, Euro-Canadians reference "African-American culture... to buttress Canadian moral superiority vis-à-vis Euro-American culture" (3). In particular, Euro-Canadians are keen to see themselves as reflected in what Clarke terms "a classical African-American discourse on Canada [that constructs] the nation as the promised land, or Canaan, for fugitive African Americans" (2). Significantly, this is a vision of Canada post-1850, as opposed to Canada pre-1834, when slavery was legal. The myth of nation that represents Canada as a place of refuge, tolerance, and equality is dependent on the careful erasure of that earlier history. Clarke's cultural memory work addresses a crisis in the discourse of multiculturalism that has dominated the last quarter of the twentieth century, and his intervention is nowhere more effective than in *Beatrice Chancy*, which explicitly challenges the historical erasure at the heart of this narrative of nation.

Beatrice Chancy is dedicated to Marie-Josèphe Angélique and Lydia Jackson, two African-Canadian women who were enslaved, one in New France, the other in Nova Scotia.[9] Their lives are recorded, however elliptically, in the archives, if not in popular histories, but the meaning of those lives is just beginning to be accounted for through the cultural memory work of African-Canadian writers like Lorena Gale (2000), Sylvia Hamilton (1994), and Clarke. Jackson's story, in particular, is germane to my discussion of the place of sexual injustice in the formation of the nation and to the function of cultural memory work that is centered on these acts. *Beatrice Chancy* is not patterned on the events of Jackson's life, but it is faithful to the history of the social formation that oppressed her. Because the occluded history of slavery in Canada is so much at stake in redressing the racism of contemporary myths of nation, and because sex and race were articulated in particularly oppressive ways in that historical moment, Jackson's story is particularly instructive. Jackson, I would go so far as to suggest, is Beatrice Chancy's historical correlate.

Jackson was a free black woman living in Nova Scotia who, having been abandoned by her husband and having no recourse under the law, found herself in dire economic straits. Her situation was exploited by a man named Henry Hedley, who "hired" her as a companion to his wife, then persuaded her to sign a contract that, in her understanding, indented her to him for a period of one year. The unscrupulous Hedley, knowing Jackson was illiterate, had in fact made the contract out for thirty-nine years. He then promptly sold Jackson to Dr. John Bulman (Bolman) of Lunenberg, Nova Scotia, for £20. Bulman was a particularly vicious master who beat Jackson frequently and raped her. Even while she was under Bulman's control, she attempted to resist this treatment, managing to file a complaint with an attorney in Lunenberg. Bulman was a powerful man, however, and successfully used his influence when the case went to court. After some three years of slavery under Bulman, Jackson managed to escape and flee to Halifax, where she again sought to obtain justice. In accordance with contemporary practices, she had a "memorial," or statement of grievances, drawn up and presented to Governor Parr, who ignored it. Some time later, she approached Chief Justice Thomas Strange, who promised to look into the matter. Strange was the first of the two successive chief justices who sought to battle slavery in the courts, to the extent that it was possible. Jackson then also met with John Clarkson, an abolitionist who was in Halifax organizing a mission to Sierra Leone of those free blacks who were dissatisfied with conditions in Nova Scotia. Clarkson took up Jackson's case himself for a time, but he decided that it could not be resolved while he was in the province and recommended that she "give it up and leave Bulman to his own reflections" (Clarkson 90). It is Clarkson's report on his mission that provides the fullest archival account of Jackson's experiences.

In her memorial and in her appeals to Strange and Clarkson, Jackson undertakes a kind of diva citizenship. Faced with the intransigence of the Loyalist Ascendancy, which Bulman represented, Jackson did not obtain the redress she sought and in all likelihood abandoned Nova Scotia for yet another "promised land," Sierra Leone. Bulman's "private" acts of sexual and racial injustice go unpunished, if not undiscovered, because of the "public" political sanction for sexual and racial inequality. Jackson's public testifying against Bulman, her repeated efforts to obtain redress for the offenses committed against her, are acts of courage in a society that scarcely acknowledged her "right" to speak. Her assumption of agency and her exposure of the connection between public and private tyranny make her an appropriate figure for comparison with Clarke's heroine. In his verse play, Clarke chooses as his vehicle for memory work another story about violence and ethics, the story of Beatrice Cènci.

Twice-told tales and surrogate acts

At the core of the original story are two acts of violence, two crimes: incest and parricide, crimes that, so named, resonate even more deeply than when they are called rape and murder because they are crimes not only against society but against the most intimate kinship structures on which patriarchal, capitalist, Western societies have been built. The incest taboo is commonly understood as the basis for the creation of social ties beyond the family unit. For Claude Lévi-Strauss, the incest prohibition is "the supreme rule of the gift" that creates mutual obligation among families. These social relations are of course gendered: in patriarchal, capitalist societies, men forge social ties through the exchange of women; that is to say, fathers give their daughters in marriage to other men in exchange for social, economic, and political gain.[10] That father-daughter incest is the most common breach of the incest taboo in patriarchal societies underscores, according to Judith Herman, the extent to which "the rights of ownership and exchange of women within the family are vested primarily in the father" (60). Francesco Cènci, in taking his daughter (for) himself, violates but also exercises a fundamental social law. In murdering her father, Beatrice also violates social law, not only by killing a member of her society but by striking at the kinship structure itself and its gendered organization. For in rising up against her father, Beatrice does the unimaginable: the object of exchange becomes an agent in her own behalf. In many tellings of this tale, the audience is asked to think differently about this act of murder, this parricide, than social law dictates. We are asked to think about Beatrice Cènci as a tragic heroine and to regard her act of parricide as a symptom of society's crime against this female individual. These are the elements of the original history and some of its literary versions that Clarke exploits in *Beatrice Chancy*.

In adapting this tale to slave-holding Nova Scotia in 1801, Clarke sets up the kinship narrative in order to tear it down. For as scholars writing about slavery have shown, this story of gender and kinship was rewritten under slavery. Not only were black families separated during the course of the notorious Middle Passage, but plantation societies throughout the Americas fundamentally disrupted African kinship relations. Hortense Spillers describes the plantation system in this way: "In effect, under conditions of captivity, the offspring of the female does not 'belong' to the Mother, nor is s/he 'related' to the 'owner,' though the latter 'possesses' it, and in the African-American instance, often fathered it, and, as often, without whatever benefit of patrimony" ("Mama's Baby" 74). Of course, this is not to say that slaves did not construct family relations anyway, imagining alternative family relations that were very powerful, but Spillers's point, and mine, is that the dominant society did not recognize those alternative family relations, and thus slaves were officially outside of kinship structures. Black women slaves were, at the same time, subjected to a process of "ungendering,"[11] first, by being assigned the same kinds of work as the men and subjected to the same acts of brutality and torture, and second, by being placed outside of a gendered moral code. Slavery as a system placed its captives outside an ethical framework by representing slaves as commodities equivalent to so many pounds sterling. At the same time that the captive body is reduced to a thing, "provid[ing] a physical and biological expression of 'otherness,'" the very otherness of the captive body "translates into a potential for pornotroping" (Spillers, "Mama's Baby" 67) that means black women can be subjected to rape without any breach of decorum.

That decorum in slavery societies depended on a deferring and differing of racial and gendered constructs is nowhere so clear as in that particularly pervasive moral discourse during the nineteenth century, the discourse of "true womanhood" (Jones; Carby). The markers of "true womanhood" were virtue, chastity, physical frailty—and whiteness. In fact, the achievement of "true womanhood" was absolutely dependent on the existence of black women slaves, who performed the strenuous physical labour that permitted white plantation mistresses to be delicate and fragile and whose stereotyped sexuality (few black women slaves had the luxury of chastity) served to guarantee the purity of their white counterparts (Carby 30). Merely to survive rape, the common lot of black women under slavery, was to contravene "true womanhood," for if the sentimental novels of the era are to be believed, no "true" woman would survive sexual assault (34). The removal of black women, under slavery, from the patriarchal kinship system was another guarantee that the category of womanhood would inevitably be bound up with whiteness, for, as Spillers observes, "the 'reproduction of mothering' [among black slaves] in this historic instance carries few of the benefits of a *patriarchilized* female gender, which, from one point of view, is the only female gender there is" ("Mama's Baby" 73). In fact, if we consider the way that this moral discourse, with its particular articulation of gender and race, depends on patriarchy, we might conclude that under slavery in North America, decorum begs the question not only of a raced and gendered morality but of kinship itself. In using father-daughter incest as a figure for unjust sexual and racial power in *Beatrice Chancy*, Clarke uses guerrilla tactics to stage an insurrection from within the structures of kinship, confronting the nation with its violence and the shame of its hypocrisy.

Another figure "restored" and reimagined in *Beatrice Chancy* is the mulatto/a, and once again we have to do with a decorous masquerade of sexual and racial injustice. Spillers argues that "the mulatto in the text of fiction provides a strategy for naming and celebrating the phallus;" that is to say, "the play and interplay of an open, undisguised sexuality are mapped on the body of the mulatto character, who allows the dominant culture to say without parting its lips that 'we have willed to sin'" ("Notes" 179). That this sexual mapping tended to conjoin "the new taboo of miscegenation" and "the old taboo of incest" (Sollors 302) makes the mulatto/a particularly apt for Clarke's cultural memory work. Spillers reads this figure for what it reveals about "gender as a special feature of racialist ideology" (181). Located between the white lady, who is maternal and reproductive but, paradoxically, "chaste," and the black woman, who is female pleasure without womanhood, the mulatta allows "the male to have his cake and eat it too, or to rejoin the 'female' with the 'woman'" (183). A figure or, in Spillers's words, an "idea-form" emanating from the perverse desires of the dominant culture, the mulatto/a has a substantial textual and performance history in the African diaspora.[12] Yet Spillers notes that "the thematic of the 'tragic mulatto/a' seems to disappear at the end of the nineteenth century" (176). It is appropriate, then, that at the end of the twentieth century, Clarke's surrogation of the theme in *Beatrice Chancy* is a rewriting that makes explicit what had, for the dominant narrating of this fiction, always to be silenced, obscured. For Spillers, the mulatto/a represented "an accretion of signs that embod[ied] the 'unspeakable,' of the Everything that the dominant culture would forget" (177), and in this respect also the figure is an appropriate one for representing the national "forgetting" of slavery. In *Beatrice Chancy*, the "idea-form" of the mulatto/a and the mixed-race historical subject are held together via a particular form of surrogation: Beatrice wears two masks, standing in at once for the historical subject and the idea-form. Her complicated agency lies in this dual status, for as historical subject she speaks and acts out against the violence and perversity of the idea-form, even as her fate (incestuous rape, murder, and hanging) is largely controlled by it.

What better way to make the point that slavery was an intimate part of the formation of Canada (however much myths of nation have sought to forget it) than to represent it as a family affair? In *Beatrice Chancy*, Beatrice is slave and daughter, and it is her ambivalent status as both that proves so troubling. The story of kinship is rewritten in the drama as Beatrice's symbolic value as Francis Chancy's daughter (and not merely the biological fact of her relation to her master) is acknowledged. In fact, as the play opens, it is her status as daughter that seems to be winning out. We learn that she is about to return home from a convent school in Halifax where she has been sent "to copy/White ladies' ways" (17). Reminiscent of the pattern laid out in *Iola Leroy*, where Eugene Leroy sends Iola's mother Marie north to be educated before he manumits and marries her, this trope in *Beatrice Chancy* becomes a means of exposing Chancy's perverse white male fantasy, his desire to eat his cake and have it too, as we shall see presently. Beatrice's status as daughter is irrevocably bound up with the acquisition of whiteness but also, as the play makes clear, with her female gender. The overseer Dice, who is also rumoured to be Chancy's offspring, has no chance of being acknowledged as Chancy's son. As Chancy himself asserts, "My son must be white and known to be white" (28). Beatrice, on the other hand, is most useful to Chancy as a daughter whom he can exchange for political gain. As he tells Reverend Peacock, when the latter suggests he sell Beatrice, "She's too expensive to waste. I'll graft her/On some slavery-endorsing Tory/To fat my interests in the Assembly" (28). The ambiguity of Beatrice's status emerges in the contradiction between Chancy's plans for her, which position her as daughter, and the language he uses to convey those plans, which is at once crudely biological ("I'll graft her") and economic—more appropriate to a slave, in other words. Strictly speaking, under slavery any child of a black mother was black. Thus Chancy's efforts to remake Beatrice in his own image ("I dispatched Beatrice to Halifax/To shape her more like us—white, modern, beautiful" [52]) suggest a deliberate reworking of kinship in a way that exposes its racial subtext.

The ambiguity of Beatrice's status, in other words, allows Clarke to expose and indict the workings of the system of slavery and the social system that condoned it. Nova Scotia, one of the slaves tells us early in the play, is a whorehouse (14). The commodification of sexual relations is the political economy of a province that allowed slavery to exist and that bartered its daughters for political patronage. The language of commodification pervades the play, informing both the slaves' understanding of their position in a plantation economy—"Father," Beatrice demands in a sharp reminder of the difference between daughters and slaves, "would you barter me like a hog,/Or wood, or a piece of machinery?" (56)—and the discourse of white society. Reverend Peacock and the Hangman both regularly remind Chancy that Beatrice is his property to dispose of as he sees fit, and they both make clear that it is more fitting that he sell her as a slave than marry her off as a daughter. These representatives of the church and the judicial system—for the Hangman will ultimately carry out Beatrice's death sentence—lend institutional support to Chancy's patriarchal power. Chancy's first speech tells of traffic in women slaves as he gives his overseer and would-be son, Dice, a shopping list:

> Buy a hogshead of stomach-stabbing rum,
> H. W. L.'s tragic Natchitoches tobacco,
> A puncheon of molasses, a keg of nails,
> One purebred *nègre* heifer and her calf

(Pay £70 for the lot, not a sou more),
And fifty-two yards of Hobbes-forged chains. (23)

The parenthetical injunction to limit costs that divides the "*nègre* heifer" from the chains in this casually rhymed-off list underscores the crude economy governing the life of bondage. The bonds of kinship form a startling contrast. When Chancy expresses surprise that Dice makes no attempt to escape bondage, the latter responds, "You've played the only father I've loved" (24). Once again, however, Chancy denies this kinship: "Your complexion's like night-exhausted stars/But go as if you could sue to be my son" (24). Chancy characterizes his slaves, stereotypically, as "childish cattle/That need unflinching mastery" (26). Paradoxically, the adjective "childish" serves to remind us once again of the question of kinship at the centre of this play, and the fact that "cattle" is so close to "chattel" reminds us that at least one and probably two of Chancy's chattel are in fact his children. The lines between property and kin refuse to remain clearly drawn. Chancy's infertile wife Lustra, who sees herself ambivalently as Beatrice's stepmother and as her rival, alternately objects to Beatrice's commodification and subscribes to it. "My only child's not for sale to your likes!" (56) she declares when the Hangman offers to buy Beatrice; later, when speaking to Beatrice, she observes sardonically, "For a piece of property, you quarrel much" (72). As it turns out, Beatrice's dual status is a threat to the system that produced her, and through her actions, tragic heroine that she is, she brings that system crashing down on herself.

If, in the context of the play, her gender gives her access to whiteness, Beatrice's mixed racial heritage imposes strict limits on that access. "True womanhood," it turns out, is not within her purview, for the virtue that characterizes "true womanhood" hangs on whiteness, as we have seen. Appropriately then, Chancy declares Beatrice chaste on her return from the convent school in Halifax, where she has been sent to acquire whiteness. That virtue is a sign of whiteness is also underscored by Chancy's overt description of the role that slaves play in the moral economy of the province, where blackness is needed to define whiteness. "How can we be beautiful, free,/Virtuous, holy, pure, *chosen*," Chancy demands, "If slaves be not our opposites?" (26). Beatrice's mixed heritage, though, makes Peacock skeptical of her proclaimed chastity. In expressing his doubts, he proffers the stereotypical view of black female sexuality: "Is Beatrix Cincia sacred? No, no./.../She'll batten on hardness like any whore./Black slave hussies are only born/To nasty, baste, breed and suckle" (38). That the slaves read the question of Beatrice's virtue very differently provides another level of commentary on the dominant discourse. Here the concern is that her convent experience might have altered her allegiances. Lead worries, "What if her heart's frostbit?/What if she craves to bed down a white boy?" (18). As it turns out, of course, Lead has nothing to worry about. But Beatrice's loyalty, her desire for Lead, makes impossible her borrowed whiteness. For while the rape of female slaves by white planters reinforced the system of slavery through what amounted to an exercise of power and control over the slave population as a whole, the notion that a white woman might actually desire a black man was inadmissible. Thus when Chancy discovers that Beatrice wishes to marry Lead, he punishes her by demoting her to slave status, declaring that "my daughter can't love some bull-thighed nigger!" (55) and treating her accordingly, first by locking her up and then by raping her.

Until Beatrice spurns his desires through her decision to marry Lead, Chancy indulges in a fantasy facilitated by Beatrice's mixed racial heritage, which makes her a candidate for the acquisition of whiteness in the first place. Beatrice's lighter skin allows Chancy to pretend that bondage is indeed kinship. "My power isn't violation, it's love" (27), he attempts to persuade Peacock on the eve of Beatrice's return from the convent school in Halifax. Peacock attempts to force Chancy into a decision about Beatrice's dual status: "Do you want Beatrice to fear or love you?" he asks, pointing out, "She is equally your daughter and your slave." Chancy persists in his equivocation: "I've sponsored her convent school for three years—/An unusual blessing for a slave./But she's my daughter" (27). Chancy appears to favour her filial status here, but he simultaneously affirms her status as slave. Moreover, on Beatrice's return "home," we begin to suspect Chancy's "love" for her may be more conjugal than paternal after all. He remarks, "Regard: rare, Demerara skin—mare's skin./Look how she denominates her mother" (53). A lighter-skinned version of her mother, Beatrice might just have other uses than fatting his interests in the Assembly. That decorum, whether conjugal or paternal, is quickly abandoned when Beatrice declares her love for another slave, which exposes the sham as well as Beatrice's real vulnerability. As mulatta, Beatrice is subjected both to white male fantasies and to the rule of sexual availability that applies to all black women under slavery. Chancy's use of rape as punishment is a sign that for him, she is no longer "white," no longer his daughter.

It is Beatrice who emphasizes her status as daughter at this point, vowing to Chancy "Tenderly, I love you, as your daughter" (69). Chancy, no longer willing to recognize Beatrice as white, insists on reading her love as lust, as evidence of her blackness: "All your lyricism, love speech, is dress/For the nakedness of longing" (70). For Chancy, such a reading is sanction for his act of rape, hardly even a crime under slavery, let alone incestuous. His meditation on the act of violence he is about to perform transfers culpability to Beatrice, who, in the terms of yet another racist fantasy, is seen as seducing her rapist:

> I tempt my brain—or she lures me—to grave
> An organ in a fresh, unscabrous cleft,
> To be darkly traduced, a prize, vicious,
> Sap-eating triangle, housing noxious
> Buzzing of incestuous insects busy
> At sex, dumping blood—swank, nervous—like Christ's. (81)

Yet this speech also acknowledges Chancy's guilt and his betrayal, as he speaks of her sex as both smooth and pure, the opposite of scabrous, and of his penetration as a misrepresentation, a defilement. The imagery of insects engaged in "noxious" activity marks the incestuous act as unnatural, the bloodletting a martyrdom, a crucifixion. Still later in his soliloquy, Chancy shifts back to the language of commodification, as he represents Beatrice as "a costly, well-kept diamond" about to be "cracked by a jeweller's chisel—/A soft, ebony jewel, split tenderly,/Then vomiting priceless ruby facets" (82). Her punishment is to move across the bar of her dual status, from daughter to slave: "My hands will speak horror to her body./She'll learn what it means to be property" (82). But Beatrice, in insisting on her status as daughter, on the injustice of Chancy's discounting of her as merchandise (70), makes possible the moral condemnation of Chancy's act by defining it as incest as well as rape. In this way, she rewrites the moral code operative under slavery, making black women the agents of moral authority rather than its negated objects.

Significantly, it is when Chancy treats Beatrice most as an object that she emerges most fully as agent, and her agency lies in her ability to expose the operations of the moral code of slavery. She indicts the false Christianity of the slaveholders even as, against the Easter setting of the play, she takes on the role of crucified Christ. More significantly, through Beatrice, Clarke makes poetry the means of rending the veil of decorum historically dropped over the most violent and gruesome acts of slavery. It is, ironically, Chancy who describes Beatrice's way with words:

> Wantonly, I'll discover her verse—
> Wet, shining, under a black bush, a language
> That is flesh webbing us, the mouth feel of poetry,
> The Word in her mouth—like salt water,
> Malicious, sad, like Clemence orchards
> Torn apart by hail. (81-82)

If the Word is phallic mastery, Beatrice swallows it up, using it to create a different language, one that speaks of the crimes committed against her. Chained and imprisoned by Chancy once she declares her love for Lead, lashed by Dice who finds her in her lover's arms, Beatrice complains to Lustra of Chancy's crimes: "he makes thieves and harlots of his slaves" (72). When Lustra chastises her for the impropriety of her speech—"To hear a woman speak thusly—so close to shame" (72), Beatrice lashes out: "Would my words stab! I'm molested/By white men's words and black men's eyes" (72). Delineating her situation in a gendered and raced system that deems her speech indecorous, Beatrice vows to use her words as a weapon in her defense. She refuses the perverted ethics of a system that justifies racial terror by blaming violation on its victims—"Your lean thighs justify your mother's slavery" (86), Chancy tells Beatrice moments before he rapes her in the chapel. Here the decorum that conventionally cloaked the worst violence of slavery is represented as censorship: as Chancy rapes her, Beatrice's speech registers a terrible silencing: "I hurt [*two words garbled*] my throat/[*Several words whited out*] a knife" (87). Decorum as whitewash, literally. What remains of Beatrice's speech after this violation—"I hurt," "my throat," "a knife"—combines pain with the source of speech and a weapon ambiguously positioned, perhaps *at* her throat, or perhaps we are to understand that her throat *is* now a knife, a weapon. In subsequent scenes, Beatrice does not hesitate to articulate the violence done her in "blunt talk." When Lustra attempts to silence her by reminding Beatrice that Chancy is her father—in a hollow appeal to the kinship system that Chancy himself destroyed—Beatrice responds, "Call him as you like. I call him my raper." And when Lustra admonishes, "These words aren't poetry, Beatrice:

They canker," Beatrice gives her what she asked for, if not exactly what she wants: "You like poetry, so here's sweetheart poetry:/He wants me for his piece of brown sugar,/ And he wants you to watch him licking it" (109). Poetry is at once what Chancy attempts to destroy and the means of representing his crimes.

Verbal niceties are the representational equivalents of the racist and sexist kinship system in the name of which Beatrice is enslaved and violated. Barred from her tenuous position as daughter, yet suffering as a daughter, Beatrice embraces the role of outlaw in order to indict the false morality of slave societies: "White men, you took away my freedom/And gave me religion./So be it: I became a devout killer" (140). Thus, she assumes agency in another, terrible guise: she becomes Chancy's judge and executioner. That we are able to read Beatrice's act of murder as the symptom of a slave society's crime against her is again due to Clarke's careful manipulation of the historical subtexts. One of the other clear limits to Beatrice's temporary and limited access to whiteness as Chancy's daughter is her inability to summon anyone to her defense. Thus, when she proposes to protect her status as daughter by summoning colonial soldiers, telling Lustra "I require that Wentworth/Field troops to warranty my father's love" (77), her stepmother quickly admonishes her: "Beatrice, you forget your low place. Troops shield/White women" (77). Having no other recourse, Beatrice acts in her own behalf, but also in behalf of the other slaves. In signing her own death warrant through her illicit act, Beatrice nonetheless succeeds in dealing a blow to slavery itself by sparking a revolt. In effect, Beatrice derives her agency from the system that oppresses her. Spillers points out that "the powers of domination succeed only to the extent that their permeation remains silent and concealed to those very historical subjects... upon whom the entire structure depends" ("Notes" 185). In *Beatrice Chancy*, we witness the breakdown of this system, insofar as Beatrice, as historical subject, becomes only too aware of how domination works and refuses to remain silent, exposing her father's actions and renaming him her "raper."

In imagining this conclusion for *Beatrice Chancy*, Clarke not only rewrites the story of the Cènci, he transforms the history that Lead early in the play deems "only good for anger" (17). Lead is responding specifically to the story of Beatrice's mother, and with her story Clarke encapsulates a diasporan history and centres it on the combined racial and sexual exploitation that was the lot of black women under slavery:

> Her name was Mafa. Thefted from Guinea,
> She washed ashore when that slaver, Fortune,
> Splintered off Peggy's crushing Cove, sinking
> Three hundred Africans. Bought as bruised goods
> By Massa, next seven years his forced wife,
> She died when I was seven, Bee was four,
> And she was herself just twenty-one years. (17)

"Fortune" is not merely the name of the ship but a synonym for the economic system that created the slave trade that "thefted [Mafa] from Guinea." Conversely, Mafa's fortune, not to mention that of her shipmates, founders in Nova Scotia where she is sold and raped. In *Beatrice Chancy*, this diasporan history is brought home, as it were, and is made to confront hegemonic national narratives that would seek to stop it at the Canada–U.S. border. In attributing unjust sexual and racial power to the nation, Clarke makes "this history [that]'s only good for anger" a testimony to the suffering of subordinated people, and in the transformation of Beatrice from commodity to agent, we can read a representation of subaltern insurgency, a claim to citizenship in the name of those historically denied it and those who continue to be asked for their passports.[13]

(Re-)Staging public memory

It remains to take account of the ways that this representation of subaltern insurgency is made to speak to the living as well as communicate with the dead. In addition to the citational practices specific to textual and operatic transmission that work to signify *Beatrice Chancy*, there are broader discursive structures that condition the reception and circulation of both. Paradoxically, in light of its support for the anodyne visions of multiethnic and interracial harmony that have helped to occlude the history of slavery in Canada, multiculturalism may be said also to offer a larger discursive structure for the entry of *Beatrice Chancy* onto the public stage in Canada.[14] That there are effectively two versions of *Beatrice Chancy* (or two formal variants, to be more precise, since cultural transmission clearly makes for a potentially infinite number of "versions") must also be taken into account, for the opera and the verse drama function as surrogates, one for the other, thus extending and reinforcing *Beatrice Chancy*'s performative possibilities. Its success as a chamber opera has led to its reproduction in other media, specifically CBC (Canadian Broadcasting Company) Radio and CBC-TV, venues that not only increase its audience considerably but, in their role as national, publicly funded media, perform the task of representing the nation to itself. That *Beatrice Chancy* is "the first Canadian opera [to be] broadcast on television in more than 30 years" (Bernstein B4) suggests, at the very least, that its impact in the public sphere has not been negligible.

Let us begin with the matter of textual transmission. While reading is most often a solitary activity, the transmission of literary texts is in fact a collective and collaborative process, thus affording a text entree into the public sphere. Via reviews in the press as well as literary magazines and academic journals, via interviews with Clarke on radio and television, via educational organizations and institutions, and via public "readings," literary texts come to have a place in the public sphere in ways that can legitimately be described as performative insofar as each of these modes of reception and circulation offers "an elaborate reiteration of a specific vision of social order" (Worthen 1097) in which the text is made to signify.[15] To date, although it was only published in 1999, *Beatrice Chancy* has enjoyed a fairly remarkable reception— remarkable because of its extent, and remarkable in view of the challenge this text poses to the dominant vision of social order in the nation.

As an opera, *Beatrice Chancy* has perhaps made an even greater impact. It opened to rave reviews in 1998 and has had three more stage productions since then, a fact that is regarded as something of a feat given that new operas are rarely revived. Clarke's libretto, with its insurgent testimony about the unjust racial and sexual power of the nation, is here mobilized by the citational practices of chamber opera performance. If, as Worthen suggests, performance "regimes can be understood to cite—or, perhaps subversively, to resignify—social and behavioral practices that operate outside the theater and that constitute contemporary social life" (1098), it is worth taking note of the social preoccupations that have surfaced in contemporary Canadian opera. Linda Hutcheon and Michael Hutcheon argue that although they do not always address explicitly Canadian themes, "the Canadian operas written in recent years go to the heart of the nation's concerns about such things as the ethics of power and the definition of the nation and of the self" (6). *Beatrice Chancy*, then, may be said to have found a national(ist) medium for its repatriation of a diasporan history.

James Rolfe's composition, described as "citational in ways which make it both resolutely contemporary and historically resonant" (Hutcheon and Hutcheon 7), quotes extensively from spirituals, gospel, the blues, and jazz, as well as Scottish strathspey and reels in an effort to evoke the historical and cultural terrain encompassed in Clarke's libretto. The music is a collage of twentieth-century operatic colors in a minimalist setting. It is scored for two violins, a viola, a cello, bass, piano, and percussion. In the primacy accorded the libretto and the theatrical elements of operatic performance, the composition resonates clearly with U.S. musical theatre in the tradition of George Gershwin, Kurt Weil, and Leonard Bernstein. It also exhibits the stylistic influences of Alban Berg and Benjamin Britten. The harmonic language, thinly orchestrated, alludes to compositions by Igor Stravinsky, Arvo Pärt, and Gershwin and occasionally offers glimpses of an older operatic style through references to Henry Purcell.[16] The opera opens with a ring shout, during which the singers play percussion instruments, and closes with the singers and the musicians standing together on the stage singing the spiritual "Oh, Freedom!" thus according prominence to the African diasporan narrative at the heart of the libretto.

The production by Queen of Puddings Music Theatre Company underscores the tensions between subaltern history and hegemonic narratives of nation that Rolfe's music and Clarke's libretto articulate.[17] The musicians are also costumed as slaves and perform at the side of the stage, in view of the audience. For one critic, this "blurring of boundaries... encourages us to contemplate our own complicity in injustice" (Bernstein B4); for another, it represents "a gesture of unity that embrace[s] the audience as well" (Kareda 89). For Bernstein, the relationship of score to libretto is also potentially conflictual: "Rolfe's deft assimilation and fusion of musical styles... seems to offer the possibility of plurality and understanding between races and classes that the story itself grimly withholds" (B4). The power of surrogation, in this instance, lies precisely in these unresolved tensions. Where the finale strives for transcendence, what emerges is perhaps best understood in terms of the ambiguous transcendence offered in the spiritual form, itself a resonant vehicle of cultural memory, where visions of a peaceful realm of freedom beyond the world of slavery present a powerful critique of the strife and lack of freedom in that world.

Through operatic performance and the collective modes of literary reception, not to mention radio and television broadcasts, *Beatrice Chancy* has entered onto the national stage and, via its eponymous heroine, undertaken an act "of risky dramatic persuasion" (Berlant 223). The tension between national narratives and subaltern memory that is, in one way or another, a feature of all citations of the work threatens to foreclose any intervention that it might make into a national self-understanding about slavery. Beatrice Chancy's performance of countermemory consists in her assumption of agency on behalf of historic and contemporary African-Canadian women, speaking of past injustice in order to call upon the nation in the present. It is a fleeting agency, to be sure, derived from suffering and the lived contradictions of her status as daughter and slave and aptly conveyed through the character's surrogation of the mulatta as both type (which, by definition, is entirely without agency [Spillers, "Notes"]) and historic subject. Yet in her performance of the wronged mixed-race daughter and the avenging spirit, Beatrice effects a kind of intervention, claiming a citizenship historically denied her.

With *Beatrice Chancy*, Clarke contributes to the growing body of contemporary African diasporan literature engaged in the process of representing the pain and trauma of the experience of slavery. In works ranging from Morrison's *Beloved* (1987) to Maryse Condé's *I, Tituba, Black Witch of Salem* (1992), from Octavia Butler's *Kindred* (1979) and Gayl Jones's *Corregidora* (1975) to Dionne Brand's *At the Full and Change of the Moon* (1999) and Lorena Gale's *Angélique* (2000), the ethical impulse to renew the self-understanding of New World Africans and to rewrite their relationship to dominant society is enacted through an abiding concern with gender, with the particular place of the black woman in the sexual economy of slavery. The peculiar national refractions of that diasporan history entail distinct mnemonic devices. In choosing the story of Beatrice Cènci, a tale of incest and parricide, Clarke strives to awaken the nation to its own repressed intimacy with racial and sexual violence. "My country needs me, and if I were not here, I would have to be invented," Spillers once observed in commenting on the overdetermined construction of black womanhood in the U.S. context ("Mama's Baby" 65). Yet in a national context that can barely conceive of an African-Canadian female subject, the need for inventing one has more to do with an overdetermined absence. In this context, what better story could one tell of unjust sexual relations than a story of incest? In effect, the national relation to slavery in the Canadian context is incestuous, not only by virtue of being a family affair but by virtue of being taboo, silenced, absent from the national imaginary. But Beatrice refuses to be silenced and, in a virtuoso performance, compels our sympathy and elicits our outrage in her behalf. That she is aiming at a diva performance is clear from her response to Deal, who advises her to play Moses to Massa's Pharaoh: "I'll play Beatrice. I'll play her beautifully" (62).

(2002)

Notes

[1] See, e.g., Jan Assmann's definition of cultural memory.

[2] A sample of the extensive feminist research on nationalism would include work by Kumari Jayawardena (1986), Nira Yuval-Davis and Floya Anthias (1989), Deniz Kandiyoti (1991), and Anne McClintock (1995).

[3] *Africadian* is a word coined by Clarke as an alternative to *African-Nova Scotian, AfroNova Scotian, black Nova Scotian,* or other possible appellations. A fusion *of Africa* and *Acadia,* this term is evocative of an imagined community. Clarke's most important poetic works to date, which in other respects are very different, have centered on "Africadia": *Whylah Falls* (1990), *One Heart Broken into Song* (1999), *Beatrice Chancy,* and *Execution Poems* (2000). Clarke was born and grew up in Nova Scotia, where, as he puts it, his "bloodlines run deep… to 1813 on [his] African-American/Mi'kmaq mother's side and to 1898 on [his] African-American/Caribbean father's side" ("Eyeing the Northern Star" xii).

[4] I have in mind here not only *Beatrice Chancy* but Clarke's poems about Lydia Jackson and Africville (1992), his commemoration of the hanging of his cousins George and Rufus Hamilton in *Execution Poems,* his commemoration of Graham Jarvis in *Whylah Falls,* and the novel *George and Rue* (2005).

[5] See "*Beatrice Chancy*: A Libretto in Four Acts" (Clarke). The full opera premiered at the Music Gallery in Toronto in 1998 and has subsequently been remounted at the Du Maurier Theatre in Toronto (June 25-26, 1999), at Alderney Landing Theatre in Halifax (August 12, 14-15, 1999), and at the Citadel Theatre in Edmonton (February 8, 10-11, 13, 2001), and it was broadcast on CBC Radio (October 25, 1998) and CBC Television (February 8, 2001).

[6] There was a "dramatic reading" of *Beatrice Chancy* at Theatre Passe Muraille in Toronto, July 10-11, 1997.

[7] The myth of the mosaic, typically counterposed to the concept of a melting pot, which is held to be American, conceives of Canadian ethnic diversity in terms of a constellation of distinct groups living amicably side by side. As Francis (1997) points out, the concept of the mosaic originates with the Euro-Canadian mainstream, its benign vision of ethnic relations masking racism and social stratification along ethnic lines.

[8] There are important differences between the discourse of multiculturalism, as it developed in the U.S. academic context in the 1980s and 1990s, and the ways that the concept of multiculturalism resonates in Canada in light of its origins in Liberal government policy and the concomitant federal funding that continues to be made available to ethnic groups across the nation. For a comparison of the discourse in the United States and Canada, see Huggan and Siemerling. Critics of the policy have

argued that it creates a two-tiered funding system that continues to marginalize the work of ethnic minorities. See Philip, Kamboureli, Wilson, Gunew, and Li.

[9] Angélique had an illicit affair with a young Frenchman at a time (1730s) when concubinage was explicitly proscribed under the Code Noir. Angélique's affair was discovered and condemned. Shortly thereafter, a fire broke out in a section of Montreal; Angélique was blamed for the fire and hanged in a public square for her crime.

[10] Gayle Rubin's careful elucidation of these issues remains an important source.

[11] See Davis, Jones, Carby, and Spillers ("Mama's Baby").

[12] A partial list would include Dion Boucicault's *The Octoroon* (1859); the novel by Mayne Reid, *The Quadroon* (1856), on which Boucicault's play is based; Richard Hildreth's *The Slave; or, Memoirs of Archy Moore* (1836); Lydia Maria Child's "The Quadroons" (1842); Elizabeth Livermore's *Zoe; or, The Quadroon's Triumph, A Tale for the Times* (1855); as well as Harper's *Iola Leroy*, Nella Larsen's *Passing* (1929); and Jessie Fauset's *Plum Bun* (1929).

[13] Both Clarke and Adrienne Shadd have written about how regularly in Canada, African Canadians are assumed to be from somewhere else, usually either the United States or the Caribbean. See Shadd and Moynagh.

[14] Press notices and television reports of the opera have assiduously referred to "Canada's dirty little secret" (Clarke, Rolfe, and Hess) or "Canada's invisible history" (CBC-TV, "Opera"), in what seems an almost obligatory gesture of expiation.

[15] For reviews, see, e.g., Beaton, Burns, Wiwa, McNeilly, Sandiford, Sealy, and Sugars. Interviews with the author include the CBC Radio interview by Tom Allen (Clarke); the CBC-TV interview, together with James Rolfe and John Hess (Clarke, Rolfe, and Hess), by Linda Griffin; and a spot on CBC-TV's national news program, "Opera Sheds Light on Canada's Invisible History."

[16] I am grateful to Daryl Burghardt of the Music Department at St. Francis Xavier University for his assistance in describing these musical styles.

[17] Queen of Puddings has mounted all the productions of *Beatrice Chancy* to date, and the same singers, including Measha Brüggergosman in the role of Beatrice, have performed each time.

Works Cited

Assmann, Jan. "Collective Memory and Cultural Identity." *New German Critique* 65 (Spring-Summer 1995): 125-33.

Beaton, Virginia. "*Beatrice Chancy* resonates with poetic grace." Review of *Beatrice Chancy*, by George Elliott Clarke. *Sunday Herald* 11 July 1999: C7.

Berlant, Lauren. *The Queen of America Goes to Washington City: Essays on Sex and Citizenship.* Durham, NC: Duke UP, 1997.

Bernstein, Tamara. "A Canadian Opera Worth Cheering About." *National Post* 8 February 2001: B4.

Burns, Kevin. Review of *Beatrice Chancy*, by George Elliott Clarke. *Quill and Quire* 65.5 (1999): 35.

Butler, Judith. *Excitable Speech: A Politics of the Performative.* New York: Routledge, 1997.

Cahill, Barry. "*Habeas Corpus* and Slavery in Nova Scotia: *R. v. Hecht ex parte Rachel*, 1798." *University of New Brunswick Law Journal* 44 (1995):179-208.

———. "Slavery and the Judges of Loyalist Nova Scotia." *University of New Brunswick Law Journal* 43 (1994): 73-134.

Carby, Hazel. *Reconstructing Womanhood: The Emergence of the Afro-American Woman Novelist.* New York: Oxford UP, 1987.

CBC-TV. "Opera Sheds Light on Canada's Invisible History." *National.* 5 October 1999.

CBC-TV and Radio Canada. "Canada: A People's History." Produced by Mark Starowicz, Hubert Gendron, and Gordon Henderson. Television series. 2000-2001.

Clarke, George Elliott. *Beatrice Chancy.* Victoria: Polestar, 1999.

———. "*Beatrice Chancy:* A Libretto in Four Acts." *Canadian Theatre Review* 96 (Fall 1998): 62-77.

———. "Contesting a Model Blackness: A Meditation on African-Canadian African Americanism, or the Structures of African Canadianité." *Essays on Canadian Writing* 63 (Spring 1998): 1-55.

———. *Execution Poems.* Wolfville, NS: Gaspereau, 2000.

———, ed. *Eyeing the North Star: Directions in African-Canadian Literature.* Toronto: McClelland & Stewart, 1997.

———, ed. *Fire on the Water: An Anthology of Black Nova Scotian Writing.* 2 vols. Lawrencetown Beach, NS: Pottersfield, 1991-92.

———. *George and Rue.* Toronto: HarperFlamingo, 2005.

———. Interview by Tom Allen. *This Morning Sunday.* CBC Radio. 25 July 1999.

———. *One Heart Broken into Song.* Digital Betacam, 90 minutes. Toronto: Telefilm Canada. 1999.

———. *Whylah Falls.* Vancouver: Polestar, 1990.

Clarke, George Elliott, James Rolfe, and John Hess. Interview by Linda Griffin. *Opening Night.* CBC-TV. February 8, 2001.

Clarkson, John. 1792. *Clarkson's Mission to America, 1791-1792.* Ed. Charles B. Ferguson. Halifax: Public Archives of Nova Scotia, 1971.

Compton, Anne. "Standing Your Ground: George Elliott Clarke in Conversation." *Studies in Canadian Literature* 23.2 (1998): 134-64.

Davis, Angela. *Women, Class, and Race.* New York: Random House, 1981.

Findlay, Len. "Always Indigenize! The Radical Humanities in the Postcolonial Canadian University." *ARIEL: A Review of International English Literature* 31.1 (1999): 307-26.

Francis, Daniel. *National Dreams: Myth, Memory, and Canadian History.* Vancouver: Arsenal Pulp, 1997.

Gale, Lorena. *Angélique.* Toronto: Playwrights Canada, 2000.

Gunew, Sneja. *Framing Marginality: Multicultural Literary Studies.* Melbourne: Melbourne UP, 1994.

Hamilton, Sylvia. "Naming Names, Naming Ourselves: A Survey of Early Black Women in Nova Scotia." *"We're Rooted Here and They Can't Pull Us Up": Essays in African Canadian Women's History.* Ed. Peggy Bristow. Toronto: U of Toronto P, 1994. 13-40.

Herman, Judith Lewis. *Father-Daughter Incest.* Cambridge, MA: Harvard UP, 1981.

Huggan, Graham, and Winfried Siemerling. "US/Canadian Writers' Perspectives on the Multiculturalism Debate." *Canadian Literature* 164 (Spring 2000): 82-111.

Hutcheon, Linda, and Michael Hutcheon. "Opera and National Identity: New Canadian Opera." *Canadian Theatre Review* 96 (Fall 1998): 5-8.

Jayawardena, Kumari. *Feminism and Nationalism in the Third World.* London: Zed, 1986.

Jones, Jacqueline. *Labor of Love, Labor of Sorrow: Black Women, Work and the Family from Slavery to the Present.* New York: Basic, 1985.

Kamboureli, Smaro. "Of Black Angels and Melancholy Lovers: Ethnicity and Writing in Canada." *Feminism and the Politics of Difference.* Ed. Sneja Gunew and Anna Yeatman, Boulder, CO: Westview, 1993. 143-56.

———. "The Technology of Ethnicity: Law and Discourse." *Open Letter* 8th ser. 5-6 (1993): 202-17.

Kandiyoti, Deniz. "Identity and Its Discontents: Women and the Nation." *Millennium: Journal of International Studies* 20.3 (1991): 429-43.

Kareda, Urjo. "The Little Company That Could." *Toronto Life*. December 1999. 81-90.

Lévi-Strauss, Claude. *The Elementary Structures of Kinship*. Boston: Beacon, 1969.

Li, Peter. "A World Apart: The Multicultural World of Visible Minorities and the Art World of Canada." *Canadian Review of Sociology and Anthropology* 31.4 (1994): 365-91.

Mannette, Joy A. "'Stark Remnants of Blackpast': Thinking on Gender, Ethnicity and Class in 1780s Nova Scotia." *Alternate Routes* 7 (1984): 102-33.

McClintock, Anne. *Imperial Leather: Race, Gender, and Sexuality in the Colonial Contest*. New York: Routledge, 1995.

McNeilly, Kevin. "Word Jazz 2." Review of *Beatrice Chancy*, by George Elliott Clarke. *Canadian Literature* 165 (Summer 2000): 176-81.

Morrison, Toni. *Beloved*. New York: Knopf, 1987.

———. "The Site of Memory." *Inventing the Truth: The Art and Craft of Memoir*. Ed. William Zinsser. Boston: Houghton Mifflin, 1987. 85-102.

Moynagh, Maureen. "Mapping Africadia's Imaginary Geography: An Interview with George Elliott Clarke." *ARIEL: A Review of International English Literature* 27.4 (1996): 71-94.

Philip, Marlene NourbeSe. "Why Multiculturalism Can't End Racism." *Frontiers: Selected Essays and Writings on Racism and Culture, 1984-1992*. Stratford, ON: Mercury, 1992. 181-86.

Roach, Joseph. *Cities of the Dead: Circum-Atlantic Performance*. New York: Columbia UP, 1996.

———. "Culture and Performance in the Circum-Atlantic World." *Performativity and Performance*. Ed. Andrew Parker and Eve Kosofsky Sedgwick. New York: Routledge, 1995. 45-63.

Rubin, Gayle. "The Traffic in Women: Notes on the 'Political Economy' of Sex." *The Second Wave: A Reader in Feminist Theory*. Ed. Linda Nicholson. New York: Routledge, 1997. 27-62.

Sandiford, Robert Edison. "Acts of Fact and Fancy." Review of *Beatrice Chancy*, by George Elliott Clarke. *Antigonish Review* 120 (Winter 2000): 161-63.

Sealy, David. Review of *Beatrice Chancy*, by George Elliott Clarke. *Canadian Review of American Studies* 30.1 (2000): 116-18.

Shadd, Adrienne. "'Where Are You Really From?' Notes of an 'Immigrant' from North Buxton, Ontario." *Talking about Difference: Encounters in Culture, Language and Identity.* Ed. Carl E. James and Adrienne Shadd. Toronto: Between the Lines, 1994. 9-15.

Singh, Amritjit, Joseph Skerrett, Jr., and Robert E. Hogan, ed. *Memory and Cultural Politics: New Approaches to American Ethnic Literatures.* Boston: Northeastern UP, 1996.

Sollors, Werner. "'Never Was Born': The Mulatto, an American Tragedy?" *Massachusetts Review* 27.2 (1986): 293-316.

Spillers, Hortense. "Mama's Baby, Papa's Maybe: An American Grammar Book." *Diacritics* 17.2 (1987): 65-81.

———. "Notes on an Alternative Model: Neither/Nor." *Year Left 2.* Ed. Michael Sprinker, Mike Davis, and Manning Marable. New York: Verso, 1987. 176-94.

Sturken, Marita. *Tangled Memories: The Vietnam War, the AIDS Epidemic, and the Politics of Remembering.* Berkeley: U of California P, 1997.

Sugars, Cynthia. Review of *Beatrice Chancy,* by George Elliott Clarke. *Books in Canada* 29 (February 2000): 13-14.

Walker, James W. St. G. *The Black Loyalists: The Search for the Promised Land in Nova Scotia and Sierra Leone.* Toronto: U of Toronto P, 1992.

Wilson, Seymour. "The Tapestry Vision of Canadian Multiculturalism." *Canadian Journal of Political Science* 26.4 (1993): 645-69.

Wiwa, Ken. "Unveiling Canada's Hidden Slave History." Review of *Beatrice Chancy,* by George Elliott Clarke. *The Globe and Mail* 3 July 1999: D16.

Worthen, W. B. "Drama, Performativity, and Performance." *PMLA* 113.5 (1998): 1093-107.

Yuval-Davis, Nira, and Floya Anthias, ed. *Women-Nation-State.* New York: St. Martin's, 1989.

Dramatic Instabilities: Diasporic Aesthetics as a Question for and about Nation

by Rinaldo Walcott

Introduction: Producing Dramatic Instabilities

Let me begin with a major claim. Black Canadian theatre is forged and performed within the context of a diasporic sensibility and/or consciousness. Thus, Black Canadian theatre sits somewhere between addressing its "nationally local" contexts and engaging in a much wider context: that wider context is the basis of what constitutes its diasporic aesthetics. So let me make one further claim: Black Canadian theatre is centrally concerned with piecing together all of the ways in which diasporic expressions of Blackness can fashion a commentary on nationally local and global conditions. What I mean by this is that the form, the performance, the texture, the content, the gesture of Black Canadian theatre engages its nationally local and its wider context. In this essay I will probe a number of Black Canadian plays to demonstrate how the execution of those plays produces a diasporic sensibility and consciousness, and thus a diasporic aesthetic, and how those plays represent a dramatic instability for nationally local concerns by reaching beyond the nationally local, as well as speaking specifically and directly to the nationally local context in uncompromising fashion. The various moves or aesthetic practices that I attempt to map from these plays are what I call dramatic instabilities. These are not negative consequences of the plays; rather, they are dramatic in their demands for a more ethical constitution of the nationally local scene and of the conditions for making a life that is Black and livable, both nationally and internationally.

When the ethical is inserted into the conversation as a form of concern, some manner of potential outcome might be expected. The philosopher of New World conditions Sylvia Wynter offers a reading of the now-classic Jamaican film, "The Harder They Come" (1973). In her reading of the film, Wynter proposes what she calls a "deciphering practice." By a deciphering practice, Wynter means to signal some rather important ways of reading and making sense of texts (broadly defined), so that we can move between and beyond the specifics of what she calls "ethno-criticism" and into a reconstituted universalism proffered from the vantage point of the subaltern or the dispossessed. Thus, for her, "a deciphering turn seeks to decipher *what* the process of rhetorical mystification *does*. It seeks to identify not what texts and their signifying practices can be interpreted to *mean* but what they can be deciphered to do, and it also seeks to evaluate the 'illocutionary force' and procedures with which they do what they do" (267). Furthermore, Wynter posits that the question of taste is important to a deciphering practice because it challenges the Western middle-class cultural imaginary in an attempt to offer a counter-politics that seeks to produce a "global popular Imaginary whose referent telos is that of the well-being of the individual human subject and, therefore, of the species" (269). Thus, a deciphering practice is about attempting to engage in a political process that concerns itself with changing our present governing orders for both individuals and the collective body politic.

The Instabilities of the Nationally Local

In attempting to think the political inside the aesthetic, Wynter is not at all trying to reduce art to a crass notion of politics. Rather, she attempts to argue and demonstrate that art always speaks for some kind of politics. I am in agreement with such an analysis. In ahdri zhina mandiela's *dark diaspora… in dub*, the opening lines immediately reference or gesture to a wide expanse of Black diasporic interests. The lines move from the individual to the collective in the following:

> & this: one
> of many/million
> dark tales (447)

But earlier, mandiela gives a nod to Langston Hughes's often-cited poem of dreams deferred, in the line "let out/blocked hopes," and gestures to the dilemma of oral performativity and the written word:

> these words are/for/ever/
> more/just fossilled:
> language (447)

This span of gesture just in the opening lines of the play is but one moment or instance of the invocation of a diasporic sensibility and/or consciousness. The play itself spans the Caribbean (Jamaica), African (Liberia) and the "white" Western world (Canada, Australia, London, etc.). The real and symbolic use of movement in the play is parallel to the forced and other forms of migration that Black diasporic people have undergone and continue to experience. The play itself is populated with all kinds of movement: migration to Canada, a poem called "blues bus," and various other forms of metaphoric and actual movement. This ongoing concern with and reference to movement is, I believe, one of the central characteristics of Black diasporic sensibilities and consciousnesses. And when these are etched into art—in this case a play—they become the bases of a diasporic aesthetics.

In the title poem from which the play takes its name, the culmination of the desires of the dark diaspora is exposed when the narrator chants "better mus come!" This chant is, in part, a counter-political act of the play, whereby politics lives in the aesthetic demand for a different world, a more ethical world. Thus, it might be suggested that *dark diaspora… in dub* is intended to do something. "Better mus come" is the plea for what that something might signify or mean. A close reading of mandiela's play can produce a wealth of references to issues and concerns that one can broadly contextualize within a diasporic framework. But one of the central concerns of the play's overall aesthetic is to affect its nationally local context. It does so by a continued return to the conditions of Black migration to Canada and the links between that migration and other Black people worldwide. A politics of trans-national identification is a signal of a Black diasporic aesthetic.

Similarly, Andrew Moodie's *Riot* offers a much more sustained concentration on the nationally local as a way to impact the national. So if mandiela begins in the wider diaspora and contracts to Canada and then moves again, Moodie begins in the nationally local, moves to the diasporic, and contracts to the nationally local again. Each of these plays is interested in clarifying something about the nationally local of Black experience and history, in relation to the national and/or as an example of diasporic conditions. Moodie's play takes its inspiration from the Rodney King beating and, more specifically, from the acquittal, in 1992, of the policemen responsible for it and the resulting riots in Los Angeles. *Riot* is, as well, a restaging of the 1992 riots that took place on Yonge Street in Toronto, in response to the acquittal of a policeman for shooting a Black man in Toronto. The ways in which the Yonge Street riots mirror the LA riots cannot be easily overlooked. While the Yonge Street riots were smaller and had less national and international impact, their nationally local significance cannot be downplayed.

Using the Yonge Street riots as the backdrop of his play, Moodie sets out to script a history and experience of Black Canadianness that would trouble previous definitions of Blackness in Canada (at least on the stage). The characters of *Riot* are a multi-ethnic cast of Black players (Jamaican, Ugandan, Canadian). This particular representation of Canadian Blackness sets into motion different kinds of attachments to the nation. Thus, what Canada means to each character is very different and is open for debate among the characters in the play, as it is among the audience. I have made two claims about *Riot* elsewhere: (1) that Blackness must be understood as internally differentiated and as a set of competing histories; and (2) that the play elaborates our understanding of Canadianness (Walcott, "Riotous"). One way to read the characters of *Riot* is to see the cast as an ensemble of diasporic characters in Canada (Walcott, "Riotous" 4). While all the characters are citizens of Canada, each has a different historical attachment to the nation and each character brings a different sensibility to what the nation means to him/her. This difference in what the nation means destabilizes how it is that both the nation and Blackness might be read. The destabilization lies in the difficult fact that neither "nation" nor Blackness can be easily pinned down, even though each is posited with a set of parameters that makes it identifiable. The boundaries of "nation" are stretched to include more than it is assumed the nation *can* include. In such an instance, for example, Moodie's *Riot* elaborates the Canadian nation by positing a range of Black characters, whose differences render any suggestion of a singular Blackness or Black community impossible. And yet the playwright is still able to produce forms of identification, so that this multi-ethnic Blackness is identified with and acts in solidarity with forms of African-American Blackness.

Moodie's *A Common Man's Guide to Loving Women* is similarly driven by a cross-border identification with the controversies, ramifications and implications of Black manhood in the midst and aftermath of the O.J. Simpson trials. *A Common Man's Guide* is, in part, an exploration of the ways in which particular representations of Black manhood circulate across North America (Walcott, "Post-OJ"). The play is, in part, concerned with historical and ongoing destabilizations of Black manhood. Without recourse to being didactic, the play concerns itself with the historical constitution of Black manhood in a post-Columbus world. The most recent instance of the overwhelming troubles of Black manhood were spectacularized in the O.J. Simpson trials, and the play makes use of this public collective memory to attempt to rescue some space for the complexities of Black manhood and, I would suggest, other (heterosexual) manhoods as well. In this way, the play does not just speak for Blackness but, in much the same way as *Riot* elaborates Canadianness, *A Common Man's Guide* forces us to confront the question of whether contemporary expressions of Black manhood can stand in for expressions of all of North American manhood and its present destabilization in the face of some important feminist gains that are remaking our patriarchal rules of governing.

A Common Man's Guide might be generously read as concerned with the destabilizations that contemporary feminism has wrought for all men in the context and practice of masculinity. In such a reading, the play is concerned with a particular set of questions and concerns about what might be a reconstituted masculinity in the face of a popular feminist consciousness. That the play launched this question through a discussion of Black manhood opens up the difficult terrain of whether subaltern experience and history can be the basis of and for a universalist understanding of human life. Thus, once again, we see how a diasporic sensibility comes to engage an aesthetic inside which a politics of some sort lives. Once again, transnational identification is evident. But to posit that the reviled, criminalized and sometimes murdered manhood of Blackness may speak for all of manhood is to destabilize modernity and universality as some of us have come to know and understand those ideas. It is my argument that diasporic sensibilities are intimately engaged in processes of destabilization that are meant to produce a different view of the world and therefore a different aesthetic. Thus, I am suggesting that part of the aesthetic of Black Canadian theatre is a question of what might constitute a universal point of view from the vantage point of the subaltern.

Because each of the plays that I have discussed above (and those that I will discuss below) take their insight, and sometimes inspiration, from events, histories, moments and other ephemera, real and imagined, from elsewhere, it is difficult to make sense of those plays without having also to think differently about the nation—in this case Canada. These plays destabilize the assumptions that produce the normative narrative of the nation as white, benevolent and just. Instead, these plays find room for Blackness and Black peoples; these plays posit a history of injustice and degradation; these plays offer forms of nationally local resistance and international political identifications and, finally, these plays refuse the notion that national contexts are the only meaningful contexts for justice, all the while holding the national context accountable, responsible and ethically implicated. These plays rethink humanity and the universal from the vantage point of the dispossessed.

The Instabilities of Modernity, Universality and Diaspora

Diasporic sensibilities are located in what we might characterize as a particular form of or insight into the universal. The idea of the universal is and remains one of the central tenets of the discourses of modernity. Because diasporic experiences might be characterized as the "b-side" of historical and contemporary discourses of globalization, diasporic experiences tend to reference and point directly to the ongoing traumas and injustices of the pre-modern, the modern, and post-modern world. Thus, diasporic insights can provide us with a perspective on the universal from a non-dominant source. In order for them to do so, those who see themselves as outside the story of suffering and pain must find ways to identify with such stories, so that the insights they permit can become a site of solidarity and ethicality. As Paul Gilroy has pointed out, using the term "strategic universalism,"

> Bolstered by the cautious, strategic universalism toward which the history of fascism inclines us, diverse stories of suffering can be recognized as belonging to anyone who dares to possess them and in good faith employ them as interpretative devices through which we may clarify the limits of our selves, the basis of our solidarities, and perhaps pronounce upon the value of our values. (230)

Diasporic experiences, thus, reference another kind of universality: the universal position of those dispossessed from the fruits of modernity. These stories of suffering can offer us a world-view for thinking differently about all of humanity. To use the insights of how vicious modernity can be and has been is, at least, one way to tell a different story of its successes and failures.

Therefore, some art that is forged within a sensibility and consciousness of Black diasporic suffering and resistance, through ongoing expressions of diasporic life, reminds us of the unfinished business of modernity—its viciousness and its promise. This art tends to make central to its narrative the ongoing business of liberty, freedom, citizenship, nation and equality. In this way, many of the important ideas and desires of modernity come under scrutiny, suspicion and question, particularly ideas of nationhood and citizenship. I am suggesting that it is from the place of instability that diasporic interventions, especially interventions through art, can constitute a form of universal insight. Black Canadian plays can be said, generally, to engage such concerns.

Since one of the central tenets of modernity is the constitution and legitimation of the nation-state and its citizen members, diasporic plays, as I am characterizing them, seem also to take as central to their articulation concerns about nation and belonging. The ongoing tensions around how Black peoples are positioned within nations, especially in regard to their citizenship, is a specific diasporic concern. Diasporic sensibilities and consciousnesses tend to make use of the ways in which Black peoples across various nations take up forms of political and cultural identification in regards to the politics of belonging. Diaspora is, therefore, an alternative to thinking and acting within the bounds of the defined nation.

An alternative to the metaphysics that "race," nation, and bounded culture code into the body, diaspora is a concept that problematizes the cultural and historical mechanics of belonging. It disrupts the fundamental power of territory to determine identity by breaking the simple sequence of explanatory links among place, location and consciousness. It destroys the naïve invocation of common memory as the basis of particularity, in a similar fashion, by drawing attention to the contingent political dynamics of commemoration (Gilroy 123).

Many of the plays I am looking at challenge how it is that one can belong to contemporary nation-states. These plays offer an explicit engagement with belonging that opens up the aesthetic to the political and the political to the aesthetic. For example, NourbeSe Philip's *Coups and Calypsos* and George Seremba's *Come Good Rain* refuse the bounded culture of nation to explore a range of issues that reverberate back onto the modern nation-state and its inadequacies. *Coups and Calypsos* is a play that explores the politics of race and race mixing, against the backdrop of a coup. Both the political and race tensions of the play reverberate back on each other to produce various forms of instability. For if nations, as imagined communities, assume a particular kind of sameness, the issues of racial, cultural and political tensions explored by Philip expose the violence that nations must practise to produce an imagined homogeneity. In the case of Philip's play, the historic tensions and the obvious mixing of Blacks and Indians in Trinidad and Tobago allow for an unsettling of continued assumptions that place these groups as poles apart. This destabilization of conversations does not resolve the situation but dramatically destabilizes politics, race and culture through race mixing and the production or evidence of the mixed-race person, in this case, expressed as the *dougla*. Furthermore, because the main characters of the play are "of" Trinidad and Tobago but are not citizens or necessarily invested in that nation—are diasporic Caribbean of British descent—further destabilizations are evident.

George Seremba's *Come Good Rain* similarly makes use of personal memory to destabilize dramatically the inadequacies of the modern nation-state of Uganda. As Modupe Olaogun has pointed out, the play is, in part, based upon Seremba's escape from Uganda after his own near murder and repression in the face of what was promised to be a democratic election. For my purposes, Seremba's telling of the tale of postcolonial disappointment from outside Uganda once again points to the ways in which the ideas of modernity continue to be the basis from which a diasporic identification can be made. Exile only makes sense in the context of the production and maintenance of the modern nation-state as something that one can be estranged and removed from. The desire and failure of the postcolonial nation to produce justice for its formerly colonized citizens is a recurring diasporic concern and may constitute a diasporic aesthetic impulse. *Come Good Rain* thematizes and dramatizes the failures of the modern and postcolonial nation to live up to the promise of freedom, democracy and liberty.

Come Good Rain is a traumatic re-memory of the postcolonial nation-state's failures. In this vein, it fits the diasporic paradigm that I am articulating, in that its performance calls us to address the unfinished promise of modernity: the promise of liberty. The particular promise that I am referring to here is the one that the nation-state, especially the nation-state forged in the context of colonial struggles, offered to Black peoples—the opportunity to participate in fashioning their own forms of liberation. *Come Good Rain* chronicles the collapse of that dream, that desire, and instead, performs its falling apart. The aesthetic-political performance of *Come Good Rain* utters the diasporic desire for justice. Seremba's performance does not remain at the level of an individual narration, as much as it (since it is based on his personal experience) moves beyond the individual to articulate the desires of an imagined nation and an imagined justice. It therefore utters the question: What should be the ethics of a nation? The play is intended to do something. And this intention was encapsulated in Seremba's desire to have the play tour various African nations. Thus Olaogun writes:

> Seremba expressed his desire to tour the play in various parts of the world. He mentioned Nigeria among the places where he would like to perform. Shortly after, Nigeria became the arena of a very repressive dictatorship under General Sani Abacha. Would a touring of *Come Good Rain* in Nigeria have made a difference? That Seremba's imaginative retelling and dramatization of his story raises a question like this one testifies to his creative and critical contributions to the important dialogues of our time. (334)

Even embedded in the critics' assessments of the play is a desire for the play to answer something about what might have happened had it toured Nigeria. One might argue that one of the central dilemmas of diasporic sensibilities and consciousness is how to articulate and perform justice and ethics. In many cases, the performance of justice and ethics is situated within a politics of what I have come to call reconnection and reparation (Walcott, "Pedagogy and Trauma").

The Politics of Reconnection and the Instabilities of Origins

Kamau Brathwaite has formulated a rather useful way of thinking about the relationship between Africa and the cultural expression and performance of New World Black people. Brathwaite articulates what he calls "a literature of rehabilitation and reconnection" (214). Such a literature, in Brathwaite's view, is evidence of African continuities in the expressive cultures of New World Black peoples. The various expressions and performances that constitute what I reformulate as the politics of reconnection and reparation consist of (1) worship, (2) rites of passage, (3) divination, (4) healing, and (5) protection. While Brathwaite is concerned with how these elements cross-reference and reinforce a continental African continuity, I am interested in how these elements appear in Black Canadian plays as the source of making reference to Africa and simultaneously finding a legitimate New World Black place in the Americas. "Reparation," in my use of the term, is a concern with making the New World a legitimate and rooted home for the expressive life of over five-hundred years of Black existence in the Americas. I am suggesting that the plays under discussion here are engaged in such a project, as those same plays pay homage to Africa as both an imagined and a real homeland. The politics of reconnection and reparation, as I reformulate it, is an attempt to come to grips with a lost or partially remembered African past and, simultaneously, work through and come to terms with the Americas as a new motherland. A number of Black Canadian plays put this actuation into performance.

Djanet Sears's *The Adventures of a Black Girl in Search of God* makes use of all five of the qualities listed above to proffer a reconnection and reparation with Canada as homeland, at the same time that it references continental Africa in its various performances. First, the diasporic identification. As Leslie Sanders writes,

> The theme of reclamation recurs in other ways. Throughout *Adventures*, Rainey eats dirt, a practice frequent especially among pregnant women in central Africa and the Southern United States…. The conflation of an action suggestive of pregnancy, mourning, loss and land resonates eloquently. At the end, her husband Michael, too, eats the dirt from Negro Creek, signalling their rootedness and their reconciliation. (488)

As Sanders so clearly points out, the play thematizes an identification with a range of Black identities, as it is concerned with affecting its nationally local—not just finding, but cementing, a place for Blackness directly in the crevice of the nation of Canada.

Sears's use of pregnancy symbolism to claim belonging to Canada is crucially important for a number of reasons. The ongoing assumption that Black peoples are recent to Canada is the most urgent and pressing problem. But additionally, as I have articulated above, the desire to reconnect and make reparation with the new homeland of the Americas as a site and home for Blackness and Black peoples is a pressing and ongoing psychic concern. The ingestion of dirt, not only by women in the play, but also by a man, is, I would argue, one of the most central claims of making reparation. In this case, the reparation is made by claiming Canada as home, with no rejection of Africa. Instead, Africa occurs in the aesthetic performances of the play. Africa occurs, in more abstract terms, in the play's texture and gesture—in song, dance, worship, healing and rites of passage. *The Adventures of a Black Girl in Search of God* is a play about memory, mourning and coming to terms with loss. Consolation for the loss of Africa is negotiated through the difficult terms of claiming a new homeland, even if that homeland must be struggled over to be claimed. Sears's play culminates, in no seductively seamless manner, among the various tensions that constitute the ongoing desires of Black diasporic people in relation to the unfinished business of belonging to various homelands.

George Boyd's *Consecrated Ground* similarly fits a number of the criteria for a politics of reconnection and reparation. Centring around the destruction of Africville, Boyd's play treats the difficult belonging to Canada of Black peoples. But as a counterpoint to Sears's play, Boyd's takes up what it means to demolish the evidence of Blackness in the homeland. The trauma of Africville, as contemporary as it is, remains an open and raw wound from the violence of the modern nation-state. Africville's destruction, and Boyd's attempt, through performance, to place it in a contemporary public memory beyond that of Black folks, is crucial to what I have been arguing. *Consecrated Ground*, in its very title, signals immediately the various expressive practices that constitute the politics and literature of rehabilitation, reconnection and reparation.

To consecrate is to seek to make something sacred. In the popular imagination of nations, many sites and moments come to mark the sacred as an emblem of national cohesion and identification. Boyd's play seeks to make Africville sacred in the Canadian popular imagination, to make art do something. But such an attempt is also in keeping with the various ways in which, both at the macro- and the micro-level, forms of ruling and governing become central to reordering life so that other moments might become evident and have some impact on our humanity. A brief example from *Consecrated Ground* is in order:

> SARAH. Gov'ment give 'em a license. The gov'ment don't put no plumbin' in here. Why the gov'ment put all the coloureds here in the first place. No jobs 'cause the gov'ment. *(beat)* Now you think Sarah Lied truss the gov'ment? You think any coloured person in he's right senses truss the gov'ment and they signs? (422)

This short discourse on the government, and Black mistrust of it, can be read in a number of ways. The actual destruction of Africville, which was the work of government, points to the ways in which, at the micro-level, governments are deeply implicated in subordinating Black people. But for my purposes, at the macro-level, it is also about how practices and processes of governing or governmentality place Black peoples in a globally subaltern position. In all of the plays that I have discussed in this essay, there are utterances that resemble or are variants of Sarah's articulation in *Consecrated Ground*. But importantly, such concerns, such utterances, also prove to be the point of diasporic identification for many Black peoples.

Recently, Africville has, in some ways, become consecrated ground. The federal government of Canada has now made the site a national treasure. Furthermore, plans to rebuild the Seaview Baptist Church on the site might signal a particular national attempt to come to terms with the trauma that the destruction of the community *is*. The rebuilding of the church should not be given short shrift, because not only does the church represent a particular cultural centre of the community but its reconstruction can, more broadly, be read as signalling yet another one of those diasporic moments of reconnection and reparation. Embedded in the practices of the Black church are many African continuities, but also embedded in the Black church are the kernels of cultural expression that can or might constitute the basis from which reparation might be made. In short, much of the expression of the "traditional" Black church continues to produce "Africa" and the New World as mutually constitutive of the kind of Blackness that I am attempting to articulate.

Conclusion: The Destabilizations of the Ethical

Finally, what these plays do is to destabilize dramatically the mythical narratives of home, nation and citizen. Because they move between nation and diaspora, homeland and imagined homeland, they productively draw on each site for advancing a politics and an aesthetics of strategic universalism. From the point of view of the dispossessed, the subaltern, these plays are intended to *do* something. I am suggesting that these plays are intended to represent the world from a vantage point from which justice and the ethical might be approached. It is the ongoing and central concern for articulating practices of and desires for justice and ethics from which emerge the strongest elements of what I have been calling diasporic sensibilities and consciousnesses. This claim can be made about a number of different plays, but what I am claiming here is that, for Black diasporic plays, even those that are not the most accomplished, justice and ethics reside inside the aesthetic-political performance of the play. Each play is intended to *do* something, and deciphering what the play intends to do is part and parcel of experiencing the play. These plays do not all announce a politics or political stance, but they perform desire, a call to justice. These plays perform an incitement to approach the ethical.

I have deliberately not given summaries of the plays being discussed. What is at stake in the argument I am making is not the total story of the plays but the ways in which the plays destabilize various assumptions. The dramatic insights of these plays put into the public sphere various questions that force us to rethink a range of concerns, issues and conditions. And even when a play is not at its most aesthetically pleasing, it can still centre a series of questions that force viewers to confront the unthought of living a life; in short to confront the ethical; in short to rethink the human.

(2004)

Works Cited

Boyd, George. *Consecrated Ground*. *Testifyin'*: *Contemporary African Canadian Drama*. Ed. Djanet Sears. Vol. 2. Toronto: Playwrights Canada, 2003. 397-483.

Brathwaite, Kamau. "The African Presence in Caribbean Literature." *Roots*. Ann Arbor: U of Michigan P, 1993. 190-258.

Gilroy, Paul. *Against Race: Imagining Political Culture Beyond the Color Line*. Cambridge: Belknap-Harvard UP, 2000.

mandiela, ahdri zhina. *dark diaspora... in dub*. *Testifyin'*: *Contemporary African Canadian Drama*. Ed. Djanet Sears. Vol. 1. Toronto: Playwrights Canada, 2000. 447-70.

Moodie, Andrew. *Riot*. *Testifyin'*: *Contemporary African Canadian Drama*. Ed. Djanet Sears. Vol. 1. Toronto: Playwrights Canada, 2000. 6-78.

———. *A Common Man's Guide to Loving Women*. *Testifyin'*: *Contemporary African Canadian Drama*. Ed. Djanet Sears. Vol. 2. Toronto: Playwrights Canada, 2003. 79-147.

Olaogun, Modupe. "The Need to Tell This Story: George Seremba's Narrative Drama, *Come Good Rain*." *Testifyin'*: *Contemporary African Canadian Drama*. Ed. Djanet Sears. Vol. 1. Toronto: Playwrights Canada, 2000. 331-35.

Sanders, Leslie. "History at Negro Creek: Djanet Sears' *The Adventures of a Black Girl in Search of God*." *Testifyin'*: *Contemporary African Canadian Drama*. Ed. Djanet Sears. Vol. 2. Toronto: Playwrights Canada, 2003. 487-89.

Sears, Djanet, ed. *Testifyin'*: *Contemporary African Canadian Drama*. 2 vols. Toronto: Playwrights Canada, 2000-03.

Sears, Djanet. *The Adventures of a Black Girl in Search of God*. *Testifyin'*: *Contemporary African Canadian Drama*. Ed. Djanet Sears. Vol. 2. Toronto: Playwrights Canada, 2003. 491-604.

Seremba, George. *Come Good Rain*. *Testifyin'*: *Contemporary African Canadian Drama*. Ed. Djanet Sears. Vol. 1. Toronto: Playwrights Canada, 2000. 337-79.

Philip, M. NourbeSe. *Coups and Calypsos*. *Testifyin'*: *Contemporary African Canadian Drama*. Ed. Djanet Sears. Vol. 1. Toronto: Playwrights Canada, 2000. 85-142.

Walcott, Rinaldo. "Post-OJ Black Men?" *Testifyin'*: *Contemporary African Canadian Drama*. Ed. Djanet Sears. Vol. 2. Toronto: Playwrights Canada, 2003. 75-77.

———. "Pedagogy and Trauma: The Middle Passage, Slavery and the Problem of Creolization." *Between Hope and Despair: Pedagogy and the Remembrance of Historical Trauma*. Ed. Roger Simon, Sharon Rosenberg, and Claudia Appert. Lanham, MD: Rowman and Littlefield, 2000. 135-51.

———. "Riotous Black Canadians." *Testifyin': Contemporary African Canadian Drama*. Ed. Djanet Sears. Vol. 1. Toronto: Playwrights Canada, 2000. 3-5.

Wynter, Sylvia. "Rethinking 'Aesthetics': Notes towards a Deciphering Practice." *Ex-Iles: Essays on Caribbean Cinema*. Ed. Mbye B. Cham. Trenton, NJ: Africa World, 1992. 237-79.

A Particular Perspective: (Re)Living Memory in George Boyd's *Wade in the Water*

by Rachael Van Fossen

In the summer of 2001, playwright George Boyd had only recently relocated to Montreal from Halifax. At about the same time I was myself embarking as the new Artistic Director of Montreal's Black Theatre Workshop. I was pleased to hear that the author of Consecrated Ground, *a play I much admire, was not only now living in Montreal, but that he wanted to come see me with a new manuscript in hand. That manuscript was an early draft of a short story entitled "Ice Nelson Johns." George Boyd wanted to know if I thought it might be worth adapting to the stage as a play for one actor. Two years and one additional actor later—in October 2003—Black Theatre Workshop (BTW) staged the premiere production of George Boyd's most recent play* Wade in the Water.[1]

George Boyd's *Wade in the Water* represents both a departure from, and an ongoing treatment of, themes explored in his earlier play *Consecrated Ground*. Both plays insist upon the importance of historical subject matter as contemporary testimony, and both stress the importance of family and community in efforts to challenge economic and political repression and marginalization. However, where *Consecrated Ground* implicitly questions the efficacy of individual agency when such initiative is not accompanied by community and family support, *Wade in the Water* instead maps the consciousness-raising journey of the play's fictional ex-slave protagonist Nelson Williams Johns, from his early days of relative privilege and political naïveté, to his so-called (and initially undesired) "liberation" in the post-Civil War south, on to a quest to reunite with his son in Nova Scotia, and ultimately to an outright rejection of North American racism through settlement in the free colony of Sierra Leone. While both plays end with death, the 70 year-old Nelson's murder by slavers in *Wade in the Water* evokes a sense of individual redemption and rebirth, and consequently of a certain inner triumph in the face of overwhelming adversity. Conversely, the highly symbolic burial of the baby Tully in *Consecrated Ground*'s dramatization of the Africville debacle emphasizes the tragedy of the demolition of a whole community: as such the play demands in a loud, angry voice that witnesses (audience) pay attention to an important cautionary tale about the dangers of paternalism masquerading as misguided liberalism (Clarke, "Making" 393). The more introspective tone of *Wade in the Water* transforms the realism of its predecessor *Consecrated Ground*, both in style and in structure, in favour of techniques of first-person direct audience address (in line with performance traditions based in orality and storytelling), and of a dream-like quality of non-linearity in a nonetheless mostly chronologically plotted play (in keeping with the play's device of events as relived in the memory of the protagonist).

In his introduction to *Consecrated Ground*, George Elliott Clarke elucidates both the meaning and the meaninglessness of the "empty triumph" of the baby's burial:

> In the last scene of the play, II.x, the Lyle family is reconstituted perhaps ephemerally—in the instance of Clarice's triumphant consecration of her son's casket with Africville soil. Still, this "triumph" is empty, given that both the scion of the Lyle household and of Clarice's inheritance is lost. Thus, the once-Promised Land of Africville becomes a graveyard and a ghost town. ("Making" 395)

Earlier in this same introduction, Clarke posits that:

> In *Consecrated Ground*, the struggle over the fate of Africville and its citizens is viewed as a political-philosophical contest between conservatism—i.e. the conservation of the "race" (to refer to an 1897 essay by the great African-American sociologist W.E.B. Du Bois)—and liberalism, or the reduction of community to an assembly of individual "consumers." When Willem Lyle signs over his wife's property to the City of Halifax, and does so on the coffin of his son, Tully (slain by rats drawn to the neighbourhood by the garbage dump that the city deliberately placed nearby), he concedes, dramatically, that a conservative regard for heritage must give way to the liberal ideal of individual, socio-economic advancement. If the life of his son means little to the City of Halifax, the life of Africville means little to Willem. (393)

On one level the story of Nelson William Johns in *Wade in the Water* is an inversion of Willem's story in *Consecrated Ground*, while still supporting the playwright's seeming indictment of "the liberal ideal of individual advancement" as George Elliott Clarke argues. Willem reveals only passing personal insight into the fallacy of his search for economic advantage (read: assimilation), whereas the underlying premise of Nelson's theatrical journey is that it leads him ultimately to an understanding of how his own privilege, whether wittingly or unwittingly (a question the playwright leaves us to consider), contributed to the economic system that nonetheless enslaved him, his family and his community.

In *Consecrated Ground* Willem's ambitions are for a "better life" than he perceives Africville can offer:

> WILLEM. It like… it like the whole universe out there, just waitin' for us to… step out into it…. Like, baby, I been thinkin'… maybe it's time we got outta Africville… and… and, well, there ain't hardly no one left here anyways. Everybody's gonna go. I'm thinkin' yeah… maybe we should take the city's offer and sell. People always movin', Leasey. White folks move all the time. Mister Clancy say we can relocate to a good, warm place in, ah, Uniacke Square. (464)

Boyd ends *Wade in the Water* with a confession of complicity, and Nelson's avowal of his own responsibility:

> NELSON. ...Ice member Ice smuggled for Young Massa ta feed da Confederate Army... Ice been entrapped in da play of da past... only ta be lookin' into tomorrah...
> ...Ice lied and Ice betrayed...
> Helpin' Young Massa ta maintain-a institution, our people and Ice...
> ...despise...
> Ice got sins ta pay fer, Ella *(pause)* ...sins... and what lies before me, sweet Ella, is the result of what went behind...
> ...Oh please baby, as Ice die, help me member da bill Ice owes ta Gawd. (45)

Alternately directing speeches to his departed wife Ella and to the audience, Nelson reveals early in his story that he was raised in a life of relative comfort and leisure, compared to the lot of most slaves in the American pre-Civil War south. No mere "field slave," Nelson was also no mere "house slave," and he seems anxious for the audience to be aware of his conferred status:

> NELSON. ...Why Ice must-a been lil' more den a pickaninny, when Ol' Massa snatch me from my Momma and tooked me into da Big House. Ice gotta whole room to mesell and Ice plays in da attic. When Ice older, Ol' Massa always took me wif him on his hoss when he went bout inspectin' Twin Oaks. He take me to town and buy me toys. Ol' Massa gimme da run of da plantation. Ice runs all ober and playin' an' talkin' to de udder coloureds as dey works in da fields. (3)

Any presumed lack of education arising from Nelson's use of slave dialect would be a false and gross assumption: not only does the Ol' Massa teach his young slave protégé to read (an illegal act in the pre-Civil War South), Nelson grows up to accompany the Young Massa, Ol' Massa's son, to attend classes at Harvard. Ostensibly and to outward appearances he is merely the Young Massa's servant, but the Ol' Massa himself tells us that the intention all along was to provide Nelson a Harvard education: "YOU, SUH, HAVE BEEN GIVEN A HARVARD EDUCATION! YOU SUH, ARE MUCH UNLIKE THESE PICKANINNIES RUNNIN' ROUND HEAH!! *(long pause)* Now you speak English—NOT SLAVE PATOIS!" (28).

Nelson replies to his owner in the King's English, "Suh!! Would Ella still love me if I spoke like this? Would I be accepted in the Slave Quarter? *(pause)* But Ice prefer ta be in da Slave Quarter with Ella, and Ice speaks dis way cause Ice choose to, suh" (28). Nelson's choice to speak in slave dialect is therefore more than simply protection from the deadly wrath of less "indulgent" whites, but is also—it seems primarily—a political act which insists upon the validity of the language itself, and its fundamental relationship to a culture and a community. Nelson's argument for speaking what Ol' Massa refers to as "slave gibberish" (28) is therefore as much a declaration of the importance of language to family, community and to identification with Black culture, as Willem's betrayal of Clarice in *Consecrated Ground* is an act of individual severance from community ties, and indicates a desire for community and individual assimilation into the dominant white society. In both plays, playwright George Boyd's implicit condemnation of this colonial, assimilationist mentality reflects a politicized stance affiliated with twentieth-century activism among Black intellectuals:

> It continues to be the painful and trying task of the black consciousness movement to destroy the ambivalence about black language and culture and replace the old pejorative [sic] assumptions with new positive ones. [...] Undoubtedly this has been in recognition of the fact that language is interwoven with culture and psychic being. Thus to deny the legitimacy of Africanized English is to deny the legitimacy of black culture and the black experience. (Geneva Smitherman, qtd. in Cook 390) [2]

George Elliott Clarke is not the least bit ambivalent:

> Since Standard English was thrust upon African diasporic peoples against their wills, it is marvelous justice that, in every exilic African culture, from New Brunswick to New Orleans, from Jamaica to California, that tongue now meets a different standard [...] Our English is, no longer, the Master's voice. ("No Language" 276)

Clarke refers to Willem in *Consecrated Ground* as "an abject example of the 'failed' Black male" ("Making" 394). *Wade in the Water* charts a male protagonist's difficult and painful path to raised personal and political consciousness. If *Consecrated Ground* demonstrates "the emasculation of Black males [...] within the inclement context of a white male-dominated society" (395), then arguably *Wade in the Water*'s exploration of the inner conflict of a slave whose biological father is also his owner is an investigation of what is behind this masculine "failure" (i.e. identification with the white man's patriarchy). By the end of the play, the protagonist asserts independence from paternalism through an act of heroism: Nelson, as a result of his process of politicization, takes a stand on freedom from slavery for his own grandson. Through his actions he is both reclaiming his own paternal responsibility and rejecting his prior acceptance of paternalism as social order:

> NELSON. Ice knows it be dangerous. As soon as Two and Ice wade in the waw-tah—as soon as we set our hooks—dese men, white men on hosses and wif swingin' nets and ropes, come racin' outa da forest. Day be slabbers, Ella…. Slabbers. *(beat)* "WEES BEES FREE!!!" *(beat)* "DIS BE FREETOWN!!" Dey don't pay me no minds and keeps coming, flashin' dere whips and swingin' dere nets. Ice look at our grand-baby Two, "RUN! TWO RUN!!" *(beat)*… We runs. *(beat)*… But hosses be faster den a character, so Ice stops and tracks dere attention to me as Ice yells at Two ta run! As Two run into dat tick forest, he bees da last ting Ice sees of our family. Dey entangle me in dere nets an drags me ober da sharp rocks a da shoreline tils Ice bleedin' into da waw-tah. Dey couldn't get Two, so dey gonna drown me… dey gots no need fer dis ol' man. (44)

Nelson has converted to a stronger identification with his Black family than with his white oppressors, despite his mixed blood ancestry.

Clarke asserts that Clarice, in *Consecrated Ground*, "emerges as the heroically obstinate articulator of Black worth and faith," where Willem—in Clarke's estimation an example of the literary syndrome of the "failed Black male"—"becomes the spokesperson for—and the symbol of—Black defeat" ("Making" 393).

Following this reasoning, in *Wade in the Water* the absence of Nelson's wife Ella allows him (or forces him) to take action, and subsequently to take responsibility for his actions. The playwright George Boyd himself states in an interview I conducted, "If Ella had been alive and said, 'Nelson, we're not going to Africa!'—they wouldn't be going to Africa." In the same interview he explains this phenomenon in his plays by referring to his own experience of growing up in Nova Scotia:

> I'm fifty years old, and the Black community I grew up in was a matriarchal community. That's not to say the men were weak, or emasculated. [But] the white community saw the Black female as less threatening than the Black male. They'd hire a Black woman to come into their homes to do domestic work, no problem. But "uh-oh!" if it's a Black male. Earlier in the last century the Black males couldn't get a job [in Nova Scotia]. The Black females got the jobs. So the female became the head of the household, really [...] That's what I've tried to depict in my plays.

Without Ella to guide him, Nelson both physically and metaphorically leaves the safety of the "known"—his Southern "home"—for the uncharted path to find his son, a journey which eventually returns him, via Nova Scotia, to his African roots: Nelson faces up to the failures of an assimilationist mentality.

Nelson's psychological journey can be considered a search for a father figure, a search that proves to be misdirected: he looks to the wrong people in the wrong places. Upon leaving the South, following the destruction of the only home he has ever known, Nelson encounters, for the second time, a white Union army officer. Nelson and the General reach a tentative, uneasy "friendship," which then progresses to a *seeming* intimacy as Nelson agrees to be employed by his former enemy and ostensible "liberator." Nelson is infuriated when a much-anticipated visit to the White House belies his alleged emancipation:

> NELSON. Ella—Ice be standin' in da White House!! I do recognize the President! And as da he and his Missus approach, I try to shake his hand but da President walk right by, like I don't matter, like I'm not a human bean. Den Ice bees rudely hustled into da White House kitchen [...] Dat kitchen be as noisy as the smithey on brandin day—a wild house; people yellin' and screamin' at one anudder. Coloured waiters dere—dey all dressed in da finest clothes Ice eber seen on a coloured. All a sudden, Ice was hussled off to a puny table in da corner [...] Ice eats alone. I neber see the General all evening.

> I looks around me. The President's kitchen, Ella, and it be no different than the kitchen at Twin Oaks. I wonder what this war was all about. Ice wonder if we gots a full membership in this here New-Knighted states cuz nothin' has changed […] It don't matter if'n you bees from da norse or south… dey all da same. (40)

For a second time Nelson walks away from the inequities of an ideology of paternalism, which has turned out to be as false in its practice in the North as it was as professed justification for slavery in the South, where slaveowners "felt more interest in enlarging their crops and their profits than in faithfully ministering to their slave 'children'" (Escott 20).

Whether or not Nelson is aware, in the fiction of the play, that Ol' Massa was his biological progenitor prior to Young Massa's revelation of the fact (the playwright leaves this question open to interpretation), the relationship in the play is clearly one of father-to-surrogate, if not actual, son. Despite Ol' Massa's seemingly genuine love for Nelson (and indeed his preference for Nelson over the profligate Young Massa) social and family constraints would have prevented the slaveowner from openly acknowledging the biological reality of the relationship. In this, the only scene between the two characters, moments where the Ol' Massa attempts to exert absolute control in his relationship to Nelson as *slave* are intermingled with the loving if sometimes reluctant indulgences of *father-to-son*. The Ol' Massa figure embodies the hypocrisies and contradictions of paternalism as theory and in its practice(s).

Although the play leaves ambiguous, in its denouement, the question of whether Nelson's feelings for the previously beloved Ol' Massa have changed, Nelson is forced to acknowledge in death what he had unconsciously acknowledged in life when he chose Ella and the Slave Quarter over a feather bed in the Big House: that the system of slavery which his "owner" both inherently and actively maintained and vehemently believed in, is precisely what prevents the older man from being a true "father," and Twin Oaks a true "home." Nelson tells Ella just prior to his capture by slavers, "Ella, Ice can't tells ya how it feels to be home. Twin Oaks was not me home. Ice was juss a tenant. My home be here in Africka, in Sierra Leone…" (43).

By ending Nelson's quest in Sierra Leone, and calling it "home," *Wade in the Water* lends credence to Clarke's assertion of Boyd's preference, in his drama, for a black nationalist option. Nelson chooses Sierra Leone over North America, and joins his beloved Ella in life-after-death: Boyd thus has Nelson reject what Clarke terms "an effete integrationism" ("Making" 394). By the end of his journey, Nelson is more closely aligned with the ideological stance of the heroic Clarice in *Consecrated Ground*, than to the "sellout" option Boyd proposes through the ultimately ineffectual Willem.

Boyd places a contradictory duality at the heart of Nelson's dramatic struggle by personalizing and complicating socio-economic inequities through a blood relationship to the Ol' Massa character, a man apparently much loved by Nelson. It is therefore not only the absence of the strong female "head of household" that distinguishes Nelson's situation from Willem's in *Consecrated Ground*: a significant part of Nelson's heritage includes both the culture and the bloodline of the plantation's white slave-owner, and the accompanying complexities of relationships and alliances add depth and layered resonances to the character's psychology. Nelson's conflict in the play is not unlike the ambivalence displayed by Pauli Murray's grandmother in her family chronicle *Proud Shoes*. As African-American scholar Ashraf H.A. Rushdy observes:

> The person who stands out in *Proud Shoes* as the most curious example of anxiety and bewildering ambivalence is Murray's maternal grandmother, who exhibits a strange mixture of commitment to her African American family and an abiding nostalgia for the glory of her slaveholding ancestors. (*Remembering* 103)

In this same chapter, Rushdy points out that "the recognition of [racial] impurity produces a difficult and wearying set of contradictions" (106). Writing about a family history by Jan Willis, he goes on to say:

> Jan Willis knew that there was no such thing as "purity" in any living race of people, yet she had difficulty confronting the complexity of her own makeup. She knew the long history of racial mixing in America but did not easily accept the fact of that mixing in her own family. As a theoretical proposition […] Willis was not pained by the idea that her "'fair' skin came from someplace." But when she discovered that it came from a "specific some*one*," that abstract idea became "living flesh" and led to "emotional turmoil." […] On the one hand, one may feel the joy of knowing precisely who one's ancestors were, while, on the other, one can feel what Willis describes as "absolute bereftness" at having to accept white ancestors. The truth may set us free, but it comes with a cost—the cost of feeling ambivalence. (*Remembering* 106)

With Ol' Massa dead, and the "Big House" in the throes of disastrous fiery destruction (notably not at the hands of Union soldiers, but in flames deliberately set by the Young Massa to prevent looting and ultimate possession of the property by the invading Northerners), Nelson and his half-brother engage in the following exchange:

> YOUNG MASSA. Nelson? Come-'ere, boy. Nelson. I never let anything happen to you, Nelson. Upon my soul to God—nothing. And nor did Pappy. Especially Pappy. *(beat)* Know why, Nelly? Know why Nelson? You're the horseman—don't you know who your sire was, boy? Don't you know why you stayed in the Big House while all the other niggers was in the Quarter?
> NELSON. *(Sarcastically)* Niggers don't rightly knows who dere daddies be. Jemney—my boy—juss one of da lucky ones.
> *Preoccupied, Nelson takes the gun out of the satchel and examines it…*
> YOUNG MASSA. You gotta go, Nelly. You're a free man.
> NELSON. What?
> YOUNG MASSA. I CAN'T FEED YA!! I HAVE NOTHING!! YOU ARE FREE!! YOU GO—YA HEAH ME—GO!!

NELSON. Where? ...Where Ice go? ...Where Ice go? Dis de only life
Ice knows—where Ice belongs. Ice be Nelson Williams Johns and
dis da Twin Oaks plantation. *(pause)* Ice knows who my pappy was.
And Ice knows who you is.
YOUNG MASSA. If you hadda been white—you would have *owned*
Twin Oaks, Nelson—YOU!!! (32-33)

This scene with the younger Johns marks the turning point in the play's plot, and hence in Nelson's "conscientization" (Paolo Freire's neologism, now widely used in popular education circles, for a transformational process toward political awareness). It is at this point in the story that Nelson begins to move toward a more strongly held identification with Black culture and community, over identification with and loyalty to a white father and a white brother who are, the character finally determines, less his family than they are his oppressors.

In an earlier scene Nelson has chosen to remain with the drunken Young Massa rather than join the chaotic Jubilee of slaves celebrating their imminent freedom: he refuses to join his son Jemney on a trek to the north. Nelson essentially abandons his son to remain with the Young Massa, and suggests that his choice reflects loyalty not to the slaveowner, but to his unacknowledged half-brother as family:

JEMNEY. —Ice goes up norse, Pappy.
NELSON. But Jemney ya bees a Johns. Yer place is on da Twin Oaks
plantation with your family.
JEMNEY. But some-a us juss bees ADOPTED family, Pappy.
NELSON. *(beat)* Yous don' know what yer family bees Jemney. No—
you stays, Jemney. You come back home wif me.
JEMNEY. It dere home, Pappy. DERE home. Ice have to find my
home—me freedom. Ice has ta bee a man.
NELSON. OH!—AND ICE AIN'T A MAN!!?? (15)

In the same scene Nelson also calls on Jemney to remain in the South out of loyalty to his Black family:

NELSON: Jemney, ya promised... when Ice die, Ice lie next to my Ella
in da Twin Oaks nigger cemetery.[...] Ice promised my gal, Ella, your
mudder, dat when Ice pass-aways Ice lie next to 'er.... And Jemney, ya
promised to put me dere. (16)

Thematically the younger man's departure signals, rather than the betrayal implied by Nelson, an affirmation of Black communalism, as Jemney joins those heading North to expected freedom. Boyd only grants Nelson his own sense of freedom (freedom from the ideology of paternalism) when he at last recognizes and accepts his own ambivalence, in addition to his confession of complicity in the enslavement of Black people. As Nelson tells Ella in his dying moments:

NELSON. Ice floats in me white Sundee robe, Ella. *(pause)* And as Ice
bees floatin', Ice see you and me and baby Jemney... Ice sees Twin

> Oaks, da Big House, Ol' Massa, da White House. Ice see flames ravagin' da fields—and Ice has one longin' image of Young Massa. Ice see his bubblin' flesh… He scream and scream and scream. Sumpin' cole run true me Ella, and Ice shot him. *(A shot rings out…)* (45)

Audience members only learn of Nelson's murder of the Young Massa in this, the final scene of the play. This late "reveal" underscores Nelson's "emotional turmoil" (Rushdy, *Remembering* 106) in the moment of the murder, since he *remembers* the moment at the end of the play, rather than *re-living* the moment in the course of the play. Most other important events play out in scenes scripted as dialogue with another character (as opposed to the storytelling in the play), and are events that Nelson "relives" in present-tense, onstage action. Nelson's emotional turmoil, evident in his attendant unwillingness to relive the moment of the murder, clearly relates in part to the loss of the only "home" he has never known, since up to this point he has invariably self-identified as a "Johns." Further layering the trauma, while fires are raging through the burning plantation mansion, Boyd has the Young Massa speak the unspeakable by revealing their shared biological father and hence shared white heritage. Ironically, then, in the same moment that Young Massa confirms Nelson's claim to the Johns name, that identity is also taken away from Nelson with the destruction of all that is familiar and beloved. But is there also an element here of "absolute bereftness" at having to accept white ancestors, and in particular at the naming of a "specific some*one*"? Boyd's preference for ambiguity leaves room for an audience to ponder the question.

When Nelson uses the Young Massa's own gun against him, he is metaphorically killing off his last remaining link to the Southern patriarchal system, even though the patriarchy—as embodied in the figure of the Young Massa and as symbolized by the Big House—is already self-destructing.

George Boyd set out to write this play because, according to his initial impulse, he wanted to explore "what did an older freed slave do?" During my interview he said:

> There was a big migration to the North after the signing of the Emancipation Proclamation, which by the way took place two full years after the war had begun. It occurred to me that the migration must have been easier for young people—they were mobile. What did the older slaves do, in the South, with no support, no money, no way of earning a living—because during Reconstruction even whites were looking for jobs. What would you do [if you were an older slave], after all that infrastructure came down?

Boyd adds layers of meaning to this conundrum of economic constraints on so-called "freedom," by tying not just Nelson's economic dependence, but also his sense of self or identity, through his mixed bloodline, to the relatively privileged existence he had previously led on the Twin Oaks plantation. The oppositional effect of the son Jemney's very different, more highly politicized perspective of a slave's relationship to plantation owner, combined with Nelson's ultimate physical relocation to and political realignment with Africa, underscores again a certain polarization in Boyd's work when it comes to this clash of ideologies—a kind of either/or scenario—yet *Wade in the Water* accomplishes this without sacrificing complexity of character.

This question of character and perspective is central to consideration of *Wade in the Water* as performance, and as dramatic literature, and all the more since it marks yet another departure from Boyd's previous, larger-cast plays, where multiple perspectives are brought to the fore (although certainly not without judgement, clearly, on the playwright's part). Take *Consecrated Ground*, where even the ambivalence of the sole white character Clancy, the representative of the City of Halifax, is given stage time, before he rationalizes to himself the "righteousness" of the City's paternalistic actions:

> CLANCY. You know, Reverend, here I am sittin' in a church in Africville. I mean, my friends would call it a "nigger" church. Here I am sittin' in this "nigger" church in Africville. I should be at the Boat Club, sipping whiskey with my buddies and laughing about the dirty niggers in Africville. But ya know Reverend? *(swigs)* I don't feel like laughing. I don't feel that way… I mean, most of the places I been to out here, you can eat off their floors they're so waxed and polished…. Look, I believed… I believe what I was told. I think what I'm doing is right. I'm doing the right thing. (455-56)

In *Wade in the Water* all secondary characters are explicitly presented through Nelson's eyes. As the first of Boyd's plays to draw largely, though not exclusively, on first-person storytelling ("Ice"), rather than primarily through dialogue enacted in relationship to other onstage characters, *Wade in the Water* makes implicit intertextual reference to the genre of the nineteenth-century slave narrative. On the other hand, by framing the story between the "bookends" of Nelson's drowning—a scene which both begins and ends the play—Boyd also invokes the memory play as theatrical tradition. *The Globe and Mail* theatre critic Kamal Al-Solaylee put this quite succinctly in his review of the Black Theatre Workshop (BTW) production:

> Boyd […] mixes the tradition of the memory play with 19th century slave narratives, using the familiar theatrical structure of a journey. He shifts the debates around the testimonial importance of slave narrative from the fictional to the theatrical […] The significance of Nelson's journey is not in its destination, but in its deconstruction of an intriguing past life—Nelson is, after all, a slave with a Harvard education. (R3)

Boyd's transformation of the "neo-slave narrative" form[3] from novel to theatrical performance is accomplished via a concomitant manipulation of the memory play tradition. The classic slave narrative is by definition a recounting of remembered experience. Boyd reconfigures the classic slave narrative convention by opening his play at the end, rather than the beginning, of his protagonist's life, ensuring that everything in between is clearly recognized as memory, rather than as fact. Boyd therefore draws simultaneously upon the authenticating convention of the slave narrative form, and the rhetorical convention of the memory play.[4] And while a significant amount of contemporary scholarship has examined the diversity of "sub-genres" among classic slave narratives,[5] it is nonetheless true that, for the most part, classic slave narratives unfold largely in chronological order, albeit often interspersed with reflections, descriptions, and some editorial commentary.[6]

Wade in the Water's non-linear narrative ordering of these past events further underlines the role of memory, and perspective, in Nelson's storytelling and, perhaps more consequentially, the role of memory in the *reliving* of scenes with the other characters. Following Jeannette R. Malkin's analysis of memory plays in the modernist canon such as Williams' *The Glass Menagerie*, and Miller's *Death of A Salesman*, we can see that *Wade in the Water* also uses the subjectivity of a protagonist to "peer" into the mind, precisely in order to construct or reconstruct that character's life and psychology, and thus provide "interpretive frameworks for personal or social failure" (Malkin 21). *Wade in the Water* additionally displays a manipulation of time that is in some ways similar to Pinter's *Betrayal*, which, as Malkin points out, "moves backward and forward at once, and although memory is never simplistic or stable or even necessarily reliable, Pinter's relentless retrospective structure retains its faith in linearity, causality, in the unified subject and the world, and in a source […] that can be recovered through memory" (22). Although a departure from *Consecrated Ground* in that it is less faithful to a "pure" realism, *Wade in the Water* remains a play with a predominantly realist aesthetic rooted in a psychological construction of character. However, unlike the retrospective structure that Malkin refers to, Boyd places an emphasis on the immediacy of the remembered events.

Nelson is both storyteller and protagonist. The scenes he re-lives as central protagonist are scenes primarily comprised of dialogue, with less reliance on storytelling and direct audience address. Notably however, even when Nelson is in storytelling mode, the character often employs the present tense and speaks to the audience (or to Ella) as if in the actual moment of the flashback. We therefore receive Nelson's story as he lived it himself (reinforcing the play's overall reliance on realism as a genre), while it is also clearly identified as memory. These memories, then, play out before an audience without their/our knowledge of Nelson's own after-the-fact awareness of his dawning politicization: we take the journey with him. This technique also reinforces for audiences the urgency of Nelson's final few moments "before God."

Since I have myself stressed the importance of subjective perspective in *Wade in the Water*, it is important to mention here the subjectivity of my own individual perspective, and no doubt bias, as the (white woman) artistic director at the theatre company that first produced the play. Prior to production, the question of how to cast this play seemed to me potentially quite tricky, given that one actor must play multiple roles: three white characters and one Black character. I consulted a number of individuals (including, of course, the playwright himself and Richard Donat, the director) who had read or were otherwise familiar with the manuscript. Interestingly, the results of this informal and entirely unscientific survey were that the white folks, with the single exception of the director of the play, responded that they would have some difficulty seeing a Black actor play the white characters. On the other hand, across the board, those of African descent, along with other individuals of colour, responded with surprise that I even posed the question: of course a Black actor can play a white man, even in a largely realistic play. My initial instinct thus confirmed, and given that the mandate of BTW is to "encourage and promote the development of a Black and Canadian theatre," I felt the company could also demonstrate to some artistic directors of other companies, and potentially (it seemed) to at least some white audience members, the untapped possibilities provided by so-called "non-traditional casting." In Canada there is apparently an ongoing resistance to such practices, where questions of equity and diversity, while they may "make sense" to people for other kinds of workplaces, are deemed not to be applicable to the theatre, the rationale provided that casting is an artistic, rather than a social, choice.[7] The director, playwright and I determined in consultation that we would cast for ability over any questions of race or ethnicity. The production went into rehearsal with two Black actors. Given the skills, versatility and virtuosity of these two (Tyrone Benskin as Nelson, and Nigel Shawn Williams in all other roles), I hope that the fallacy of the above "artistic" rationale can be more easily exposed for the false dichotomy it sets up. In retrospect, even my posing of the initial question seems silly and naïve.

In discussions with the playwright and director, we furthermore considered that casting Black actors to play the white characters could actually reinforce elements of memory and perspective in the play, by saying implicitly: "This is how Nelson remembers the people he knew." The casting would in this way work against any conception or perception (coming back to questions of perspective) of whiteness as "the Norm," and Black people as "the Other." Indeed George Boyd, as a result of the resonances from the BTW production, has decided to specify this casting choice as the playwright's suggestion when the play is published.

A no less interesting factor playing into this decision around casting was the playwright's oft-stated preference for ambiguity in his plays. Since in Canada we rarely see non-traditional casting of lead roles in contemporary plays (even more rarely do we see this in a play that deals specifically with questions of race), it seemed likely that audience members not in the habit of accepting this convention might have to reflect for themselves on what basis the casting decision was made. In my interview, George Boyd says:

> I prefer ambiguity because I think theatre is a venue of thought, and I don't think an author's point of view should dictate someone making up their own mind about particular issues. It's easy for someone to come and see one of my plays, and see it differently than I do. They might come away with a whole different conclusion than what I thought it was about. I welcome that, because those are the kind of plays I like to see.

In other words, George Boyd prefers to leave audiences still posing questions at the end of his plays. He does not want to "connect all the dots" for people. In *Consecrated Ground*, for instance, audiences do not know after the final scene whether

Clarice and Willem will, or will not, be able to reconcile or work through their opposing ideologies and his betrayal of her values.

Despite the principal character's choice in *Wade in the Water* to return to African roots, family and community, Boyd still wishes to leave us pondering the protagonist's inner struggles, i.e. his feelings of ambivalence. To take but one example, following Nelson's confession that he murdered the Young Massa, he says:

> Ice kilt Young Massa. Because Ice took pity or because Ice hated him so? *(long pause)* ...Ice don't rightly knows... (45)

As another example, consider the play's title: while *Wade in the Water* refers implicitly to the coded slave song of the same name (reinforcing an intertextual relationship to flights to freedom, and hence to slave narrative form) the song itself is not explicitly referred to in the text, nor does the playwright include it in his suggestions for music. Audiences are left to make these connections for themselves, presumably with the intent that the resonances will be all the stronger for not being made explicit. Water imagery is ubiquitous in the play, and can be received as referring both to its cleansing or purification powers (baptism), and the power water held to conceal the escaping slave's route north by limiting the possibility that humans could follow the tracks, or dogs the scent. Through the several and various references to water, Boyd ensures that the character Nelson's relationship to the precious, vital, life-giving substance is as sacred and multi-layered as Clarice's relationship to the community and the geography of Africville in *Consecrated Ground*.

Both of these plays bring to light aspects of Black Nova Scotian history/ies. Although some may, at first glance, see *Wade in the Water* as dealing with primarily American subject matter, to do so would be to deny, or to betray ignorance of, the historical movement of Black Loyalists to Canada. Both plays expose and condemn governments and white society for repressive politics and deceitful tactics. Perhaps most significantly, both plays interrogate the role of personal responsibility in family relationships and community alliances. In an interesting new direction in the context of his work overall, Boyd accomplishes *Wade in the Water*'s affirmation of the collectivity of Black community through adherence to a single perspective in first-person narrative form, where *Consecrated Ground*, despite its representations of multiple perspectives, in a highly realistic "fourth wall" playing style, tends to accentuate tragedy over celebration.

(2004)

Notes

1. *Wade in the Water* is forthcoming from Playwrights Canada Press, March 2005.
2. Cook lists the original source as Geneva Smitherman, *Talkin and Testifyin* (Boston: Houghton Mifflin, 1977) 174-75.
3. Ashraf H.A. Rushdy has written extensively on neo-slave narratives, his term for "contemporary novels that assume the form, adopt the conventions, and take on the first-person voice of the antebellum slave narrative" (*Neo-slave Narratives* 3). Rushdy's analysis provided me with much insight in the formulation of my own thinking around *Wade in the Water*. I also referred to Elizabeth Ann Beaulieu's *Black Women Writers and the American Neo-Slave Narrative*.
4. Baz Kershaw, in *The Politics of Performance: Radical Theatre as Cultural Intervention*, expands on an earlier theoretical framework proposed by Elizabeth Burns in which these "two different types of convention govern the audience's reading of perform-ance" (Kershaw 25). According to Kershaw, "the notion that there is a category of theatrical sign directly engaged with the ideology of the 'real' extra-theatrical world is crucial to an account of performance efficacy. Authenticating conventions or signs are the key to the audience's successful decoding of the event's significance to their lives. They determine the audience's reading of performance by establishing more or less transparent relationships between the fictionality of performance, the 'possible worlds' created by performance, and the 'real world' of the audience's socio-political experience outside theatre. In terms of my [Kershaw's] theoretical perspective, they enable an audience to perceive the specific ideological meanings of the show in relatively explicit ways" (26). I find it especially interesting to consider *Wade in the Water*'s implicit reference to slave narrative form as an authenticating convention, given the original importance assigned to establishing authenticity in classic slave narratives, since, "in the antebellum period, slave narratives, whether self-authored or ghostwritten, almost always contained authenticating documents that established the credibility of the narrator" (Heglar 36).
5. See especially Charles J. Heglar's *Rethinking the Slave Narrative*.
6. James Olney, perhaps somewhat reductively, outlines the usual conventions of classic ante-bellum slave narrative (152-53).
7. Journalist Steve Jones's article in *NOW* Magazine is an eye-opener when it comes to the slow pace of non-traditional casting practices in Canada. He quotes one prominent artistic director as saying that the "work doesn't always lend itself to a racially mixed cast. If you're doing something set in an English drawing room, it's difficult not to reflect that in the casting."

Works Cited

Al-Solaylee, Kamal. "On the Cold Road to the Promised Land." *The Globe and Mail* 6 November 2003: R3.

Beaulieu, Elizabeth Ann. *Black Women Writers and the American Neo-Slave Narrative: Femininity Unfettered.* Westport, Conn: Greenwood, 1999.

Boyd, George Elroy. *Wade in the Water* (unpublished manuscript).

———. Personal Interview. 27 August 2004.

———. *Consecrated Ground.* Testifyin': Contemporary African Canadian Drama. Ed. Djanet Sears. Vol. 2. Toronto: Playwrights Canada, 2003. 397-483.

Clarke, George Elliott. "Making the 'Damn' Nation the Race's 'Salvation': The Politics of George Elroy Boyd's *Consecrated Ground.*" *Testifyin': Contemporary African Canadian Drama.* Ed. Djanet Sears. Vol. 2. Toronto: Playwrights Canada, 2003. 393-96.

———. "No Language is Neutral: Seizing English for Ourselves." *Odysseys Home: Mapping African-Canadian Literature.* Toronto: U of Toronto P, 2002. 275-76.

Cook, William W. "Members and Lames: Language in the Plays of August Wilson." *Black Theatre: Ritual Performance in the African Diaspora.* Ed. Paul Carter Harrison, Victor Leo Edwards and Gus Edwards. Philadelphia: Temple UP, 2002. 388-96.

Escott, Paul D. *Slavery Remembered: A Record of Twentieth-Century Slave Narratives.* Chapel Hill: U of North Carolina P, 1979.

Freire, Paulo. *Pedagogy of the Oppressed.* New York: Continuum, 2000.

Heglar, Charles J. *Rethinking the Slave Narrative.* Westport, CT: Greenwood, 2001.

Jones, Steve. "Casting Aspersions: Bypassing minorities for key roles shows failure of the imagination." *NOW* Aug 28-Sep 3, 2003: 22-23.

Kershaw, Baz. *The Politics of Performance: Radical Theatre as Cultural Intervention.* New York: Routledge, 1992.

Malkin, Jeannette R. *Memory-Theater and Postmodern Drama.* Ann Arbor: U of Michigan P, 1999.

Murray, Pauli. *Proud Shoes: The Story of an American Family.* 1956. New York: Harper & Row, 1978.

Olney, James. "'I Was Born.'" *The Slave's Narrative.* Ed. Charles T. Davis and Henry Louis Gates, Jr. New York: Oxford UP, 1985. 148-75.

Rushdy, Ashraf H.A. *Remembering Generations: Race and Family in Contemporary African American Fiction.* Chapel Hill: U of North Carolina P, 2001.

———. *Neo-slave Narratives: Studies in the Social Logic of a Literary Form.* New York: Oxford UP, 1999.

Sex and the Nation: Performing Black Female Sexuality in Canadian Theatre

by Andrea Davis

> DINAH. *Let me tell you once and for all. You are a blasted jagabat and will be so all your life. I have my pride and I ent letting you drag my Black, blind arse through the streets of Port-of-Spain on this Carnival Monday for nobody, nobody, no focking body. You understand? I have my dignity.* (Tony Hall, *Jean and Dinah* 165)

The black female body has become the object of significant research over the last several years. This interest has been encouraged, in part, by the rise of postcolonial, feminist and postmodernist theories. Against this background, black women, given their race, gender and postcolonial condition, have been appropriated as the most valuable commodities of all. Positioned as the ultimate victims, black women and black women's bodies can be used to theorize multiple oppressions, while critics continue to privilege dominant western discourses about whiteness and difference. Often viewed outside of relevant social and historical contexts, the black female subject/object has been examined and re-examined in an attempt to designate the evils of the postcolonial condition and "nation." Even where this "viewing" takes place within a liberal and progressive western feminist agenda, black women's agency is often ignored and black women's right to their own bodies is violated (Collins, *Black Feminist Thought*; hooks, *Feminist Theory, Talking Back*, "Black Women;" Mohammed; Mohanty). As Kumari Jayawardena has pointed out, these racialized, gendered and, inevitably, sexualized representations of black women's and other non-white women's experiences rely on the legitimization of political and economic global hierarchies that position the "Third World" as culturally backward and industrially incompetent (11-12). The black female body is, thus, made to take on important cultural, political and economic functions.

In response to this simultaneous insertion and erasure of the black female body within western discourse, there is another "body" of research that seeks to offer more sensitive and complex examinations of black women. These examinations attempt a retrieval of the non-white, "non-ideal" female body and offer alternative ways of conceptualizing black women's experiences. In the African diaspora in the Americas, this research begins, of necessity, with an examination of the racist and gendered construction and exploitation of black women's bodies during slavery and the recuperation of that body as an act of slave resistance (Bush, "White 'Ladies';" Shepherd; Stevenson). The research also engages varying debates about black women's bodies in the contemporary period, including discussions about alternative and criminalized sexualities (Alexander; Brand; Kempadoo and Doezema; Kempadoo *Sun, Sex and Gold* and *Sexing the Caribbean*; Lorde), and representations and negotiations of black women's bodies and sexualities in popular culture and the family (Collins, *Black Feminist Thought* and *Black Sexual Politics*; Cooper, *Noises in the Blood* and *Sound Clash*; Rose, *Black Noise* and *Longing to Tell*). Importantly, some aspects of this research also critically interrogate nationalist discourses that seem, on the one hand, to disrupt the colonizing agenda while, on the other hand, subordinating women's bodies into a discourse of racial liberation and autonomy premised on male political and economic empowerment (Alexander; Alexander and Mohanty; Jayawardena; McClintock, Mufti, and Shohat).

Drawing on this oppositional research, I wish to open up a discussion about black women's sexualities that locates that discussion within a shared, but often ignored, Caribbean-Canadian context, in order to complicate questions about identity and national belonging. Tony Hall's *Jean and Dinah* (1994) and debbie young and naila belvett's *yagayah: two.womyn.black.griots* (2001) both allow us to examine the ways in which African-Caribbean women's bodies often find themselves inscribed within a patriarchal and nationalist discourse of (un)belonging and are made to bear the scars of their nations' frustrated desires and fears. Both plays, in fact, attempt to engage a historical debate about nationhood from a radical perspective that writes the nation not only as female but as an empowered, sexualized and spiritual black femininity. By expanding the discussion beyond the Caribbean and locating it also within the Caribbean diaspora in Canada, debbie young and naila belvett further problematize questions of identity and belonging. For them black women's bodies become the bridge that can connect nations across geographic, political and cultural divides. Yet these divides also threaten black women's existence—black women's bodies are often damaged, ruptured, torn apart by these cultural crossings. In examining two plays that, themselves, reside outside of mainstream Canadian theatre, we are able to engage important alternative discussions about the dramatization of Canadian identities.

***

JEAN. Home? Where the fock is home? (166)

Tony Hall's play *Jean and Dinah… Who Have Been Locked Away in a World Famous Calypso Since 1956 Speak Their Minds Publicly* provides one opportunity for the critical (re)examination of African-Caribbean nationalist narratives of the 1950s and 1960s that articulated a liberatory project for blacks in the region, even while they set clear boundaries around who could have full rights to citizenship within these newly constituted nations. The play is a stunning response both to Sparrow's popular calypso, which won him the 1956 Calypso Crown, and the gendered nationalism that the calypso represents. The play provides a necessary glance backward, over almost forty years, through the memories of the two women trapped and exploited in Sparrow's calypso. In an attempt to give these women agency, to retrieve their maligned bodies and rejected sexualities, the play revisits pre-independence debates about political autonomy and national identity-formation from the women's radical perspective.

To uncover the theoretical tools that can help us unpack Hall's play, I want to turn briefly to some of the important work already done in the critical interrogation of postcolonial nationalist discourses. Kumari Jayawardena, in her exploration of postcolonial nationalisms within a crisis of cultural identity, argues that national independence and decolonization for many countries in Africa and Asia involved the twin processes of an internal reorganization of pre-capitalist structures and an external challenge of imperialism (4). Because the internal reorganization was itself made necessary for the local bourgeoisie by the reality of western economic development, the nationalist project found itself torn between a desire for and a rejection of the west, which could also be read through an opposite impulse: the desire for and rejection of the past.

This simultaneous desire to both contest and mimic western economic development and white global patriarchal power could most easily be reconciled by a self-conscious (re)positioning of women's social relationships within the family and wider society and by the control and management of women's bodies. As Jayawardena illustrates in her discussion of nationalist movements in Asia, since the status of women in society was an important indicator of "civilization"—that is, equality to the west— women were often made to function as the signs of their country's economic and political progress and transformation:

> This new consciousness demanded an "enlightened" woman. The new bourgeois man, himself a product of Western education or missionary influence, needed as his partner a "new woman," educated in the relevant foreign language, dressed in the new styles and attuned to Western ways—a woman who was "presentable" in colonial society yet whose role was primarily in the home. (12)

By seeming to give middle-class women more autonomy and freedom in the public sphere, while ensuring their cooperation in the private sphere, these strategies made women serve both an economic and cultural function. Women of the peasantry and working class could continue to function in the public sphere as cheap labourers, and middle-class women could be used to legitimize the local patriarchy's desire for economic and political equality with the west without a complete sacrifice of "cultural traditions." Precisely because economic and political equality with the west was never really possible, the preservation of cultural traditions became absolutely essential as a necessary challenge to the overwhelming power of western imperialism. In this function of a dual, politicized role

> ...the new woman could not be a total negation of traditional culture. Although certain obviously unjust practices should be abolished, and women involved in activities outside the home, they still had to act as the guardians of national culture, indigenous religion and family traditions—in other words, to be both "modern" and "traditional." (14)

Women's social relationships and women's bodies could be manipulated to both challenge imperialism and comply with it.

In a similar argument, Cynthia Enloe suggests that women's bodies are often eroticized and exoticized both to justify imperial domination and to privilege masculinized memory and hope (44). Interestingly, Partha Chatterjee in his critique of Benedict Anderson in "Whose Imagined Community?" positions this masculinized memory in a more positive way as the colonial nation's only tool of imagining community (217). Unlike Jayawardena and Enloe, he does not go on to critically analyze the ways in which gendered nationalisms work to oppress women. As Jayawardena insists, the internal reorganization of national cultures almost always relies on a western ideal of monogamy in order to ensure women's subordination within the family (15).

> DINAH. *Brown skin gyal, stay home and mind baby.*
> *Brown skin gyal, stay home and mind baby.*
> *Ah going away in a sailing boat*
> *And if I don't come back,*
> *Stay home and mind baby.* (194)

What Jacqui Alexander contributes to the ideas offered by Jayawardena and Enloe is a positioning of the discussion of gendered nationalisms within a specifically Caribbean context of naturalized heterosexuality and hyper-masculinity. In so doing, she offers a powerful critique of the Caribbean (nation) state and its assumed authority to manage and control alternative and "transgressive" sexualities. In her article "Not Just (Any) Body can be a Citizen" Alexander argues that this management and control result from an "internal crisis of authority" precipitated by the region's relationship to the rest of the world (6). While this crisis of authority is, in some ways, similar to that identified in Jayawardena's discussion of internal cultural reorganization, Alexander goes further by insisting that in the Caribbean this crisis has to be negotiated, out of necessity, through a management and reorganization of sexual relationships. Because black sexualities in the Caribbean were marked as untamed and unmanageable and even demonized during slavery, the post-slavery, post-independence project has had self-consciously to find ways to manage this "unruly" black sexuality in order to prove the middle class's civility and consolidate its right and power to rule. In an argument similar to Jayawardena's, Alexander explains:

> Women were to fiercely defend the nation by protecting their honour, by guarding the nuclear, conjugal family, "the fundamental institution of the society," by guarding "culture" defined as the transmission of a fixed set of proper values to the children of the nation, and by mobilizing on the party's behalf into the far reaches of the country. (13)

Women, then, were expected not only to accept but be complicit within political systems that denied them agency and control over their bodies. While this role as guardian of the national culture was largely reserved for middle-class women, working-class women and peasant women would have been equally involved, if not more so, in political campaigns and service. Despite their loyalty to the nation, however, these working-class women were seen as embodying the very sexuality that threatened the nation's stability:

> …Black nationalist masculinity needed to demonstrate that it was now capable of ruling…. It also required distancing itself from, while simultaneously attempting to control, Black working-class femininity that ostensibly harboured a profligate sexuality: the "Jezebel" and the whore who was not completely socialized into housewifery, but whose labour would be mobilized to help consolidate popular nationalism. (Alexander 13)

But if Caribbean nationalisms feel compelled to manage unruly heterosexuality, Alexander argues, they feel even more compelled to manage lesbian and other forms of non-procreative sexual activity. These "transgressive" sexualities cannot simply be confined within the rule of the family, which still offers some kind of national identity, however unsatisfactory, but are marked as criminalized and, therefore, as standing completely outside of the boundaries of the nation (5). "'Homosexual' difference," Alexander goes on to demonstrate, "is indispensable to the creation of the putative heterosexual norm" (6):

> JEAN. *Then it was just me and small boy Toto alone, left in the house… All of a sudden, he start calling me jamette to my face. He and he little Junior Secondary hangman friends. I try with him and give him everything. By that time ah had was to go back to work. Next thing I know, I see he pick up with some white men, strange looking white people. They always just passing through.*
> DINAH. *(She sits up in disbelief.) Toto is a macomé man?* (181)

While Tony Hall's play *Jean and Dinah* does not fully engage in a discussion of lesbian or gay sexuality, it is concerned with another kind of criminalized sexuality, that of the female sex worker. This socially threatening female working-class sexuality, which is echoed literally in the racist historical construction of the Jezebel and the whore, can "shame" the nation. The women's labour, thus, marks them as inimical to the nation's development. Forced outside of the real boundaries of the nation, the women's bodies are made to bear the deep scars of their alienation and abuse: Dinah has been blinded in one eye and one of Jean's hands has been disfigured. Yet, in this play Jean and Dinah manage to challenge the social inscriptions that deny them full citizenship and redefine their role within the wider society.

Act 1, which is framed around a series of questions, repeatedly forces the women back into their past and offers them the opportunity to (re)examine their friendship and life choices. Their friendship, which is presented in some instances as a kind of mother-daughter relationship, demonstrates and summarizes the problems encoded within an elitist patriarchal nationalist discourse of exclusion and sexual management. As a testament to the power of the colonizing and nationalist agendas, Dinah, who had initially been safely entrenched within the protective space of the "respectable" lower-middle class family with her husband, house and children, is never able to truly reconcile her marginalized position as a criminalized sexual being. As a surrogate mother to Jean she in fact feels compelled to manage Jean's sexuality by trying to reinsert her into a nationally accepted, but sexually abusive, patriarchal family. Dinah, in fact, desperately afraid of her potential erasure in a national discourse that says she should not exist, refuses to admit that she is a sex worker. But on the Carnival Monday on which the play opens, a search for the truth pulls the women deeper and deeper into the past to face important questions about the meanings of their lives.

In act 2 the women are, thus, literally transported through memory across thirty-five years of their lives to confront the realities of their past and the hopes of the then burgeoning nation. In making the journey back when they are older and wiser and less constrained by middle-class rules of sexual respectability, the women can examine their own painful past through a critical examination of the very nation that has been committed to their silencing and erasure. It is in this act that the women are more successfully able to challenge the nationalist narrative of exclusion and begin to reposition themselves as valuable and necessary citizens. This journey backwards and the acts of resistance that it facilitates are performed through a series of skits in traditional masquerade roles. The women, however, rewrite these roles from a radical woman-centred perspective that can reinvent the Baby Doll and Midnight Robber carnival characters with a new kind of resisting stance, located within a rich continuum of Caribbean women's resistance. Jean, thus, indicts her community for its complicity in the irresponsible behaviour of men, the exoticization of brown and light skin, and the social legislation of middle-class values that oppress all women. Perhaps, more importantly, she rewrites her own history of sexual and emotional abuse by charting a historical narrative that connects her to a line of powerful female warriors.

> JEAN. *Well, I descend from the seed of Petite Belle Lily and Alice Sugar the Former. I trod the centuries from Na Na Yah come down. I is woman. Watch form. Ebony. From that one seed, I stand up. I grow to these proportions.* (203)

In revisiting her own familial history, itself located in the cultural tradition of carnival, Dinah is able to identify culture and tradition as empowering and healing rather than as marginalizing and controlling. By rewriting carnival as a shared female space rather than an exclusively male and authoritarian space, she writes herself not as marginal, but as indispensable to the nation's survival and articulation of itself. Dinah, like Jean, charts a female tradition of warriorhood, this time by disrupting the traditional male character of the Midnight Robber and redefining it as part of a female tradition. Her personal history, in fact, establishes her as one of the brave early women of carnival, and she is thus able to retrace carnival's history as part of her own historical memory and through a feminine, rather than masculine line: "I am the mother of the warrior musician, the Pan Man and I prepared for war, the Pan Man prepared for war, I prepare him for war. My son" (204). She names herself, then, as the source of carnival, as the female muse on which male performers must rely. But since carnival has come to represent in Trinidad and Tobago such an important function of national identity, Dinah, by disrupting the patriarchal power of carnival, is even more importantly inscribing herself as essential to this national identity. There can, indeed, be no national narrative without women. The play seems to be suggesting that an honest recognition of this mutual relationship may actually facilitate more equal social relationships between men and women.

This revisioning of the cultural tradition of carnival from a female perspective is also achieved in the play through a re-examination of Sparrow's 1956 calypso that first indicted Jean and Dinah's sexuality as detrimental to the national agenda. In Trinidad and Tobago, calypsonians like Sparrow, of course, have been recognized as important national spokespersons for the ordinary Caribbean folk. Assumed to have clear, unobstructed access through national culture to all aspects of Trinidadian life—economic, political and social concerns—calypsonians often function as political mediators. In this sense, calypsos are often read as resisting cultural narratives that can challenge oppressive middle-class values or political corruption. Because of their enormous national value and appeal, however, the social inventions and interventions offered within calypsos can also come to represent a kind of unchallenged nationalist discourse—a discourse that is assumed to speak not only on behalf of the national community it represents, but to speak the "truth" about that community. As an internal tool of cultural management, the calypso and calypsonian can, therefore, come not only to constitute another kind of oppressive hegemonic discourse, but to articulate that discourse in specifically gendered and even sexualized ways.

Denyse Plummer, a female calypsonian, describes one of the ways in which calypso and carnival as nationalist discourses attempted to manage women. The few women, she explains, who dared to defy the social norms and participate in carnival before the 1960s were labelled "as prostitutes, as whores, people you didn't want your children to associate with" (qtd. in Mason 141). As part of a nationalist reinvention of gender, therefore, women's participation in carnival was actively discouraged. Those women who chose to participate were made to take on certain types of constructed sexualities that marked them, along with their class, as external to or inimical to the nation's prosperity and development. But not only was women's participation in carnival discouraged, calypsos often portray women with ridicule, even contempt. According to Merle Hodge, this devalorization of women within calypsos is part of a national ethos that encourages the embarrassment of women (117). In *Jean and Dinah*, it is the women on whom respectable Trinidadian society looks down, the "prostitutes" and "whores" who play mas, who perform their lives. In so doing brave, bold women, like Dinah, not only critically challenge the dominant male discourse of the 1950s, but also re-inhabit the tradition of carnival with a vibrant female sensibility.

Sparrow's calypso, appearing at a significant juncture in the history of Trinidad and Tobago, clearly encapsulates this function of calypsos as both nationalist discourse and male-centered narrative. 1956 is enormously important in Trinidad's historical memory as the year when the People's National Movement (PNM) came to power under the leadership of Eric Williams. This initiated a period of strong nationalist sentiment that culminated in the gaining of independence in 1962. Sparrow's career, in many ways, was built on this political platform and his popularity grew enormously during this period, as he functioned as a primary supporter of the new government (Regis 4). Before and after independence, Sparrow would explore in many of his calypsos the preoccupation with the question of national identity as Trinidad and Tobago struggled to name itself within a wider region and more powerful world.

> DINAH. *That useless good for nothing. You know if you give them fellas a chance they will give you a bad name. They sing on you, just so. He and Little Sparrow. Next thing you know, people jumping to the tune of you on Carnival day.* (167)

Jean and Dinah is an important commentary on this quest toward nationhood and women's subordination within the national agenda. The presence of the US military in Trinidad during World War II dramatically increased employment opportunities for Trinidadians, but also sharpened their awareness of the outside world and their position within it, and acerbated class and color conflicts (van Koningsbruggen 53-56). By 1956 and the coming to power of the PNM, the Americans had come to represent in the political discourse an exploitative foreign interest that, like the British, was inimical to the development of the emerging nation (Rohlehr 527). This opinion was voiced clearly in Sparrow's calypso as he expressed the new emerging national self-confidence. As in other black nationalist discourses, the reinsertion of the political power of Trinidadian men coincides in the calypso with a celebration of male heterosexuality and the denial of women's independent sexual power: "It's the glamour boys again/We are going to rule Port of Spain/no more Yankees to spoil the fete/Dorothy have to take what she get." Sparrow suggests that the "new Trinidad" had to be reconstituted not only in political, but also in gendered terms. National growth depended on the dismantling of the economic and political power of foreign, white men and the subordination and control of women's bodies and sexualities. As sex workers involved in socially transgressive sexual relationships with the very representatives of white, external economic and political power, the women are doubly indicted. They come to represent a historical betrayal of black masculinity by black women in which the sexual abuse of black women's bodies gets rewritten as their seeming willingness to privilege their own economic survival over that of black men. While black women's bodies can be exoticized and sold as sexual commodities on behalf of the nation in order to exploit that very same historical narrative of colonial obedience and servility, women can as easily be punished for that exoticization. In the calypso, therefore, it is the women who are conceived as a threat to the nation's development—the morality of the local men, who now have free access to their labour, is never questioned. The calypso's condemnation of the women in moral terms designates them, in fact, as standing outside of the newly constituted citizenship. They cannot legitimately take part in the project of nation building. The primary impetus of Hall's play is, precisely, a reinsertion of Jean and Dinah as legitimate citizens by the rewriting of their histories and the assertion of their human rights as sex workers, mothers and wives.

> JEAN: *Now you hear what I have to say. You feel because I is a whore, I must go with any and everybody. That little pissin' tail man who want to pay me a little $2 and a little $3. I don't go with them kind of man. That little half man from behind the bridge. He can't give me stick. Cave man come to town. I don't want to see he. And every time he see me, he only ridiculing me, that now the Yankees gone I have to take what I get. That good for Dorothy so. Not me. You mad or what? You crazy? For what? Eh? For what? I is Jean you know.* (199)

The two women contest the roles of carnival and calypso as male-centered discourse precisely by challenging stereotypes about black women's sexuality. As active agents in the project of nation building, they insist on their right to make independent economic and sexual choices. In an attempt to recuperate their bodies from a place of simultaneous erasure and cultural over-exploitation, they refuse to occupy the socially condemnatory roles of "immoral" sex workers and non-citizens reserved for them in Sparrow's calypso. The women, instead, redefine their identities by critically discussing the socio-economic realities of 1950s Trinidad and Tobago, which severely restricted income-earning opportunities for poor women. These women insist, therefore, on their right to fair wages and define their labour as part of their familial and communal responsibilities. The women, abandoned and abused by the men in their lives, willingly care for families and children on their own, and for each other, and see sex work as one economically viable option. They argue, in fact, that their labour as sex workers cannot be separated from their roles as mothers and even wives. This assertion is, indeed, radical in Caribbean societies where: "the discouragement of autonomous expressions of female sexuality as transgressing gender ideals… results in the maintenance of a discursive distinction between prostitution and family life that denies any correspondence between the two realms" (Red Thread 273). By insisting on their own agency and by reclaiming power over their bodies, Jean and Dinah challenge not only the management of women's sexualities within nationalist agendas, but also the exploitation of the working class by elitist, exclusionary nationalist movements that pretend to represent the interests of the poor, while continuing to support a hidden colonialist project that ensures the working class's political and economic subordination. In challenging these oppressive middle-class and patriarchal values, Hall's play urges the wider society to critically re-examine its understanding of family and community.

In giving us access to their lives, the women, therefore, challenge us to rethink many of our own assumptions. Yet, in some ways, the play doesn't seem to take this challenge far enough. While defending the sexual choices of these women, the play is unable to offer any useful defence of small boy Toto's homosexuality. By refusing to engage this discussion in any meaningful way and by writing him as cruel and emotionally sterile, the play, in fact, seems to be suggesting that his sexuality is the one that is legitimately perverse. In his sexual relationships with white men, which also appear to have an economic function, he is presented as the one most threatening to the nation by his seemingly uncritical acceptance of external and corrupting values. It is his selfishness that really threatens the community represented in the play. Again, while the two women celebrate and justify their choices, this play remains ultimately sad—the women's bodies bear the scars of years of emotional and physical violence and abandonment. If Dinah's death brings relief, it is because the violence can no longer be played out on her subjected body. Dinah's plea to Jean throughout the play makes us hesitate over the extent to which she really believes in her own sexual empowerment: "Watch me. Hush, listen to me…. If, as I did tell you to go home, you did go home, today you wouldn't be in this position" (195).

JEAN. *Home? Where the fock is home?* (166)

***

yagayah: two.womyn.black.griots by debbie young and naila belvett is equally concerned with questions of home, nation and belonging. Structured similarly to *Jean and Dinah,* this play is a running dialogue between two Caribbean women and is very much concerned, like the earlier play, with memory as an exploration of black women's desires. By expanding the discussion outside of the Caribbean and into its diaspora, the play is able to address questions about national (un)belonging in even more complicated ways. These questions are explored in the tensions the play creates between the ideal romanticized and spiritual love of yemoja and ogun and lived sexual abuse, as well as the play's treatment of the search for belonging that writes the Caribbean and Canada simultaneously as both desired and undesirable spaces.

> *dear yemoja*
> *do not be anxious*
> *our tribulation is*
> *short-lived*
> *fate*
> *an unusual friend of mine*
> *promised our eventual*
> *hereafter*
> *i believe him* (364)

From the very beginning of this play, danger hovers beneath the surface, behind the games and the songs and the laughter. As these two young best friends take various journeys toward and away from each other, they are forced to admit the illusiveness of their childhood dreams: even their love for each other is not perfect. Played out against two seemingly distinct and even culturally-competing national landscapes—Jamaica and Canada—the girls' and women's friendship is influenced by the nature of these differing national narratives. These narratives, which go unchallenged in the Caribbean, rely on a political and economic hierarchy that positions the region as incapable of real economic progress and, thus, marks Caribbean citizens as suspect within the Canadian national landscape.

In engaging a specifically Jamaican nationalist discourse, this play, like *Jean and Dinah*, suggests a necessary intersection between the categories of nation, class, gender and sexuality. Again like the earlier play, *yagayah* argues that the subjugation of women's bodies is necessary to entrench male middle-class power. Black women's bodies repeatedly, then, are scarred by the violence of masculinized power and sexuality. The play gestures toward the violent nature of this heteronormative and hyper-masculine sexuality very early in the performance of the children's game, emmanuel road. In this game, the bodies of black girls can feel pain, and fear, and bleed, and the sources of pain can come from the most unexpected places. The sexual abuse of imogene by her uncle disrupts the tidy middle-class *façade* that her family wears. Yet, the pain of sexual abuse and incest, the terrifying damage of black children's bodies by black men, cannot really be spoken in this play, not even between friends: "if yuh do it wid a man an yuh was a likkle gyal/yuh was in di wrong yuh mek it happen" (360). After her long painful soliloquy in which imogene fantasizes her uncle's death, mary consoles us by reminding us that we don't have to speak or even imagine this kind of betrayal and pain. The audience is made complicit in the children and community's silence: "memba a play we a play" (361).

mary, who embodies the working-class ambition in this play, hopes to break out of her family's cycle of poverty, but finds herself entrapped, like generations of women before her, by too-early pregnancy and an absence of any real life chances. The black working-class masculinity represented in the play is in some ways equally trapped within Caribbean nationalist narratives that deny young black men the means to economic empowerment, reserved only for middle-class men. This deliberate refusal by middle-class men to share economic and political power encourages the performance of a hyper-sexualized masculine identity that the middle class can punish and use to legitimize the continued disempowerment of black working-class masculinity. As Jacqui Alexander points out, it is not just black working-class female sexuality that is managed by nationalist discourses:

> …Black nationalist masculinity needed to demonstrate… moral rectitude, particularly on questions of paternity. This required distancing itself from irresponsible Black working-class masculinity that spawned the "bastard," the "illegitimate," and thus had to be criminalized for irresponsible fatherhood by the British. (13)

It is this nationalist masculinity that traps both tyrone and mary and distorts the fantasy of the Shakespeare play they performed as children. It is mary, however, who must bear the social repercussions of the sexual and economic competition between the men in her society: "him sweet me up wid him lyrics/den him pyzen mi wid him seed/tell mi big man nuh fi wear latex/end a month cum an mi still neva bleed" (380). In a rejection of herself and her corrupted sexuality, mary now fantasizes the destruction of a baby she fears she cannot care for, and her black female body and its poisoned womb. Her childhood dreams of an ideal, romanticized love offered in *Romeo and Juliet* are located outside of a Jamaican reality. Increasingly replacing that protected past in which girls can dream is a present of terrifyingly real masculine violence:

> mek mi si—johnny dead, harry dead, clive an barry dead. police kill two a dem, gunman kill di odda two. dem kill horrett cause him wouldn't tell dem where one a di twin dem live. dem tek juney frock from off di clothes line, wrap it roun' him head suh dat nobody woulda hear and shot him dead two time—rain di fall di morning. jamaica is quite fine, tek care of yuhself an write me back. (370)

When imogene moves to Canada, she seems to have escaped both this daily physical violence and her uncle's sexual aggression, but as she tries to explain to mary, "jamaica hard but in foreign there is a new set of battles" (371).

> *dear ogun*
> *i had a dream*
> *you kissed me with*
> *chalk on your lips*
> *my tongue searched*
> *powder thick hoping*
> *to find home in*
> *familiar*
> *you covered white across*
> *my face into and*
> *under my eyes. they burnt*
> *you smiled*
> *i dreamt*
> *you tasted disgust and hate* (378)

imogene finds both her blackness and womanhood erased in Canada—a society in which blackness is not only left unvalued but is rendered invisible. In her class, Feminism 101, there is no space to articulate or contextualize her specific experiences. Her alienation and invisibility in the classroom are mirrored, even more dangerously, in a wider societal dismissal of the black female presence as physically deviant. Her physical difference, her revised social class and her immigrant status mark her as a clear outsider in a privileged "First World" nation, where privilege, as in the Caribbean, is guarded and reserved only for a few. Like mary, imogene, in search of an idealized, romanticized love that can displace the loneliness she experiences in Canada, mistakes the desire for feminine compliance as love and finds that the sexual offering of her black female body is never enough: "pawning self-respect/selling identity and beliefs/just to get a fix/thinking a little dick can heal a loveless heart/addicted to love/I want to rap myself in your skin/'cause mine hurts" (384).

Running parallel to the women's frustrated desire for love is the spiritual love of yemoja and ogun that is framed within an identifiable African-Caribbean context that valorizes and worships black femininity and offers a wholesome, unthreatened, black masculinity. It is noteworthy that in the move to Canada, however, even this love is much harder to realize. Intended, in fact, to form a parallel to imogene and mary's relationship, the love story of yemoja and ogun begins to fragment in the face of Canada's racist rejection, which imogene understands not as a rejection of African Caribbean masculinity but as a rejection of black women's bodies, black women's sexualities and black women's beauty: "why don't you cover your face cause you come from an ugly race/and like a festering sore/keep wanting more and more" (387). The difficulty in explaining this complete devaluing of her body and self to mary, who sees the "First World" only in economic terms, results in the increasing fragmentation of the women's friendship.

young and belvett's play, thus, forces a critical conversation between the Caribbean and Canada. Because the play, itself, does not create a physical disruption between the two places, so that imogene and mary are both on stage at the same time, even when they are in different geographical locations, this conversation is made immediate and more urgent. By allowing both women to speak to each other as through a mirror, the play emphasizes not only the cultural (although sometimes competing) connections between both places, but also the deep diasporic linkages that connect black women's lives across borders and cultures in ways they may not even understand. *yagayah* attempts a critical intervention into Canadian national identity by insisting that that identity be expanded to make space for the multiple identities that share this national space.

In using black female sexuality as an essential entry point into the discussion of national belonging in black and other communities, these plays argue that social and political constructions of black women depend on the ways in which communities imagine themselves. In offering what bell hooks describes as an "oppositional gaze," these plays seek to distort and disrupt stereotypical images of black women. Rather than facilitating a project of cultural recuperation for men, white women and some black middle-class women through the bodies of black women, these plays disrupt the received images of black women, so those images are increasingly transgressive, unmanageable and unrecognizable.

> *yemoja*
> *if only i could have touched you*
> *then*
> *my tongue*
> *your personal hair bush comb*
> *to tidy pearl black nipples*
> *zimbezi river deep belly button*
> *thick bush at the centre*
> *yemoja I thought you*
> *in a dream* (364)

(2005)

Works Cited

Alexander, M. Jacqui and Chandra Talpade Mohanty, ed. *Feminist Genealogies, Colonial Legacies, and Democratic Futures.* New York: Routledge, 1997.

Alexander, Jacqui. "NOT JUST (ANY)BODY CAN BE A CITIZEN: The Politics of Law, Sexuality and Postcoloniality in Trinidad and Tobago and the Bahamas." *Feminist Review* 48 (1994): 5-23.

Brand, Dionne. *Bread out of Stone: Recollections, Sex, Race, Dreaming, Politics.* Toronto: Coach House, 1994.

Bush, Barbara. *Slave Women in Caribbean Society: 1650-1838.* Bloomington: Indiana UP, 1990.

———. "White 'Ladies,' Coloured 'Favourites' and Black 'Wenches'." *Slavery and Abolition* 2.2 (1981): 245-62.

Chatterjee, Partha. "Whose Imagined Community?" *Mapping the Nation.* Ed. Gopal Balakrishnan. London: Verso, 1996. 214-25.

Collins, Patricia Hill. *Black Sexual Politics: African Americans, Gender and the New Racism.* New York: Routledge, 2004.

———. *Black Feminist Thought.* New York: Routledge, 2000.

Cooper, Carolyn. *Sound Clash: Jamaican Dancehall Culture from Lady Saw to Dancehall Queen.* New York: Palgrave Macmillan, 2004.

———. *Noises in the Blood: Orality, Gender and the "Vulgar" Body of Jamaican Popular Culture.* Durham, North Carolina: Duke UP, 1995.

Enloe, Cynthia. *Bananas, Beaches and Bases: Making Feminist Sense of International Politics.* Berkeley: U of California P, 2000.

Hall, Tony. *Jean and Dinah... Who Have Been Locked Away in a World Famous Calypso Since 1956 Speak Their Minds Publicly. Testifyin': Contemporary African Canadian Drama.* Ed. Djanet Sears. Vol. 2. Toronto: Playwrights Canada, 2003. 149-213.

Hodge, Merle. "The Shadow of the Whip: A Comment on Male-Female Relationships in the Caribbean." *Is Massa Day Dead?* Ed. Orde Coombs. New York: Anchor Books, 1974. 111-18.

hooks, bell. "Black Women: Shaping Feminist Theory." *The Black Feminist Reader.* Malden, MA: Blackwell, 2000. 131-45.

———. *Feminist Theory: From Margin to Center.* Boston: South End, 1984.

———. "The Oppositional Gaze." *Black Looks: Race and Representation.* Toronto: Between the Lines, 1992. 115-32.

———. *Talking Back: Thinking Feminist, Thinking Black.* Boston: South End, 1989.

Jayawardena, Kumari. *Feminism and Nationalism in the Third World.* London; Atlantic Highlands, NJ: Zed Books, 1986.

Kempadoo, Kamala. *Sexing the Caribbean: Gender, Race and Sexual Labour.* New York: Routledge, 2004.

———, ed. *Sun, Sex and Gold: Tourism and Sex Work in the Caribbean.* Lanham, MD: Rowman and Littlefield, 1999.

Kempadoo, Kamala and Jo Doezema, ed. *Global Sex Workers: Rights, Resistance, and Redefinition.* New York: Routledge, 1998.

Lorde, Audre. *Sister Outsider: Essays and Speeches.* New York: The Crossing Press, 1984.

Mason, Peter. *Bacchanal! The Carnival Culture of Trinidad.* Philadelphia: Temple UP, 1998.

McClintock, Anne, Aamir Mufti and Ella Shohat, ed. *Dangerous Liaisons: Gender, Nation, and Postcolonial Perspectives.* Minneapolis: U of Minnesota P, 1997.

Mighty Sparrow. "Jean and Dinah." Rec. 1956. Vol. 1–Mighty Sparrow. Ice Records, 2000.

Mohammed, Patricia. "Towards Indigenous Feminist Theorizing in the Caribbean." *Feminist Review* 59 (1998): 6-33.

Mohanty, Chandra Talpade. "Under Western Eyes: Feminist Scholarship and Colonial Discourses." *Dangerous Liaisons: Gender, Nation, and Postcolonial Perspectives.* Ed. Anne McClintock, et al. Minneapolis: U of Minnesota P, 1997. 255-77.

Red Thread Women's Development Programme. "'Givin' Lil' Bit fuh Lil' Bit': Women and Sex Work in Guyana." *Sun, Sex and Gold: Tourism and Sex Work in the Caribbean.* Ed. Kamala Kempadoo. Lanham, MD: Rowman and Littlefield, 1999. 263-90.

Regis, Louis. *The Political Calypso: True Opposition in Trinidad and Tobago 1962-1987.* Barbados: UP of the West Indies, 1999.

Rohlehr, Gordon. *Calypso and Society in Pre-independence Trinidad.* Port of Spain, Trinidad: Gordon Rohlehr, 1990.

Rose, Tricia. *Black Noise: Rap Music and Black Culture in Contemporary America.* Hanover, NH: UP of New England, 1994.

———. *Longing to Tell: Black Women Talk about Sexuality and Intimacy.* New York: Farrar, Straus and Giroux, 2003.

Shepherd, Verene. *Engendering History: Caribbean Women in Historical Perspective.* New York: St. Martin's, 1995.

Stevenson, Brenda E. "Gender Convention, Ideals, and Identity Among Antebellum Virginia Slave Women." *Black Women and Slavery in the Americas: More Than Chattel.* Ed. David Barry Gaspar and Darlene Clark Hine. Bloomington: Indiana UP, 1996. 169-90.

Van Koningsbruggen, Peter. *Trinidad Carnival: A Quest for National Identity.* London: Macmillan, 1997.

young, debbie and naila belvett. *yagayah: two.womyn.black.griots. Testifyin': Contemporary African Canadian Drama.* Ed. Djanet Sears. Vol. 2. Toronto: Playwrights Canada, 2003. 349-90.

Suggested Further Reading

Collections

Nolan, Yvette, Betty Quan, and George Bwanika Seremba, ed. *Beyond the Pale: Dramatic Writing from First Nations Writers and Writers of Colour.* Toronto: Playwrights Canada, 1996.

Nolan, Yvette, ed. *Beyond the Pale: Dramatic Writing from First Nations Writers and Writers of Colour.* Revised Edition. Toronto: Playwrights Canada, 2004.

Sears, Djanet, ed. *Testifyin': Contemporary African Canadian Drama.* 2 Vols. Toronto: Playwrights Canada, 2000, 2003.

———, ed. *Tellin' It Like It Is: A Compendium of African Canadian Monologues for Actors.* Toronto: Playwrights Union of Canada, 2000.

Special Issues on African-Canadian Writing and Performance

Ballantyne, Darcy, et al., ed. *Women and the Black Diaspora.* Spec. issue of *Canadian Woman Studies/les cahiers de la femme* 23.2 (Winter 2004): 1-179.

Clarke, George Elliott, ed. *Special Africadian Issue.* Spec. issue of *The Dalhousie Review* 77.1 (Summer 1997): 149-304.

Coleman, Daniel and Donald Goellnicht, ed. *Race.* Spec. issue of *Essays on Canadian Writing* 75 (Winter 2002): 1-246.

Fisher, Susan, ed. *Black Writing in Canada.* Spec. issue of *Canadian Literature* 182 (Autumn 2004). 1-202.

Hudson, Peter, ed. *North: New African Canadian Writing.* Spec. issue of *West Coast Line* 31.1 (Spring/Summer 1997): 5-120.

Lee, Angela with Natalie Rewa, ed. *Back Theatre in Canada/African Canadian Theatre.* Spec. issue of *Canadian Theatre Review* 83 (Summer 1995): 1-84.

Sears, Djanet and Ric Knowles, ed. *African-Canadian Theatre: Honouring the Word.* Spec. issue of *Canadian Theatre Review* 118 (Spring 2004): 1-123.

Secondary Materials on Theatre and Drama

Benson, Eugene and L. W. Conolly. *English-Canadian Theatre*. Toronto: Oxford UP Canada, 1987.

Benston, Kimberly W. *Performing Blackness: Enactments of African-American Modernism*. London; New York: Routledge, 2000.

Breon, Robin. "Blackface: Thoughts on Racial Masquerade [Minstrel Shows]." *Canadian Theatre Review* 98 (1999): 60-62.

Clarke, George Elliott. "Raising Raced and Erased Executions in African-Canadian Literature: Or, Unearthing Angélique." *Essays on Canadian Writing* 75 (2002): 30-61.

Crow, Brian and Chris Barnfield. *An Introduction to Post-Colonial Theatre*. Cambridge: Cambridge UP, 1996.

Dickinson, Peter. "Duets, Duologues, and Black Diasporic Theatre: Djanet Sears, William Shakespeare, and Others." *Modern Drama* 45.2 (2002): 188-208.

Elam, Harry J. Jr. and David Krasner, ed. *African American Performance and Theater History: A Critical Reader*. Oxford; New York: Oxford UP, 2001.

Fabre, Genevieve. *Drumbeats, Masks and Metaphor: Contemporary Afro-American Theatre*. Trans. Melvin Dixon. Cambridge: Cambridge UP, 1983.

Filewod, Alan. *Performing Canada: The Nation Enacted in the Imagined Theatre*. Kamloops, BC: Textual Studies in Canada Monograph Series, 2002.

Gilbert, Helen. *(Post) Colonial Stages: Critical & Creative Views on Drama, Theatre & Performance*. London: Dangaroo, 1999.

Gilbert, Helen and Joanne Tompkins, ed. *Post-Colonial Drama: Theory, Practice, Politics*. London; New York: Routledge, 1996.

Glaap, Albert-Reiner and Sherrill Grace, ed. *Performing National Identities: International Perspectives on Contemporary Canadian Theatre*. Vancouver: Talonbooks, 2003.

Glaap, Albert-Reiner and Rolf Althof, ed. *On-Stage and Off-Stage: English Canadian Drama in Discourse*. St. John's, NF&L: Breakwater, 1995.

Harrison, Paul Carter, Victor Leo Walker II, and Gus Edwards, ed. *Black Theatre: Ritual Performance in the African Diaspora*. Philadelphia: Temple UP, 2002.

Knowles, Ric. "The Nike Method." Interview with Djanet Sears and Alison Sealy Smith. *Canadian Theatre Review* 97 (1998): 24-30.

———. "*Othello* in Three Times." *Shakespeare and Canada: Essays on Production, Translation, and Adaptation*. Brussels: P.I.E. Peter Lang, 2004. 137-64. (Reprinted from Diana Brydon and Irena Makaryk, ed. *Shakespeare in Canada: A World Elsewhere?* Toronto: U of Toronto P, 2002. 371-94.

———. *The Theatre of Form and the Production of Meaning: Contemporary Canadian Dramaturgies*. Toronto: ECW, 1999.

Maufort, Marc, and Franca Bellarsi, ed. *Siting the Other: Re-Visions of Marginality in Australian and English-Canadian Drama*. Bruxelles; New York: P.I.E.-Peter Lang, 2001.

Olaniyan, Tejumola. *Scars of Conquest/Masks of Resistance: The Invention of Cultural Identities in African, African-American, and Caribbean Drama*. New York; Oxford: Oxford UP, 1995.

Olaogun, Modupe. "Dramatizing Atrocities: Plays by Wole Soyinka, Francis Imbuga, and George Seremba Recalling the Idi Amin Era." *Modern Drama* 45.3 (2002): 430-48.

Omotoso, Kole. *The Theatrical into Theatre: A Study of the Drama and Theatre of the English-Speaking Caribbean*. London; Port of Spain: New Beacon, 1982.

Rebeiro, Angela, ed. *Theatre in Society: Politics, Plays & Performance*. Toronto: Playwrights Union of Canada, 2002.

Sanders, Leslie. *The Development of Black Theater in America: From Shadows to Selves*. Baton Rouge: Louisiana State UP, 1988.

Wagner, Anton, E. *Contemporary Canadian Theatre: New World Visions*. Toronto: Simon and Pierre, 1985.

Wallace, Robert. *Producing Marginality: Theatre and Criticism in Canada*. Saskatoon: Fifth House, 1990.

———. *Staging a Nation: Evolutions in Contemporary Canadian Theatre*. Canada House Lecture Ser. 69. London: Canada House, Canadian High Commission, 2002.

———. *Theatre and Transformation in Contemporary Canada*. Robarts Centre for Canadian Studies Lecture Ser. Toronto: Robarts Centre for Canadian Studies, York University, 1999.

Waters, Harold A. *Black Theater in French: a Guide*. Collection Bibliographies 2. Sherbrooke, QC: Editions Naaman, 1978.

Wilson, Ann. "*Beatrice Chancy*: Slavery, Martyrdom and the Female Body." *Siting the Other: Re-Visions of Marginality in Australian and English-Canadian Drama*. Ed. and introd. Marc Maufort and Franca Bellarsi. Bruxelles; New York: P.I.E.-Peter Lang, 2001. 267-78.

Secondary Materials on African-Canadian Writing

Brydon, Diana. "Detour Canada: Rerouting the Black Atlantic, Reconfiguring the Postcolonial." *Reconfigurations: Canadian Literatures and Postcolonial Identities.* Ed. Marc Maufort and Franca Bellarsi. Bruxelles: P.I.E. Peter Lang, 2002. 109-22.

———. "Black Canadas: Rethinking Canadian and Diasporic Cultural Studies." *Revista Canaria De Estudios Ingleses* 43 (2001): 101-17.

Chariandy, David. "'Canada In Us Now': Locating the Criticism of Black Canadian Writing." *Essays on Canadian Writing* 75 (2002): 196-216.

Clarke, George Elliott. *Odysseys Home: Mapping African-Canadian Literature.* Toronto: U of Toronto P, 2002.

Compton, Wayde. *Bluesprint: Black British Columbian Literature and Orature.* Vancouver: Arsenal Pulp, 2001.

Dabydeen, Cyril. "Places We Come From: Voices of Caribbean Canadian Writers (in English) and Multicultural Contexts." *World Literature Today* 73.2 (1999): 231-37.

Dorscht, Susan R. "Decolonizing Canadian Writing: Why Gender? Whose English? When Canada?" *Essays on Canadian Writing* 54 (1994): 124-52.

Fiamengo, Janice. "Painting the Maple: Essays on Race, Gender, and the Construction of Canada." *BC Studies* 124 (2000): 124-25.

Gadsby, Meredith M. "'I Suck Coarse Salt': Caribbean Women Writers in Canada and the Politics of Transcendence." *Modern Fiction Studies* 44.1 (1998): 144-63.

Makeda, Silvera. *The Other Woman: Women of Colour in Contemporary Canadian Literature.* Toronto: Sister Vision, 1995.

Moynagh, Maureen. "Eyeing the North Star? Figuring Canada in African-Canadian Postslavery Fiction and Drama." *Comparative American Studies* 3.1 (March 2005): 15-27.

———. "Africville, an Imagined Community." *Canadian Literature* 157 (Summer 1998): 14-34.

Padolsky Enoch. "Ethnicity and Race: Canadian Minority Writing at a Crossroads." *Journal of Canadian Studies* 31.3 (1996): 129-47.

Sanders, Leslie. "'The Mere Determination to Remember': M. Nourbese Phillip's 'Stop Frame.'" *West Coast Line* 22.1.31 (1997): 134-42.

———. "Marlene Nourbese Philip's 'Bad Words.'" *Tessera* 12 (1992): 81-89.

———. "'I Am Stateless Anyway': The Poetry of Dionne Brand." *Zora Neale Hurston Forum* 3.2 (1989): 19-29.

Verduyn, Christl. "Disjunctions: Place, Identity and Nation in 'Minority' Literatures in Canada." *Canadian Issues* 20 (1998): 164-75.

Vevaina, Coomi S. and Barbara Godard. *Intersexions: Issues of Race and Gender in Canadian Women's Writing.* New Delhi: Creative Books, 1996.

Walcott, Rinaldo. *Black Like Who? Writing Black Canada.* Rev. 2nd ed. Toronto: Insomniac, 2003.

———, ed. *Rude: Contemporary Black Canadian Cultural Criticism.* Toronto: Insomniac, 2000.

Winks, Robin. *The Blacks in Canada: A History.* 2nd ed. Montreal; Kingston: McGill Queen's UP, 1997.

Notes on Contributors

Robin Breon is an arts and cultural writer who often focusses on equity issues as they affect the arts. He is a founding member of the Canadian Theatre Critics Association and a regular reviewer for AisleSay.com.

George Elliott Clarke is a pioneer scholar of African-Canadian Literature. His landmark work, *Odysseys Home: Mapping African-Canadian Literature*, appeared in 2002. He is the E.J. Pratt Professor of Canadian Literature at the University of Toronto.

Andrea Davis is an Assistant Professor in the Division of Humanities at York University where she teaches courses in Black Canadian, African American and Caribbean Literatures and Cultural Studies. She also directs the Latin American and Caribbean Studies Program (LACS) and is a fellow of the Centre for Research on Latin America and the Caribbean (CERLAC). She serves on the Board of Directors for the Centre for the Study of Black Cultures in Canada.

Alan Filewod teaches in the School of English and Theatre Studies at the University of Guelph. He has published widely on Canadian drama and theatre history, political theatre and postcolonialism. His books include *Collective Encounters: Documentary Theatre in English Canada* (University of Toronto Press, 1987), *Performing "Canada": The Nation Enacted in the Imagined Theatre* (*Textual Studies in Canada*, 2002), and, with David Watt, *Workers' Playtime: Theatre and the Labour Movement since 1970* (Currency Press, 2001).

Margaret Jane Kidnie, Associate Professor of English at the University of Western Ontario, is the editor of *Ben Jonson: The Devil is an Ass and Other Plays*, and Philip Stubbes, *The Anatomie of Abuses*. She has co-edited with Lukas Erne *Textual Performances: The Modern Reproduction of Shakespeare's Drama*, and published articles on bibliography, textual theory, and performance. She is currently editing *A Woman Killed with Kindness* for the Arden Early Modern Drama series, and writing a book on late-twentieth century performance and adaptation.

Maureen Moynagh is Associate Professor in the English Department at St. Francis Xavier University where she teaches postcolonial literature and does research in the areas of modernism and empire, nationalism/transnationalism, and the literature of the African Diaspora. Recent publications include *Nancy Cunard: Essays on Race and Empire* (Broadview Press, 2002). She is currently working on a study of political tourism, and on contemporary African-Canadian postslavery literature.

A professional playwright and theatre director, **Rachael Van Fossen** is currently the Artistic Director of Black Theatre Workshop in Montreal, and teaches part-time in the Theatre and Development programme at Concordia University. Rachael was Founding Artistic Director of Common Weal in Regina from 1992-1999. Her play *Ka'ma'mo'pi cik/The Gathering*, co-written with Darrel Wildcat in 1992, was recently published in the anthology *The West of All Possible Worlds*. Rachael's other produced plays include *A North Side Story (or two)*, *Dene Suline Ho Ni Ye*, and *City Flats*. She has contributed to *Canadian Theatre Review*, and co-authored with ahdri zhina mandiela the introduction to the play *yagayah: two.womyn.black.griots* in *Testifyin': Contemporary African Canadian Drama: Volume II* (edited by Djanet Sears). Rachael has also produced and directed several radio dramas for the CBC.

Rinaldo Walcott is an Associate Professor in the Department of Sociology and Equity Studies at the Ontario Institute for Studies in Education, University of Toronto. He is Canada Research Chair of Social Justice and Cultural Studies. His next book is titled *Disturbing the Peace: The Impossible Dream of Black Canadian Studies*.